THE
SACRED BOOKS OF THE EAST

Translated by

VARIOUS ORIENTAL SCHOLARS

Edited by

F. MAX MÜLLER

PART I DHAMMAPADA

PART II SUTTA-NIPĀTA

Vol. 10

SACRED BOOKS OF THE EAST

(50 VOLUMES)

Series Editor : *F. Max-Müller*

ISBN: 978-81-208-0101-1 (Set) Rs. 15000 (Each Vol. Rs. 350)

These volumes of the Sacred Books of the East series incl..de translations of all the most important works of the seven non-Christian religions that have exercised a profound influence on the civilisations of the continent of Asia. The Vedic Brahmanic system claims 21 volumes, Buddhism 10, and Jainism 2; 8 volumes comprise Sacred Books of the Parsis; 2 volumes represent Islam; and 6 the two main indigenous systems of China. Translated by twenty leading authorities in their respective fields, the volumes have been edited by the late F. Max Müller. The inception, publication and the compilation of these books cover almost 34 years.

I. BUDDHISM

Vol. 49: Buddhist Mahayana Texts (2 Parts)
Vol. 11: Buddhist Suttas
Vol. 10: The Dhammapada and Sutta Nipata
Vols. 35 & 36: The Questions of King Milinda (2 Parts)
Vol. 21: The Saddharma Pundarika or the Lotus of the True Law
Vols. 13, 17 & 20: Vinaya Texts (3 Parts)

II. CHINESE

Vol. 19: The Fo-Sho-Hing-Tsan-King
Vols. 3, 16, 27, 28, 39 & 40: The Sacred Books of China (6 Parts)

III. A GENERAL INDEX

Vol. 50: A General Index to the Names and Subject-matter of the Sacred Books of the East

IV. ISLAM

Vols. 6 & 9: The Qur'an (2 Parts)

V. JAINISM

Vols. 22 & 45: The Jaina Sutras (2 Parts)

VI. PARSIS

Vols. 5, 18, 24, 37 & 47: Pahlavi Texts (5 Parts)
Vols. 4, 23 & 31: The Zend-Avesta (3 Parts)

VII. VEDIC-BRAHMANIC SYSTEM

Vol. 8: The Bhagavadgita with the Sanatsujatiya and the Anugita
Vols. 29 & 30: The Grihya-Sutras: Rules of Vedic Domestic Ceremonies (2 Parts)
Vol. 42: Hymns of the Atharva Veda together with Extracts from the Ritual Books and the Commentaries
Vol. 7: The Institutes of Vishnu
Vol. 25: The Laws of Manu
Vol. 33: The Minor Law Books
Vols. 2 & 14: The Sacred Laws of the Aryas as Taught in the Schools of Apastamba, Gautama, Vasishtha and Baudhayana (2 Parts)
Vols. 12, 26, 41, 43 & 44: The Satapatha Brahmana According to the Text of the Madhyandina School (5 Parts)
Vols. 1 & 15: The Upanishads (2 Parts)
Vols. 34 & 38: The Vedanta Sutras (2 Parts)
Vol. 48: The Vedanta-Sutras (with the commentary by Ramanuja)
Vols. 32 & 46: Vedic Hymns (2 Parts)

THE DHAMMAPADA

A COLLECTION OF VERSES

Being One of the Canonical Books of the Buddhists

Translated from Pāli by
F. MAX MÜLLER

MOTILAL BANARSIDASS PUBLISHERS
PRIVATE LIMITED • DELHI

9th Reprint: Delhi, 2013
First Indian Edition: Delhi, 1965
(First Published by the Oxford University Press, 1881)

ISBN: 978-81-208-0111-0

MOTILAL BANARSIDASS
41 U.A. Bungalow Road, Jawahar Nagar, Delhi 110 007
8 Mahalaxmi Chamber, 22 Bhulabhai Desai Road, Mumbai 400 026
203 Royapettah High Road, Mylapore, Chennai 600 004
236, 9th Main III Block, Jayanagar, Bangaluru 560 011
Sanas Plaza, 1302 Baji Rao Road, Pune 411 002
8 Camac Street, Kolkata 700 017
Ashok Rajpath, Patna 800 004
Chowk, Varanasi 221 001

UNESCO COLLECTION OF REPRESENTATIVE WORKS— Indian Series
This book has been accepted in the Indian Translation Series of the UNESCO Collection of Representative Works, jointly sponsored by the United Nations Educational Scientific and Cultural Organization (UNESCO) and the Government of India

Printed in India

by RP Jain at NAB Printing Unit,
A-44, Naraina Industrial Area, Phase I, New Delhi–110028
and published by JP Jain for Motilal Banarsidass Publishers (P) Ltd,
41 U.A. Bungalow Road, Jawahar Nagar, Delhi-110007

Rashtrapati Bhavan,
New Delhi-4
June 10, 1962

I am very glad to know that the Sacred Books of the East, published years ago by the Clarendon Press, Oxford, which have been out-of-print for a number of years, will now be available to all students of religion and philosophy. The enterprise of the publishers is commendable and I hope the books will be widely read.

S. Radhakrishnan

PREFATORY NOTE TO THE NEW EDITION

Since 1948 the United Nations Educational, Scientific and Cultural Organization (UNESCO), upon the recommendation of the General Assembly of the United Nations, has been concerned with facilitating the translation of the works most representative of the culture of certain of its Member States, and, in particular, those of Asia.

One of the major difficulties confronting this programme is the lack of translators having both the qualifications and the time to undertake translations of the many outstanding books meriting publication. To help overcome this difficulty in part, UNESCO's advisers in this field (a panel of experts convened every other year by the International Council for Philosophy and Humanisitic Studies), have recommended that many worthwhile translations published during the 19th century, and now impossible to find except in a limited number of libraries, should be brought back into print in low-priced editions, for the use of students and of the general public. The experts also pointed out that in certain cases, even though there might be in existence more recent and more accurate translations endowed with a more modern apparatus of scholarship, a number of pioneer works of the greatest value and interest to students of Eastern religions also merited republication.

This point of view was warmly endorsed by the Indian National Academy of Letters (Sahitya Akademi), and the Indian National Commission for UNESCO.

It is in the spirit of these recommendations that this work from the famous series "Sacred Books of the East" is now once again being made available to the general public as part of the UNESCO Collection of Representative Works.

PUBLISHER'S NOTE

First, the man distinguished between eternal and perishable. Later he discovered within himself the germ of the Eternal. This discovery was an epoch in the history of the human mind and the *East was the first to discover it.*

To watch in the Sacred Books of the East the dawn of this religious consciousness of man, must always remain one of the most inspiring and hallowing sights in the whole history of the world. In order to have a solid foundation for a comparative study of the Religions of the East, we must have before all things, complete and thoroughly faithful translation of their Sacred Books in which some of the ancient sayings were preserved because they were so true and so striking that they could not be forgotten. They contained eternal truths, expressed for the first time in human language.

With profoundest reverence for Dr. S. Radhakrishnan, President of India, who inspired us for the task; our deep sense of gratitude for Dr. C. D. Deshmukh & Dr. D. S. Kothari, for encouraging assistance; esteemed appreciation of UNESCO for the warm endorsement of the cause ; and finally with indebtedness to Dr. H. Rau, Director, Max Müller Bhawan, New Delhi, in procuring us the texts of the Series for reprint, we humbly conclude.

CONTENTS.

PREFACE

TO NEW EDITION.

It has been a great and unexpected pleasure to me to have to bring out a new, the third edition of my translation of the Dhammapada. The first was published in 1870, the second in 1881. I cannot indeed pretend to have improved the present edition very much, for I have not had any time left during the last few years to continue my study of Pâli. Nor has Pâli ever been more than a *parergon* to me. I began it in 1845 during my stay at Paris with Burnouf, who was then almost the only scholar who could read Pâli texts, and I still have a letter of his in which he apologises for his imperfect knowledge of the language. At that time Pâli scholarship had not yet become a special and independent study, but it was a kind of annexe to Sanskrit. Men like Bopp and Burnouf were expected to teach not only Sanskrit and Comparative Philology, but at the same time, Zend, the Prâkrit dialects, and, as one of them, Pâli. Clough's Pâli Grammar (Colombo, 1824 and 1832) and Turnour's Mahâvanso (1837) were all that we had to depend on. Some advance was made by Spiegel and Westergaard, but the real impulse to an independent and scholarlike study of Pâli literature came from my friend Childers, the author of the first Pâli Dictionary, published in 1875. Before that time the only names to be mentioned in Pâli scholarship were those of James D'Alwis, Spence Hardy, Spiegel, E. Kuhn, Minayeff, Senart, Weber, and last, not least, Fausböll. After the publication of Childers' Dictionary, the progress of Pâli scholarship has been very rapid, and the number of Pâli texts and translations has increased very considerably. As the most active among the new generation of Pâli scholars deserve to be mentioned Rhys Davids, the founder of the Pâli Text Society, Oldenberg, the editor of the Vinaya-pi*t*aka, Trenckner, E. Senart, Féer, Morris and the translators of the *G*âtaka, Professor E. B. Cowell, Messrs. R. Chalmers, W. H. D. Rouse, H. T. Francis, and R. H. Neil.

The most favourite Pâli text seems to have been the Dhammapada. It is certainly a most interesting collection of verses, giving a trustworthy picture of Buddhist thought, particularly in its practical and moral character. Consisting of short sentences it seems at first an easy book to translate, but the very fact that these *versus memoriales* stand by themselves without any context to throw light on them creates a peculiar difficulty, much the same as that with which the readers of another elementary book, the Hitopade*s*a, are well acquainted. Like the Hitopade*s*a, the Dhammapada also may be called an easy and at the same time a very difficult book. The verses being often torn from the context to which they originally belonged, may indeed be rendered word by word, but they leave us often in the dark, particularly where two readings are possible, which of the two we ought to choose; while if we knew what preceded and followed them in their original context, we should find our choice much easier. Though many difficult and obscure passages in the Dhammapada have now by a succession of translators and commentators been elucidated, many more still remain which require renewed study. It may seem strange to outsiders that there should still be so much uncertainty as to the exact meaning of many Pâli words. The meaning of the very title of our book, the Dhammapada, is still contested. I have produced whatever arguments I could collect in support of the meaning of 'Path of Virtue' or 'Path of the Law.' But I am far from saying that the translation 'Collection of Texts of the Law,' 'Worte der Wahrheit,' is impossible. What we want to settle the point is some ancient Buddhist authority to tell us with what intention this title was originally given. For titles are often fanciful, and mere scholarship is not sufficient to enable us to speak with magisterial assurance.

Let us take another instance. One of the commonest words in Buddhist philosophy is sańkhâro. It corresponds to Sanskrit sa*m*skâra. The meanings of the Sanskrit word are difficult enough. It means the forming of matter, it can mean refining, polishing, embellishing, also the preparing of food and the moulding of clay. Purifying rites also are called sa*m*skâra and the impressions of the mind as well as the result of them, the dispositions, tastes, talents or inclinations, may go by the same name. In Pâli, however, the growth of the meanings of sańkhâro becomes far more complicated. It means there also preparing, but the Buddhist, as if remembering that sa*m*skâra meant etymologically putting together, and then what has been put together, uses sańkhâro in the sense of anything that has been made and will therefore perish. According to Hindu philosophy whatever has been put together or made can be put asunder or unmade, and thus sańkhâro came to be used not only for what we should call the created or material world, but for anything in it that is anitya or perishable. Thus sańkhâro may sometimes be rendered by matter in general, though chiefly by organised or living matter, except that sańkhâro includes what we should call attributes also. Lastly, like sa*m*skâra, sańkhâro may mean the impressions left on the mind, and the resulting states of the mind predispositions, talents or character, in which sense it is often used by the Sâńkhya philosophers. If then we read v. 368 that the quiet place or Nirvâ*n*a is sańkhârupasama*m* sukha*m* or happiness arising from the quieting of the sańkhâras, we may translate either 'from the cessation of all existing things,' or 'from the calming of all desires or affections.' Hence Fausböll translates 'naturarum sedatio;' Weber, 'wo aufhören die Einkleidungen;' Gray, 'life-ending;' Hu, 'où cessent les existences;' v. Schroeder, 'wo alles Ding zur Ruhe kommt,' whereas I prefer to take upasama in the sense of calming, and sańkhâro in the sense of all states of the mind, more particularly the calming of all desires and affections.

If such a verse occurred in a text treating either of the end of the world and all created things or of the subduing of all affections or passions, we should know at once which meaning to choose, while in our case we may, I think, allow ourselves to be guided by the word sukha, happiness, which seems to point to the quieting of the affections of the mind rather than to the destruction of the world.

In looking at the literature devoted to the Dhammapada, we may read very clearly the steady progress of Pâli scholarship. Fausböll's edition of the text with a Latin translation, and with extracts from the native commentary, which was published in 1855, marked indeed an epoch, if we may use such a hackneyed expression of a work of real importance and permanent value. It was indeed a work *sui generis*, and there was no other scholar living at the time who would have ventured on such new ground as that chosen by that young Danish scholar. It ought never to be forgotten that the publication of an Oriental text never published before, and the translation of an Oriental text never translated before, requires a kind of scholarship quite different from that of the patient follower who is satisfied with *jurare in verba magistri.* There is between a scholar such as Fausböll and the ordinary scholars who can read what has been read and translated before, about the same difference as between a Stanley exploring the darkest Africa and a tourist who now goes to Egypt personally conducted by Messrs. Cook & Co. Naturally the pioneer is apt to lose his way and to make mistakes. These very mistakes, however, are sometimes most creditable, just as the bold adventures of those who did not discover the sources of the Nile have often required greater efforts and entailed more severe sufferings than the successful discoveries of later comers. But be that as it may, no true Pâli scholar will ever forget what we owe to Fausböll's adventurous daring, no one pointing out improvements in his text and translation would not feel ashamed to blame or to ridicule him. In that respect Pâli scholarship may indeed be proud for having always preserved the temper of the true Buddhist or the gentleman, and it seems almost as if the best Pâli scholars had been those who were most thoroughly imbued with the true spirit of Buddha himself, and to whom nothing seemed so offensive as *pharusham*, which—sit venia—one might almost translate by *langage farouche ou grossier*.

After the first editor and translator followed—but longo intervallo—those who for the first time translated the text into a new language, whether German, English or French. To this class belong the translations of Weber (German), myself (English), Hu (French). No one who has not himself tried to translate Oriental thought into any European language can have any idea of the almost impossible task of finding words in any of these modern languages exactly corresponding to the ancient terms of Eastern religion or philosophy. To find terms exactly corresponding to the varied terminology of Buddhism is simply impossible. They do not exist, as little as there are modern coins corresponding exactly to a kârshâpa*n*a. Here nothing remains but to use terms of more general meaning which at all events are not wrong, and which, though they do not exactly cover the Pâli terms, yet include them. This is the rule I have tried to follow throughout. It is not very satisfactory, but it is better at all events than to use a word which is actually wrong or covers but a small segment of the original term.

In some cases the native commentary is of great help, and scholars who formerly despised the help of native interpreters, such as Sâya*n*a or Buddhaghosa, are now agreed that they form a *sine qua non* in a critical study of ancient texts. How, for instance, should we know the right meaning of such a verse as 353, where we read:

'I have conquered all, I know all, in all conditions of life I am free from taint; I have left all, and through the destruction of thirst I am free; having learnt myself, whom should I teach?'

It is true we know now, and might have known before, that Pâli uddis is not used in the sense of teaching, but means pointing towards a person or a thing. In Sanskrit also upadis means teaching (anweisen), but not uddis, which means to point to.

A very similar verse occurs in the Suttanipâta 210:

Sabbâbhibhu*m* sabbavidu*m* sumedha*m*
Sabbesu dhammesu anupalitta*m*
Sabba*ñg*aha*m* ta*m*hakkhaya vimutta*m*
Ta*m* vâpi dhîrâ muni*m* vedayanti,

which Fausböll translates: 'The man who has overcome everything, who knows everything, who is possessed of a good understanding, undefiled in all things (dhamma), abandoning all things, liberated in the destruction of desire (nibbâna), him the wise style a Muni.'

Here all traces of the event which gave rise to the utterance of the verse have disappeared. But the commentator tells us that it was uttered originally by Buddha when on his way to Benares he met an Upa*g*îvaka who asked him who it was that ordained him, and who was the teacher whose doctrine he taught. It was then that Buddha declared that he could point to no one as his teacher, but that he was his own teacher. After this all becomes clear, and we see that the verb uddis is the right verb to use for pointing out. We have only to refer to the Lalita-vistara XXVI, to see the story of the native commentator confirmed. Here kasmin Gautama brahma*k*aryam u*k*yate corresponds to kam uddissa pabba*g*ito, that is, who gave thee leave to become a bhikshu or a pabba*g*ita?

I subjoin a list of books containing translations or notes on the Dhammapada, published after the publication of my own translation, so far as they have become known to me:

(1) Le Dhammapada, par Fernand Hu, Paris, 1878.

(2) The Dhammapadam or Scriptural Texts translated from Pâli on the basis of Burmese MSS., by James Gray, 1881; sec. ed. Calcutta, 1887.

(3) Das Dhammapadam, Ein Vers. sammlung, aus der Englischen Übersetztung von Professor M. M.: metrisch ins Deutsch übersetzt, Leipzig, 1885.

(4) Der Wahrheitsphad, übersetzt von K. E. Neumann, 1893.

(5) A translation from a Chinese translation of the Dhammapada by Samuel Beal was published in 1878, and is useful sometimes by the subjoined narratives.

Difficult passages have been discussed not only by Childers in his Dictionary and in his 'Notes on the Dhammapada,' but likewise by Morris in his valuable contributions to the Journal of the Pâli Text Society, by Kern in his Bijdrage tot de Verklaring van eenige woorden in Pali-geschriften voorkomende (Verhandelingen der Kon. Akademie van Wetenschappen, Amsterdam, 1886), and by Fausböll in his Nogle Bemærkninger om enkelte vanskelige Pâli-Ord i Jâtaka-Bogen, 1888.

I have also to thank Prof. Fausböll, as formerly Childers, for help given me in my translation. What I said in my introduction to my former edition, that 'I can claim for myself no more than the name of a very humble gleaner in this field of Pâli literature,' applies with equal truth to the new edition. I have gleaned whatever grains seemed to me valuable in these later publications, and have consulted several of the translators whenever there seemed to be some points left that required to be cleared up.

F. M. M.

INTRODUCTION

TO

THE DHAMMAPADA.

THE DHAMMAPADA, A CANONICAL BOOK.

The Dhammapada forms part of the Pâli Buddhist canon, though its exact place varies according to different authorities, and we have not as yet a sufficient number of complete MSS. of the Tipi*t*aka to help us to decide the question[1].

Those who divide that canon into three Pi*t*akas or baskets, the Vinaya-pi*t*aka, Sutta-pi*t*aka, and Abhidhamma-pi*t*aka, assign the Dhammapada to the Sutta-pi*t*aka. That Pi*t*aka consists of five Nikâyas: the Dîgha-nikâya, the Ma*ggh*ima-nikâya, the Sa*m*yutta-nikâya, the Aṅguttara-nikâya, and the Khuddaka-nikâya. The fifth, or Khuddaka-nikâya, comprehends the following works: 1. Khuddaka-pâ*th*a; 2. DHAMMAPADA; 3. Udâna; 4. Itivuttaka; 5. Sutta-nipâta; 6. Vimânavatthu; 7. Petavatthu; 8. Theragâthâ; 9. Therîgâthâ; 10. *G*âtaka; 11. Niddesa; 12. Pa*t*isambhidâ; 13. Apadâna; 14. Buddhava*m*sa; 15. *K*ariyâ-pi*t*aka.

According to another division[2], however, the whole Buddhist canon consists of five Nikâyas: the Dîgha-nikâya, the Ma*ggh*ima-nikâya, the Sa*m*yutta-nikâya, the Aṅguttara-nikâya, and the fifth, the Khuddaka-nikâya, which Khuddaka-nikâya is then made to comprehend the whole of the Vinaya (discipline) and Abhidhamma (metaphysics), together with the fifteen books beginning with the Khuddaka-pâ*th*a.

The order of these fifteen books varies, and even, as it would seem, their number. The Dîghabhâ*n*aka school

[1] See Feer, Journal Asiatique, 1871, p. 263. There is now at least one complete MS. of the Tipi*t*aka, the Phayre MS., at the India Office, and Professor Forchhammer has just published a most useful List of Pâli MSS., collected in Burma, the largest collection hitherto known.

[2] See Childers, s. v. Nikâya, and extracts from Buddhaghosa's commentary on the Brahma*g*âla-sutta.

admits twelve books only, and assigns them all to the Abhidhamma, while the Ma*ggh*imabhâ*n*akas admit fifteen books, and assign them to the Sutta-pi*t*aka. The order of the fifteen books is: 1. *G*âtaka [10]; 2. Mahâniddesa [11]; 3. *K*ullaniddesa [11]; 4. Pa*t*isambhidâmagga [12]; 5. Suttanipâta [5]; 6. DHAMMAPADA [2]; 7. Udâna [3]; 8. Itivuttaka [4]; 9. Vimânavatthu [6]; 10. Petavatthu [7]; 11. Theragâthâ [8]; 12. Therîgâthâ [9]; 13. *K*ariyâpi*t*aka [15]; 14. Apadâna [13]; 15. Buddhava*m*sa [14][1].

The Khuddaka-pâ*th*a is left out in the second list, and the number is brought to fifteen by dividing Niddesa into Mahâ-niddesa and *K*ulla-niddesa.

There is a commentary on the Dhammapada in Pâli, and supposed to be written by Buddhaghosa[2], in the first half of the fifth century A.D. In explaining the verses of the Dhammapada, the commentator gives for every or nearly every verse a parable to illustrate its meaning, which is likewise believed to have been uttered by Buddha in his intercourse with his disciples, or in preaching to the multitudes that came to hear him.

DATE OF THE DHAMMAPADA.

The only means of fixing the date of the Dhammapada is trying to ascertain the date of the Buddhist canon of which it forms a part, or the date of Buddhaghosa, who wrote a commentary on it. This, however, is by no means easy, and the evidence on which we have to rely is such that we must not be surprised if those who are accustomed to test historical and chronological evidence in Greece and Rome, decline to be convinced by it. As

[1] The figures within brackets refer to the other list of books in the Khuddaka-nikâya. See also p. xxxvi.

[2] M. Léon Feer in the Journal Asiatique, 1871, p. 266, mentions another commentary of a more philosophical character, equally ascribed to Buddhaghosa, and having the title Vivara Bra Dhammapada, i. e. L'auguste Dhammapada devoilé. Professor Forchhammer in his 'List of Manuscripts,' 1879–80, mentions the following works in connection with the Dhammapada: Dhammapada-Nissayo; Dh. P. A*tth*akathâ by Buddhaghosa; Dh. P. A*tth*akathâ Nissayo, 3 vols., containing a complete translation of the commentary; Dh. P. Va*tth*u. Of printed books he quotes: Kayanupassanakyam, a work based on the *G*arâvaggo, Mandalay, 1876 (390 pages), and Dhammapada-desanakyam, printed in 'British Burma News.'

a general rule, I quite agree that we cannot be too sceptical in assigning a date to ancient books, particularly if we intend to use them as documents for tracing the history of human thought. To the initiated, I mean to those who have themselves worked in the mines of ancient Oriental literature, such extreme scepticism may often seem unscientific and uncalled for. They are more or less aware of hundreds of arguments, each by itself, it may be, of small weight, but all combined proving irresistible. They are conscious, too, of having been constantly on the look out for danger, and, as all has gone on smoothly, they feel sure that, in the main, they are on the right road. Still it is always useful to be as incredulous as possible, particularly against oneself, and to have before our eyes critics who will not yield one inch beyond what they are forced to yield by the strongest pressure of facts.

The age of our MSS. of the canonical books, either in Pâli or Sanskrit, is of no help to us. All Indian MSS. are comparatively modern, and one who has probably handled more Indian MSS. than anybody else, Mr. A. Burnell, has lately expressed his conviction that 'no MS. written one thousand years ago is now existent in India, and that it is almost impossible to find one written five hundred years ago, for most MSS. which claim to be of that date are merely copies of old MSS. the dates of which are repeated by the copyists [1].' This applies, however, to MSS. only which are written in the ordinary Devanâgarî alphabet.

Nor is the language, whether Sanskrit or Pâli, a safe guide for fixing dates. Both languages continue to be written to our own time, and though there are some characteristic marks to distinguish more modern from more ancient Buddhist Sanskrit and Pâli, this branch of critical scholarship requires to be cultivated far more extensively and accurately before true scholars would venture to fix the date of a Sanskrit or Pâli text on the strength of linguistic evidence alone [2].

[1] Indian Antiquary, 1880, p. 233.

[2] See some important remarks on this subject in Fausböll's Introduction to Sutta-nipâta, p. xi.

The Buddhists themselves have no difficulty in assigning a date to their sacred canon. They are told in that canon itself that it was settled at the First Council, or immediately after the death of Buddha, and they believe that it was afterwards handed down by means of oral tradition, or, according to other authorities, actually written down in books by order of Kâsyapa, the president of the First Council [1]. Buddhaghosa, a learned and in some respects a critical scholar, living in the beginning of the fifth century A.D., asserts that the canon which he had before him, was the same as that fixed by the First Council [2].

Several European students have adopted the same opinion, and, so far as I know, no argument has yet been advanced showing the impossibility of the native view, that some collection of Buddha's doctrines was made immediately after his death at Râgagaha, and that it was finally settled at what is called the Second Council, or the Council of Vesâlî. But what is not impossible is not therefore true, nor can anything be gained by appealing to later witnesses, such as, for instance, Hiouen Thsang, who travelled through India in the seventh century, and wrote down anything that he could learn, little concerned whether one statement tallied with the other or not [3]. He says that the Tipitaka was written down on palm leaves by Kâsyapa at the end of the First Council. But what can be the weight of such a witness, living more than a thousand years after the event, compared with that, for instance, of the Mahâvamsa, which dates from the fifth century of our era, and

[1] Bigandet, Life of Gaudama (Rangoon, 1866), p. 350; but also p. 120 note.

[2] See Childers, s. v. Tipitaka. There is a curious passage in Buddhaghosa's account of the First Council. 'Now one may ask,' he says, 'Is there or is there not in this first Parâgika anything to be taken away or added?' I reply, There is nothing in the words of the Blessed Buddha that can be taken away, for the Buddhas speak not even a single syllable in vain, yet in the words of disciples and devatâs there are things which may be omitted, and these the elders who made the recension, did omit. On the other hand, additions are everywhere necessary, and accordingly, whenever it was necessary to add anything, they added it. If it be asked, What are the additions referred to? I reply, Only sentences necessary to connect the text, as 'at that time,' 'again at that time,' 'and so forth.'

[3] Pèlerins Bouddhistes, vol. i, p. 158.

tells us in the account of Mahinda's missionary journey to Ceylon (241/318), that the son of Asoka had to spend three years in learning the Tipi*t*aka by heart from the mouth of a teacher[1]? No mention is then made of any books or MSS., when it would have been most natural to do so[2]. At a later time, during the reign of King Va*tt*agâmani[3] (88–76 B.C.), the same chronicle, the Mahâva*m*sa, tells us that 'the profoundly wise priests had theretofore orally (mukhapâ*th*ena) perpetuated the Pâli of the Pi*t*akattaya and its A*tth*akathâ (commentary), but that at this period the priests, foreseeing the perdition of the people assembled, and in order that the religion might endure for ages, recorded the same in books (potthakesu likhâpayu*m*)[4].'

No one has yet questioned the dates of the Dîpava*m*sa, about 400 A.D., or of the first part of the Mahâva*m*sa, between 459–477 A.D., and though no doubt there is an interval of nearly 600 years between the composition of the Mahâva*m*sa and the recorded writing down of the Buddhist canon under Va*tt*agâmani, yet we must remember that the Ceylonese chronicles were confessedly founded on an older A*tth*akathâ preserved in the monasteries of the island, and representing an unbroken line of local tradition.

My own argument therefore, so long as the question was only whether we could assign a pre-Christian date to the Pâli Buddhist canon, has always been this. We have the commentaries on the Pâli canon translated from Sinhalese into Pâli, or actually composed, it may be, by

---

[1] Mahâva*m*sa, p. 37; Dîpava*m*sa VII, 28–31; Buddhaghosha's Parables, p. xviii.

[2] Bigandet, Life of Gaudama, p. 351.

[3] Dr. E. Müller (Indian Antiquary, Nov. 1880, p. 270) has discovered inscriptions in Ceylon, belonging to Devanapiya Maharâga Gâmi*n*i Tissa, whom he identifies with Va*tt*agâmani.

[4] The same account is given in the Dîpava*m*sa XX, 20, and in the Sârasaṅgraha, as quoted by Spence Hardy, Legends, p. 192. As throwing light on the completeness of the Buddhist canon at the time of King Va*tt*agâmani, it should be mentioned that, according to the commentary on the Mahâva*m*sa (Turnour, p. liii), the sect of the Dhammaru*k*ikas established itself at the Abhayavihâra, which had been constructed by Va*tt*agâmani, and that one of the grounds of their secession was their refusing to acknowledge the Parivâra (thus I read instead of Pariwána) as part of the Vinaya-pi*t*aka. According to the Dîpava*m*sa (VII, 42) Mahinda knew the Parivâra.

Buddhaghosa. Buddhaghosa confessedly consulted various MSS., and gives various readings, just as any modern scholar might do. This was in the beginning of the fifth century A.D., and there is nothing improbable, though I would say no more, in supposing that some of the MSS., consulted by Buddhaghosa, dated from the first century B.C., when Va*tt*agâmani ordered the sacred canon to be reduced to writing.

There is one other event with reference to the existence of the sacred canon in Ceylon, recorded in the Mahâva*m*sa, between the time of Buddhaghosa and Va*tt*agâmani, viz. the translation of the Suttas from Pâli into the language of Ceylon, during the reign of Buddhadâsa, 339-368 A.D. If MSS. of that ancient translation still existed, they would, no doubt, be very useful for determining the exact state of the Pâli originals at that time[1]. But even without them there seems no reason to doubt that Buddhaghosa had before him old MSS. of the Pâli canon, and that these were in the main the same as those written down at the time of Va*tt*agâmani.

BUDDHAGHOSA'S AGE.

The whole of this argument, however, rested on the supposition that Buddhaghosa's date in the beginning of the fifth century A.D. was beyond the reach of reasonable doubt. 'His age,' I had ventured to say in the Preface to Buddhaghosha's Parables (1870), 'can be fixed with greater accuracy than most dates in the literary history of India.' But soon after, one of our most celebrated Pâli scholars, the great Russian traveller, Professor Joh. Minayeff, expressed in the Mélanges Asiatiques (13/25 April, 1871) the gravest doubts as to Buddhaghosa's age, and thus threw the whole Buddhist chronology, so far as it had then been accepted by all, or nearly all scholars, back into chaos. He gave as his chief reason that Buddhaghosa was

[1] A note is added, stating that several portions of the other two divisions also of the Pi*t*akattaya were translated into the Sinhalese language, and that these alone are consulted by the priests, who are unacquainted with Pâli. On the other hand, it is stated that the Sinhalese text of the A*tth*akathâ exists no longer. See Spence Hardy, Legends, p. xxv, and p. 69.

not, as I supposed, the contemporary of Mahânâma, the author of the Mahâva*m*sa, but of another Mahânâma, the king of Ceylon.

Professor Minayeff is undoubtedly right in this, but I am not aware that I, or anybody else, had ever questioned so palpable a fact. There are certainly two Mahânâmas; one, the king who reigned from 410–432 A.D.; the other, the supposed author of the Mahâva*m*sa, the uncle and protector of King Dhâtusena, 459–477. 'Dhâtusena,' I had written, 'was the nephew of the historian Mahânâma, and owed the throne to the protection of his uncle. Dhâtusena was in fact the restorer of a national dynasty, and after having defeated the foreign usurpers (the Damilo dynasty) "he restored the religion which had been set aside by the foreigners"' (Mahâv. p. 256). Among his many pious acts it is particularly mentioned that he gave a thousand, and ordered the Dîpava*m*sa to be promulgated. As Mahânâma was the uncle of Dhâtusena, who reigned from 459–477, he may be considered as a trustworthy witness with regard to events that occurred between 410 and 432. Now the literary activity of Buddhaghosa in Ceylon falls in that period[1]'

These facts being admitted, it is surely not too great a stretch of probability to suppose, as I did, that a man whose nephew was king in 459–477, might have been alive in 410–432, that is to say, might have been a contemporary of Buddhaghosa. I did not commit myself to any further theories. The question whether Mahânâma, the uncle of Dhâtusena, was really the author of the Mahâva*m*sa, the question whether he wrote the second half of the 37th chapter of that work, or broke off his chronicle in the middle of that chapter, I did not discuss, having no new materials to bring forward beyond those on which Turnour and those who followed him had founded their conclusions, and which I had discussed in my History of Sanskrit Literature (1859), p. 267. All I said was, 'It is difficult to determine whether the 38th as well as the (whole of the) 37th chapter came from the pen of Mahânâma, for

[1] 'Ungefähr 50 Jahre älter als Mahânâma ist Buddhaghosha,' see Westergaard, Über Buddha's Todesjahr, p. 99.

the Mahâva*m*sa was afterwards continued by different writers, even to the middle of the last century. But, taking into account all the circumstances of the case, it is most probable that Mahânâma carried on the history to his own time, to the death of Dhâtusena, 477 A.D.'

What I meant by 'all the circumstances of the case' might easily be understood by any one who had read Turnour's Preface to the Mahâva*m*sa. Turnour himself thought at first that Mahânâma's share in the Mahâva*m*sa ended with the year 301 A.D., and that the rest of the work, called the Sulu Wansé, was composed by subsequent writers [1]. Dharmakîrti is mentioned by name as having continued the work to the reign of Prâkrama Bâhu (A.D. 1266). But Turnour afterwards changed his mind [2]. Considering that the account of Mahâsena's reign, the first of the Seven Kings, terminates in the middle of a chapter, at verse 48, while the whole chapter is called the Sattarâ*g*iko, 'the chapter of the Seven Kings,' he naturally supposed that the whole of that chapter, extending to the end of the reign of his nephew Dhâtusena, might be the work of Mahânâma, unless there were any strong proofs to the contrary. Such proofs, beyond the tradition of writers of the MSS., have not, as yet, been adduced [3].

But even if it could be proved that Mahânâma's own pen did not go beyond the 48th verse of the 37th chapter, the historical trustworthiness of the concluding portion of that chapter, containing the account of Buddhaghosa's literary activity, nay, even of the 38th chapter, would be little affected thereby. We know that both the Mahâva*m*sa and the somewhat earlier Dîpava*m*sa were founded on the Sinhalese A*tth*akathâs, the commentaries and chronicles preserved in the Mahâvihâra at Anurâdhapura. We also know that that Vihâra was demolished by Mahâsena, and deserted by nearly all its inmates for the space of nine years (p. 235), and again for the space of nine months

[1] Introduction, p. ii. The *K*ûlava*m*sa is mentioned with the Mahâva*m*sa, both as the works of Mahânâma, by Professor Forchhammer in his List of Pâli MSS.

[2] Introduction, p. xci.

[3] See Rhys Davids, Journal of the Royal Asiatic Society, 1875, p. 196.

(p. 237). We can well understand therefore why the older history, the Dîpava*m*sa, should end with the death of Mahâsena (died 302 A. D.), and why in the Mahâva*m*sa too there should have been a break at that date. But we must not forget that, during Mahânâma's life, the Mahâvihâra at Anurâdhapura was restored, that some kind of chronicle, called the Dîpava*m*sa, whether it be a general name of any 'chronicle of the island,' or of our Dîpava*m*sa, or, it may be, even of our Mahâva*m*sa, was ordered to be published or promulgated (dîpetum) under Dhâtusena, the nephew and protegé of Mahânâma. Therefore, even if we do not insist on the personal authorship of Mahânâma, we may certainly maintain that historical entries had been made in the chronicles of Anurâdhapura during Dhâtusena's reign, and probably under the personal auspices of Mahânâma, so that if we find afterwards, in the second half of the 37th chapter of his Mahâva*m*sa, an account of events which had happened between the destruction of the Mahâvihâra and the reign of Dhâtusena, and among them an account of so important an event as the arrival of Buddhaghosa from Magadha and his translation of the Sinhalese A*tth*akathâ into the language of Magadha, we may well suppose that they rest on the authority of native chronicles, written not long after the events, and that therefore, 'under all the circumstances of the case,' the age of Buddhaghosa can be fixed with greater accuracy than most dates in the literary history of India.

There is one difficulty still remaining with regard to the date of the historian Mahânâma which might have perplexed Turnour's mind, and has certainly proved a stumbling-block to myself. Turnour thought that the author of the commentary on the Mahâva*m*sa, the Va*m*satthappakâsinî, was the same as the author of the Mahâva*m*sa, viz. Mahânâma. The date of that commentary, however, as we know now, must be fixed much later, for it speaks of a schism which took place in the year 601 A. D., during the reign of Agrabôdhi (also called Dhâtâpatisso). Turnour[1] looked

[1] Introduction, p. liii.

upon that passage as a later interpolation, because he thought the evidence for the identity of the author and the commentator of the Mahâva*m*sa too strong to be set aside. He trusted chiefly to a passage in the commentary, and if that passage had been correctly rendered, the conclusion which he drew from it could hardly be resisted. We read in the Mahâva*m*sa (p. 254):

'Certain members of the Moriyan dynasty, dreading the power of the (usurper) Subho, the bâlattho, had settled in various parts of the country, concealing themselves. Among them there was a certain landed proprietor Dhâtusena, who had established himself at Nandivâpi. His son named Dhâtâ, who lived at the village Ambiliyâgo, had two sons, Dhâtusena and Sîlatissabodhi, of unexceptional descent. Their mother's brother (Mahânâma), devoted to the cause of religion, continued to reside (at Anurâdhapura) in his sacerdotal character, at the edifice built by the minister Dîghasandana. The youth Dhâtusena became a priest in his fraternity, and on a certain day, while he was chaunting at the foot of a tree, a shower of rain fell, and a Nâga, seeing him there, encircled him in his folds, and covered him and his book with his hood. . . . Causing an image of Mahâ Mahinda to be made, and conveying it to the edifice (Ambamâlaka) in which the thera's body had been burnt, in order that he might celebrate a great festival there, and that he might also promulgate the contents of the Dîpava*m*sa, distributing a thousand pieces, he caused it to be read aloud [1].'

If we compare with this extract from the Mahâva*m*sa a passage from the commentary as translated by Turnour, we can well understand how he arrived at the conclusion that it was written by the same person who wrote the Mahâva*m*sa.

Turnour translates (p. liv):

'Upon these data by me, the thera, who had, with due

[1] Mr. Turnour added a note in which he states that Dîpava*m*sa is here meant for Mahâva*m*sa, but whether brought down to this period, or only to the end of the reign of Mahâsena, to which alone the *T*îkâ extends, there is no means of ascertaining (p. 257).

solemnity, been invested with the dignified title of Mahânâma, resident at the pariven*n*a founded by the minister Dîghasandana, endowed with the capacity requisite to record the narrative comprised in the Mahâva*m*sa, in due order, rejecting only the dialect in which the Singhalese A*tth*akathâ are written, but retaining their import and following their arrangement, the history, entitled the Palapadôruva*m*sa (Padyapadânuva*m*sa), is compiled. As even in times when the despotism of the ruler of the land, and the horrors arising from the inclemencies of the seasons, and when panics of epidemics and other visitations prevailed, this work escaped all injury; and moreover, as it serves to perpetuate the fame of the Buddhas, their disciples, and the Paché Buddhas of old, it is also worthy of bearing the title of Va*m*satthappakâsinî.'

As the evidence of these two passages in support of the identity of the author and the commentator of the Mahâva*m*sa seemed to me very startling, I requested Mr. Rhys Davids to copy for me the passage of the commentary.

The passage runs as follows:

Yâ ettavatâ mahâva*m*satthânusârakusalena Dîghasandasenâpatinâ kârâpita-mahâpariveṇavâsinâ Mahânâmo ti garûhi gahitanâmadheyyena there*n*a pubba-Sîhala-bhâsitâya Sîhala*tth*akathâya bhâsantara*m* eva va*gg*iya atthasâram eva gahetva tantinayânurûpena katassa imassa Padyapadânuva*m*sassa atthava*nn*anâ mayâ tam eva sannissitena âraddhâ, padesissariya-dubbu*tth*ibhaya-rogabhayâdi-vividha-antarâya-yuttakâle pi anantarâyena ni*tth*ânam upagatâ, sâ buddha-buddhasâvaka-pa*kk*ekabuddhâdîna*m* porâ*n*âna*m* ki*kk*a*m* pubbava*m*satthappakâsanato aya*m* Va*m*satthappakâsinî nâmâ ti dhâretabbâ. . . . Padyapadânuva*m*sava*nn*anâ Va*m*satthappakâsinî ni*tth*itâ.

Mr. Rhys Davids translates this:

'The commentary on this Padyapadânuva*m*sa, which (latter work) was made (in the same order and arrangement, and retaining the sense, but rejecting the dialect, of the Sinhalese commentary formerly expressed in the Sinhalese tongue) by the elder who bore the name of Mahânâma, which he had received from the venerable, who resided at the Mahâparivena built by the minister Dîghasanda, and who was well able to conform to the sense of the Mahâvamsa—(this commentary) which was undertaken by me out of devotion to that (history), and which (though thus undertaken) at a time full of danger of various kinds—such as the danger from disease, and the danger from drought, and the danger from the government of the province—has been safely brought to a conclusion—this (commentary), since it makes known the meaning of the history of old, the mission of the ancients, of the Buddhas, of their disciples, and of the Pakkeka Buddhas, should bear the name Vamsatthappakâsinî. . . .

'End of the Vamsatthappakâsinî, the commentary on the Padyapadânuvamsa.'

This shows clearly that Turnour made a mistake in translating this exceedingly involved, yet perfectly intelligible, passage, and that so far from proving that the author of the commentary was the same person as the author of the text [1], it proves the very contrary. Nay, I feel bound to add, that we might now argue that as the commentator must have lived later than 601 A.D., the fact that he too breaks off at verse 48 of chapter 37, seems to show that at his time also the Mahâvamsa did not extend as yet beyond that verse. But even then, the fact that with the restoration of the Mahâvihâra of Anurâdhapura an interest in historical studies revived in Ceylon, would clearly show that we may trust the date of Buddhaghosa, as fixed by the second part of the 37th chapter of the Mahâvamsa, at all events till stronger evidence is brought forward against such a date.

Now I am not aware of any such evidence [2]. On the contrary, making allowance for a difference of some ten or twenty years, all the evidence which we can gain from other quarters tends to confirm the date of Buddha-

[1] Dr. Oldenberg informs me that the commentator quotes various readings in the text of the Mahâvamsa.

[2] The passage, quoted by Professor Minayeff from the Sâsanavamsa, would assign to Buddhaghosa the date of 930 − 543 = 387 A.D., which can easily be reconciled with his accepted date. If he is called the contemporary of Siripâla, we ought to know who that Siripâla is.

ghosa[1]. I therefore feel no hesitation in here reprinting that story, as we find it in the Mahâva*m*sa, not free from legendary ingredients, it is true, yet resting, I believe, on a sound foundation of historical fact.

'A Brâhman youth, born in the neighbourhood of the terrace of the great Bo-tree (in Magadha), accomplished in the "vi*gg*â" (knowledge) and "sippa" (art), who had achieved the knowledge of the three Vedas, and possessed great aptitude in attaining acquirements; indefatigable as a schismatic disputant, and himself a schismatic wanderer over *G*ambudîpa, established himself, in the character of a disputant, in a certain vihâra[2], and was in the habit of rehearsing, by night and by day with clasped hands, a discourse which he had learned, perfect in all its component parts, and sustained throughout in the same lofty strain. A certain Mahâthera, Revata, becoming acquainted with him there, and (saying to himself), "This individual is a person of profound knowledge, it will be worthy (of me) to convert him;" enquired, "Who is this who is braying like an ass?" The Brâhman replied to him, "Thou canst define, then, the meaning conveyed in the bray of asses." On the Thera rejoining, "I can define it;" he (the Brâhman) exhibited the extent of the knowledge he possessed. The Thera criticised each of his propositions, and pointed out in what respect they were fallacious. He who had been thus refuted, said, "Well, then, descend to thy own creed;" and he propounded to him a passage from the Abhidhamma (of the Pi*t*akattaya). He (the Brâhman) could not divine the signification of that passage, and enquired, "Whose manta is this?"—"It is Buddha's manta." On his exclaiming, "Impart it to me;" the Thera replied, "Enter the sacerdotal order." He who was desirous of acquiring the knowledge of the Pi*t*akattaya, subsequently coming to this conviction, "This is the sole road" (to salvation), became a convert to that faith. As he was as profound in his eloquence (ghosa) as Buddha himself, they conferred on him the appellation of Buddhaghosa (the

[1] See Bigandet, Life of Gaudama, pp. 351, 381.

[2] On this vihâra, its foundation and character, see Oldenberg, Vinaya, vol. i, p. liii; Hiouen-thsang, III, p. 487 seq.

voice of Buddha); and throughout the world he became as renowned as Buddha. Having there (in *G*ambudîpa) composed an original work called *Ñ*ânodaya (Rise of Knowledge), he, at the same time, wrote the chapter called A*tth*asâlinî, on the Dhammasaṅgani (one of the commentaries on the Abhidhamma).

'Revata Thera then observing that he was desirous of undertaking the compilation of a general commentary on the Pi*t*akattaya, thus addressed him: "The text alone of the Pi*t*akattaya has been preserved in this land, the A*tth*akathâ are not extant here, nor is there any version to be found of the schisms (vâda) complete. The Sinhalese A*tth*akathâ are genuine. They were composed in the Sinhalese language by the inspired and profoundly wise Mahinda, who had previously consulted the discourses (kathâmagga) of Buddha, authenticated at the three convocations, and the dissertations and arguments of Sâriputta and others, and they are extant among the Sinhalese. Preparing for this, and studying the same, translate them according to the rules of the grammar of the Mâgadhas. It will be an act conducive to the welfare of the whole world."

'Having been thus advised, this eminently wise personage rejoicing therein, departed from thence, and visited this island in the reign of this monarch (i.e. Mahânâma, 410–432). On reaching the Mahâvihâra (at Anurâdhapura), he entered the Mahâpadhâna hall, the most splendid of the apartments in the vihâra, and listened to the Sinhalese A*tth*akathâ, and the Theravâda from the beginning to the end, propounded by the Thera Saṅghapâla; and became thoroughly convinced that they conveyed the true meaning of the doctrines of the Lord of Dhamma. Thereupon paying reverential respect to the priesthood, he thus petitioned: "I am desirous of translating the A*tth*akathâ; give me access to all your books." The priesthood, for the purpose of testing his qualifications, gave only two gâthâs, saying, "Hence prove thy qualification; having satisfied ourselves on this point, we will then let thee have all our books." From these (taking these gâthâ for his text), and consulting the Pi*t*akattaya, together with the A*tth*akathâ, and condensing them into an abridged form, he composed the work called the Visuddhimagga. Thereupon, having assembled the priesthood, who had acquired a thorough knowledge of the doctrines of Buddha, at the Bo-tree, he commenced to read out the work he had composed. The devatâs, in order that they might make his (Buddhaghosa's) gifts of wisdom celebrated among men, rendered that book invisible. He, however, for a second and third time re-composed it. When he was in the act of producing his book for the third time, for the purpose of propounding it, the devatâs restored the other two copies also. The assembled priests then read out the three books simultaneously. In those three versions there was no variation whatever from the orthodox Theravâdas in passages, in words, or in syllables. Thereupon, the priesthood rejoicing, again and again fervently shouted forth, saying, "Most assuredly this is Metteya (Buddha) himself," and made over to him the books in which the Pi*t*akattaya were recorded, together with the A*tth*akathâ. Taking up his residence in the secluded Ganthâkara-vihâra (at Anurâdhapura), he translated, according to the grammatical rules of the Mâgadhas, which is the root of all languages, the whole of the Sinhalese A*tth*akathâ (into Pâli). This proved an achievement of the utmost consequence to all beings, whatever their language.

'All the Theras and Â*k*âriyas held this compilation in the same estimation as the text (of the Pi*t*akattaya). Thereafter, the objects of his mission having been fulfilled, he returned to *G*ambudîpa, to worship at the Bo-tree (at Uruvelâya, or Uruvilvâ, in Magadha).'

Here [1] we have a simple account of Buddhaghosa [2] and

[1] Mahâva*m*sa, p. 250, translated by Turnour.

[2] The Burmese entertain the highest respect for Buddhaghosa. Bishop Bigandet, in his Life or Legend of Gaudama (Ṛangoon, 1866), writes: 'It is perhaps as well to mention here an epoch which has been, at all times, famous in the history of Budhism in Burma. I allude to the voyage which a Religious of Thaton, named Budhagosa, made to Ceylon, in the year of religion 943 = 400 A.D. The object of this voyage was to secure a copy of the scriptures. He succeeded in his undertaking. He made use of the Burmese, or rather Talaing

his literary labours written by a man, himself a priest, and who may well have known Buddhaghosa during his stay in Ceylon. It is true that the statement of his writing the same book three times over without a single various reading, partakes a little of the miraculous; but we find similar legends mixed up with accounts of translations of other sacred books, and we cannot contend that writers who believed in such legends are therefore altogether unworthy to be believed as historical witnesses.

But although the date which we can assign to Buddhaghosa's translation of the commentaries on the Pâli Tipi*t*aka proves the existence of that canon, not only for the beginning of the fifth century of our era, but likewise, though it may be, with less stringency, for the first century before our era, the time of Va*tt*agâmani, the question whether Buddhaghosa was merely a compiler and translator of old commentaries and more particularly of the commentaries brought to Ceylon by Mahinda (241 B.C.), or whether he added anything of his own[1], requires to be more carefully examined. The Buddhists themselves have no difficulty on that point. They consider the A*tth*akathâs or commentaries as old as the canon itself. To us, such a supposition seems improbable, yet it has never been proved to be impossible. The Mahâva*m*sa tells us that Mahinda, the son of Asoka, who had become a priest, learnt the whole of the Buddhist canon, as it then was, in three years (p. 37)[2]; and that at the end of the Third Council he was despatched to Ceylon, in order to establish there the religion of Buddha (p. 71). The king of Ceylon, Devânampiya Tissa, was converted, and Buddhism soon became the dominant

characters, in transcribing the manuscripts, which were written with the characters of Magatha. The Burmans lay much stress upon that voyage, and always carefully note down the year it took place. In fact, it is to Budhagosa that the people living on the shores of the Gulf of Martaban owe the possession of the Budhist scriptures. From Thaton, the collection made by Budhagosa was transferred to Pagan, six hundred and fifty years after it had been imported from Ceylon.' See ibid. p. 392.

[1] He had written the *Ñ*ânodaya, and the A*tth*asâlinî, a commentary on the Dhamma-sangani, before he went to Ceylon. Cf. Mahâva*m*sa, p. 251.

[2] He learnt the five Nikâyas, and the seven sections (of the Abhidhamma); the two Vibhangas of the Vinaya, the Parivâra and the Khandhaka. See Dîpava*m*sa VII, 42.

religion of the island. The Tipi*t*aka and the A*tth*akathâ, such as they had been collected or settled at the Third Council in 242 B.C., were brought to Ceylon by Mahinda, who promulgated them orally, the Tipi*t*aka in Pâli, the A*tth*akathâ in Sinhalese, together with an additional A*tth*akathâ of his own. It does not follow that Mahinda knew the whole of that enormous literature by heart, for, as he was supported by a number of priests, they may well have divided the different sections among them, following the example of Ânanda and Upâli at the First Council. The same applies to their disciples also. But the fact of their transmitting the sacred literature by oral tradition[1] was evidently quite familiar to the author of the Mahâva*m*sa. For when he comes to describe the reign of Va*tt*agâmani (88–76 B.C.) he simply says: 'The profoundly wise priests had heretofore orally perpetuated the Pâli Pi*t*akattaya and its A*tth*akathâ (commentaries). At this period these priests, foreseeing the perdition of the people (from the perversions of the true doctrines), assembled; and in order that the religion might endure for ages, wrote the same in books.' No valid objection has yet been advanced to our accepting Buddhaghosa's A*tth*akathâs as a translation and new redaction of the A*tth*akathâs which were reduced to writing under Va*tt*agâmani[2], and these again as a translation of the old A*tth*akathâs brought to Ceylon by Mahinda[3]. There is prima facie evidence in favour of the truth of historical events vouched for by such works as the Dîpava*m*sa and the Mahâva*m*sa so far back at least as Mahinda, because we know that historical events were recorded in the monasteries of Ceylon long before Mahânâma's time. Beyond Mahinda we move in legendary history, and must be ready to surrender every name and every date as soon as rebutting evidence has been produced, but not till then.

I cannot, therefore, see any reason why we should not treat the verses of the Dhammapada, if not as the utterances of Buddha, at least as what were believed by the

[1] On the importance of oral tradition in the history of Sanskrit literature see the writer's Ancient Sanskrit Literature, 1859, pp. 497–524.

[2] Mahâva*m*sa, p. 207; Dîpava*m*sa XX, 20.

[3] Mahâva*m*sa, p. 251.

members of the Council under A*s*oka, in 242 B.C., to have been the utterances of the founder of their religion; nor can I see that even Professor Minayeff has shaken the date of Buddhaghosa and the general credibility of the Ceylonese tradition, that he was the translator and editor of commentaries which had existed in the island for many centuries, whether from the time of Va*tt*agâmani or from the time of Mahinda.

Date of the Buddhist Canon.

We now return to the question of the date of the Buddhist canon, which, as yet, we have only traced back to the first century before Christ, when it was reduced to writing in Ceylon under King Va*tt*agâmani. The question is, how far beyond that date we may trace its existence in a collected form, or in the form of the three Pi*t*akas or baskets. There may be, and we shall see that there is, some doubt as to the age of certain works, now incorporated in the Tipi*t*aka. We are told, for instance, that some doubt attached to the canonicity of the *K*ariyâ-pi*t*aka, the Apadâna, and the Buddhava*m*sa[1], and there is another book of the Abhidhamma-pi*t*aka, the Kathâvatthu, which was reported to be the work of Tissa Moggaliputta, the president of the Third Council. Childers, s. v., stated that it was composed by the apostle Moggaliputtatissa, and delivered by him at the Third Mahâsaṅgîti. The same scholar, however, withdrew this opinion on p. 507 of his valuable Dictionary, where he says: 'It is a source of great regret to me that in my article on Kathâvatthuppakara*n*a*m* I inadvertently followed James D'Alwis in the stupendous blunder of his assertion that the Kathâvatthu was a d d e d by Moggaliputtatissa' at the Third Convocation. The Kathâvatthu is one of the Abhidhamma books, mentioned by Buddhaghosa as having been rehearsed at the First Convocation, immediately after Gotama's death; and the passage in Mahâva*m*sa upon which D'Alwis rests his assertion is as follows, Kathâvatthuppakarara*n*a*m* paravâdappamaddana*m* abhâsi Tissatthero *k*a tasmi*m* saṅgîtima*nd*ale, which simply means 'in that Convocation-assem-

[1] See Childers, s. v. Nikâya.

bly the Thera Tissa also recited (Buddha's) heresy-crushing Kathâvatthuppakara*n*a.'

This mistake, for I quite agree with Childers that it was a mistake, becomes however less stupendous than at first sight it would appear, when we read the account given in the Dîpava*m*sa. Here the impression is easily conveyed that Moggaliputta was the author of the Kathâvatthu, and that he recited it for the first time at the Third Council. 'Wise Moggaliputta,' we read[1], 'the destroyer of the schismatic doctrines, firmly established the Theravâda, and held the Third Council. Having destroyed the different (heretical) doctrines, and subdued many shameless people, and restored splendour to the (true) faith, he proclaimed (pakâsayi) (the treatise called) Kathâvatthu.' And again: 'They all were sectarians[2], opposed to the Theravâda; and in order to annihilate them and to make his own doctrine resplendent, the Thera set forth (desesi) the treatise belonging to the Abhidhamma, which is called Kathâvatthu[3].'

At present, however, we are not concerned with these smaller questions. We treat the canon as a whole, divided into three parts, and containing the books which still exist in MSS., and we want to find out at what time such a collection was made. The following is a short abstract of the Tipi*t*aka, chiefly taken from Childers' Pâli Dictionary:

I. Vinaya-pi*t*aka.

1. Vibhaṅga[4].
    - Vol. I, beginning with Pârâ*g*ika, or sins involving expulsion.
    - Vol. II, beginning with Pâ*k*ittiya, or sins involving penance.
2. Khandhaka.
    - Vol. I, Mahâvagga, the large section.
    - Vol. II, *K*ullavagga, the small section.
3. Parivârapâ*th*a, an appendix and later resumé (25 chapters). See p. xxi, n. 4; p. xxxii, n. 2.

[1] Dîpava*m*sa VII, 40. [2] Dîpava*m*sa VII, 55.

[3] Dr. Oldenberg, in his Introduction to the Vinaya-pi*t*aka, p. xxxii.

[4] Oldenberg, Vinaya-pi*t*aka I, p. xvi, treats it as an extended reading of the Pâtimokkha.

II. Sutta-pi*t*aka.

1. Dîgha-nikâya, collection of long suttas (34 suttas)[1].
2. Ma*ggh*ima-nikâya, collection of middle suttas (152 suttas).
3. Sa*m*yutta-nikâya, collection of joined suttas.
4. Aṅguttara-nikâya[2], miscellaneous suttas, in divisions the length of which increases by one.
5. Khuddaka-nikâya[3], the collection of short suttas, consisting of—
    1. Khuddakapâ*th*a, the small texts[4].
    2. Dhammapada, law verses (423)[5].
    3. Udâna, praise (82 suttas).
    4. Itivuttaka, stories referring to sayings of Buddha.
    5. Suttanipâta, 70 suttas[6].
    6. Vimânavatthu, stories of Vimânas, celestial palaces.
    7. Petavatthu, stories of Pretas, departed spirits.
    8. Theragâthâ, stanzas of monks.
    9. Therîgâthâ, stanzas of nuns.
    10. *G*âtaka, former births (550 tales)[7].
    11. Niddesa, explanations of certain suttas by Sâriputta.

---

[1] The Mahâparinibbâna-sutta, ed. by Childers, Journal of the Royal Asiatic Society, translated with other Suttas by Rhys Davids (S. B. E. vol. xi). Sept Suttas Palis, par Grimblot, Paris, 1876.

[2] The first four are sometimes called the Four Nikâyas, the five together the Five Nikâyas. They represent the Dharma, as settled at the First and Second Councils, described in the *K*ullavagga (Oldenberg, I, p. xi).

[3] Sometimes Khuddaka-nikâya stands for the whole Vinaya and Abhidhamma-pi*t*aka, with the fifteen divisions here given of Khuddaka-nikâya. In the commentary on the Brahmagâla-sutta it is said that the Dîghanikâya professors rehearsed the text of the *G*âtaka, Mahâ and *K*ulla Niddesa, Pa*t*isambhidâmagga, Suttanipâta, Dhammapada, Udâna, Itivuttaka, Vimâna, and Petavatthu, Thera and Therî Gâthâ, and called it Khuddakagantha, and made it a canonical text, forming part of the Abhidhamma; while the Ma*ggh*imanikâya professors assert that, with the addition of the *K*ariyâpi*t*aka, Apadâna, and Buddhava*m*sa, the whole of this Khuddakagantha was included in the Suttapi*t*aka. See Childers, s.v. Nikâya. See also p. xviii.

[4] Published by Childers, Journal of the Royal Asiatic Society, 1869.

[5] Published by Fausböll, 1855.

[6] Thirty translated by Sir Coomâra Swâmy; the whole by Fausböll, in Sacred Books of the East, vol. x.

[7] Published by Fausböll, translated by Rhys Davids.

12. Patisambhidâmagga, the road of discrimination, and intuitive insight.
13. Apadâna[1], legends.
14. Buddhavamsa[1], story of twenty-four preceding Buddhas and of Gotama.
15. *K*ariyâpitaka[1], basket of conduct, Buddha's meritorious actions[2].

III. Abhidhamma-pitaka.

1. Dhammasangani, numeration of conditions of life[3].
2. Vibhanga, disquisitions (18).
3. Kathâvatthupakarana, book of subjects for discussion (1000 suttas).
4. Puggalapaññatti or pannatti, declaration on puggala, or personality.
5. Dhâtukathâ, account of dhâtus or elements.
6. Yamaka, pairs (ten divisions).
7. Patthânapakarana, book of causes.

Taking this collection as a whole we may lay it down as self-evident that the canon, in its collected form, cannot be older than any of the events related therein.

There are two important facts for determining the age of the Pâli canon, which, as Dr. Oldenberg[4] has been the first to show, should take precedence of all other arguments, viz.

1. That in the Tipitaka, as we now have it, no mention is made of the so-called Third Council, which took place at Pâtaliputta, under King Asoka, about 242 B.C.

2. That in the Tipitaka, as we now have it, the First Council of Râgagaha (477 B.C.) and the Second Council of Vesâlî (377 B.C.) are both mentioned.

From these two facts it may safely be concluded that the Buddhist canon, as handed down to us, was finally closed

[1] Buddhaghosa does not say whether these were recited at the First Council.
[2] Partly translated by Gogerly, Journal of the Asiatic Society of Ceylon, 1852.
[3] Cf. Gogerly, Journal of the Asiatic Society of Ceylon, 1848, p. 7.
[4] See Oldenberg's Vinaya-pitaka, Introduction, p. xxv. The kings Agâtasatru (485–453 B.C.), Udâyin (453–437 B.C.), and Munda (437–429 B.C.) are all mentioned in the Tipitaka. See Oldenberg, Zeitschrift der D. M. G., XXXIV, pp. 752, 753.

after the Second and before, or possibly at, the Third Council. Nay, the fact that the description of the two Councils stands at the very end of the *K*ullavagga may be taken, as Dr. Oldenberg remarks, as an indication that it was one of the latest literary contributions which obtained canonical authority, while the great bulk of the canon may probably claim a date anterior to the Second Council.

This fact, namely, that the collection of the canon, as a whole, must have preceded the Second Council rests on an argument which does great credit to the ingenuity of Dr. Oldenberg. The Second Council was convoked to consider the ten deviations[1] from the strict discipline of the earliest times. That discipline had been laid down first in the Pâtimokkha rules, then in the commentary now included in the Vibhaṅga, lastly in the Mahâvagga and *K*ullavagga. The rules as to what was allowed or forbidden to a Bhikkhu were most minute[2], and they were so firmly established that no one could have ventured either to take away or to add anything to them as they stood in the sacred code. In that code itself a distinction is made between the offences which were from the first visited with punishment (pârâ*g*ika and pâ*k*ittiya) and those misdemeanours and crimes which were put down as punishable at a later time (dukka*t*a and thulla*kk*aya). With these classes the code was considered as closed, and if any doubt arose as to the criminality of certain acts, it could be settled at once by an appeal to the Vinaya-pi*t*aka. Now it so happens that, with one exception, the ten deviations that had to be considered at the Second Council, are not provided for in the Vinaya-pi*t*aka; and I quite agree with Dr. Oldenberg's argument that, if they had been mentioned in the Vinaya-pi*t*aka, the Second Council would have been objectless. A mere appeal to chapter and verse in the existing Pi*t*aka would then have silenced all dissent. On the other side, if it had been possible to add anything to the canon, as it then existed, the ten, or nine, deviations might have been con-

[1] Oldenberg, Introduction, p. xxix.

[2] Oldenberg, loc. cit. p. xx.

demned by a few additional paragraphs of the canon, without convoking a new Council.

I think we may be nearly certain, therefore, that we possess the principal portion of the Vinaya-pi*t*aka as it existed before the Council of Vesâlî.

So far I quite agree with Dr. Oldenberg. But if he proceeds to argue[1] that certain portions of the canon must have been finally settled before even the First Council took place, or was believed to have taken place, I do not think his arguments conclusive. He contends that in the Parinibbâna-sutta, which tells of the last days of Buddha's life, of his death, the cremation of his body, and the distribution of his relics, and of Subhadda's revolt, it would have been impossible to leave out all mention of the First Council, if that Council had then been known. It is true, no doubt, that Subhadda's disloyalty was the chief cause of the First Council, but there was no necessity to mention that Council. On the contrary, it seems to me that the unity of the Parinibbâna-sutta would have been broken if, besides telling of the last days of Buddha, it had also given a full description of the Council. The very title, the Sutta of the Great Decease, would have become inappropriate, if so important a subject as the first Saṅgîti had been mixed up with it. However, how little we may trust to such general arguments, is best shown by the fact that in some very early Chinese renderings of the Hînayâna text of the Mahâparinibbâna-sutta the story is actually carried on to the First Council, two (Nos. 552 and 119) mentioning the rehearsal under Ka*s*yapa, while the third (No. 118) simply states that the Tipi*t*aka was then collected[2].

[1] Loc. cit. pp. xxvi–xxviii.

[2] There are several Chinese translations of Sûtras on the subject of the Mahâparinirvâ*n*a. Three belong to the Mahâyâna school: 1. Mahâparinirvâ*n*a-sûtra, translated by Dharmaraksha, about 414–423 A. D.; afterwards revised, 424–453 (Nos. 113, 114). 2. Translation by Fa-hian and Buddhabhadra, about 415 A. D.; less complete (No. 120). 3. Translation (vaipulya) by Dharmaraksha I, i. e. *K*u Fa-hu, about 261–308 A. D. (No. 116). Three belong to the Hînayâna school: 1. Mahâparinirvâ*n*a-sûtra, translated by Po-fa-tsu, about 290–306 A. D. (No. 552). 2. Translation under the Eastern Tsin dynasty, 317–420 A.D. (No. 119). 3. Translation by Fa-hian, about 415 A. D. (No. 118).

We must be satisfied therefore, so far as I can see at present, with fixing the date, and the latest date, of a Buddhist canon at the time of the Second Council, 377 B.C. That some works were added later, we know; that many of the treatises included in the canon existed before that Council, can hardly be doubted. The second chapter of the Dhammapada, for instance, is called the Appamâda-vagga, and if the Mahâva*m*sa (p. 25) tells us that at the time when Asoka was converted by Nigrodha, that Buddhist priest explained to him the Appamâda-vagga, we can hardly doubt that there existed then a collection (vagga) of verses on Appamâda, such as we now possess in the Dhammapada and in the Sa*m*yutta-nikâya[1].

With regard to the Vinaya, I should even feel inclined to admit, with Dr. Oldenberg, that it must have existed in a more or less settled form before that time. What I doubt is whether such terms as Pi*t*aka, basket, or Tipi*t*aka, the three baskets, i.e. the canon, existed at that early time. They have not been met with, as yet, in any of the canonical books; and if the Dîpava*m*sa (IV, 32) uses the word 'Tipi*t*aka,' when describing the First Council, this is due to its transferring new terms to older times. If Dr. Oldenberg speaks of a Dvi-pi*t*aka[2] as the name of the canon before the third basket, that of the Abhidhamma, was admitted, this seems to me an impossible name, because at the time when the Abhidhamma was not yet recognised as a third part of the canon, the word pi*t*aka had probably no existence as a technical term[3].

We must always, I think, distinguish between the three portions of the canon, called the basket of the Suttas, the

---

[1] Feer, Revue Critique, 1870, No. 24, p. 377. [2] Introduction, pp. x, xii.

[3] Dr. Oldenberg informs me that pi*t*aka occurs in the *K*aṅkîsuttanta in the Ma*gg*hima Nikâya (Turnour's MS., fol. the), but applied to the Veda. He also refers to the tipi*t*akâ*k*âryas mentioned in the Western Cave inscriptions as compared with the Pa*ñk*anekâyâka in the square A*s*oka character inscriptions (Cunningham, Bharhut, pl. lvi, No. 52). In the Sûtrak*ri*d-aṅga of the *G*ainas, too, the term pi*d*aga*m* occurs (MS. Berol. fol. 77 a). He admits, however, that pi*t*aka or tipi*t*aka, as the technical name of the Buddhist canon, has not yet been met with in that canon itself, and defends Dvipi*t*aka only as a convenient term.

basket of Vinaya, and the basket of Abhidhamma, and the three subjects of Dhamma (sutta), Vinaya, and Abhidhamma, treated in these baskets. The subjects existed and were taught long before the three baskets were definitely arranged. Dhamma had originally a much wider meaning than Sutta-pi*t*aka. It often means the whole teaching of Buddha; and even when it refers more particularly to the Sutta-pi*t*aka, we know that the Dhamma there taught deals largely with Vinaya and Abhidhamma doctrines. Even the fact that at the First Council, according to the description given in the *K*ullavagga, the Vinaya and Dhamma only were rehearsed, though proving the absence at that time of the Abhidhamma, as a separate Pi*t*aka, by no means excludes the subject of the Abhidhamma having been taught under the head of Dhamma. In the Mahâkaru*n*âpu*nd*arîka-sûtra the doctrine of Buddha is divided into Dharma and Vinaya; the Abhidharma is not mentioned. But the same text knows of all the twelve Dharmaprava*k*anâni[1], the 1. Sûtra; 2. Geya; 3. Vyâkara*n*a; 4. Gâthâ; 5. Udâna; 6. Nidâna; 7. Avadâna; 8. Itiv*ri*ttaka; 9. *G*âtaka; 10. Vaipulya; 11. Adbhutadharma; 12. Upade*s*a; some of these being decidedly metaphysical.

To my mind nothing shows so well the historical character both of the *K*ullavagga and of Buddhaghosa in the Introduction to his commentary on the Dîgha-nikâya, as that the former, in its account of the First Council, should know of the Vinaya only, as rehearsed by Upâli, and the Dhamma, as rehearsed by Ânanda, while the much later Buddhaghosa, in his account of the First Council[2], divides the Dhamma into two parts, and states that the second part, the Abhidhamma, was rehearsed after the first part, the Dhamma. Between the time of the *K*ullavagga and the time of Buddhaghosa the Abhidhamma must have assumed its recognised position by the side of Vinaya and Sutta. It must be left to further researches to determine, if possible,

[1] See Academy, August 28, 1880, Division of Buddhist Scriptures.

[2] Oldenberg, Introduction, p. xii; Turnour, Journal of the Asiatic Society of Bengal, vi, p. 510 seq.

the time when the name of pi*t*aka was first used, and when Tipi*t*aka was accepted as the title of the whole canon.

Whenever we see such traces of growth, we feel that we are on historical ground, and in that sense Dr. Oldenberg's researches into the growth of the Vinaya, previous to the Second Council, deserve the highest credit. He shows, in opposition to other scholars, that the earliest elements of Vinaya must be looked for in the short Pâtimokkha rules, which were afterwards supplemented by explanations, by glosses and commentaries, and in that form answered for some time every practical purpose. Then followed a new generation who, not being satisfied, as it would seem, with these brief rules and comments, wished to know the occasion on which these rules had been originally promulgated. What we now call the Vibhaṅga, i. e. the first and second divisions of the Vinaya-pi*t*aka, is a collection of the stories, illustrating the origin of each rule, of the rules themselves (the Pâtimokkha), and of the glosses and comments on these rules.

The third and fourth books, the Mahâvagga and *K*ullavagga, are looked upon as possibly of a slightly later date. They treat, in a similar manner as the Vibhaṅga, on the rules not included in that collection, and give a general picture of the outward life of the monks. While the Vibhaṅga deals chiefly with the original so-called pârâ*g*ika, saṅghâdisesa, and pâ*k*ittîya offences, the Khandhaka, i. e. the Mahâvagga and *K*ullavagga, treats of the so-called dukka*t*a and thullaa*kk*aya crimes. The arrangement is the same, story, rule, and comment succeeding each other in regular sequence.

If we follow the guidance of the Vinaya-pi*t*aka, we should be able to distinguish the following steps in the growth of Buddhism before the Second Council of Vesâlî:

1. Teaching of Buddha and his disciples (543/477 A.D. Buddha's death).
2. Collection of Pâtimokkha rules (first code).
3. Comment and glosses on these rules.
4. Stories in illustration of these rules (vibhaṅga).
5. Mahâvagga and *K*ullavagga (Khandhaka).

6. Council of Vesâlî for the repression of ten abuses (443/377 A.D.)

7. Description of First and Second Councils in *K*ullavagga. The *K*ullavagga ascribes the settlement of the canon to the First Council, and does not even claim a revision of that canon for the Second Council. The Dîpava*m*sa claims a revision of the canon by the 700 Arhats for the Second Council.

CHRONOLOGY.

In order to bring the Council of Vesâlî in connection with the chronology of the world, we must follow the Buddhist historians for another century. One hundred and eighteen years after the Council of Vesâlî they place the anointment of King Asoka, during whose reign a Third Council, under the presidency of Tissa Moggaliputta, took place at Pâ*t*aliputta, the new capital adopted by that king, instead of Râ*g*agaha and Vesâlî. This Council is chiefly known to us through the writings of the southern Buddhists (Dîpava*m*sa, Mahâva*m*sa, and Buddhaghosa), who belong to the school of Moggalîputta (Theravâda or Vibha*gg*avâda), which ruled supreme at Pâ*t*aliputta, while Upagupta, the chief authority of the northern Buddhists, is altogether ignored in the Pâli chronicles.

Now it is well known that Asoka was the grandson of *K*andagutta, and *K*andagutta the contemporary of Alexander the Great. Here we see land, and I may refer to my History of Sanskrit Literature, published in 1859, for the process by which the storm-tossed ship of Indian chronology has been landed in the harbour of real historical chronology. We are told by the monks of the Mahâvihâra in Ceylon that Asoka was crowned, according to their computation, 146 + 18 years before the accession of Du*tth*agâmani, 161 B.C., i. e. 325 B.C.; that between his coronation and his father's death four years had elapsed (329 B.C.); that his father Bindusâra had reigned twenty-eight years[1] (357–329 B.C.), and Bindusâra's father, *K*an-

[1] Mahâva*m*sa, p. 21.

dagutta, twenty-four years (381–357). As we know that *K*andagutta, whom the Ceylonese place 381–357 B.C., was king of India after Alexander's conquest, it follows that Ceylonese chronology is wrong by more than half a century. For reasons stated in my History of Sanskrit Literature, I fix the exact fault in Ceylonese chronology as sixty-six years, assigning to *K*andagutta the dates 315–291, instead of 381–357. This gives us 291–263 for Bindusâra, 259 for Asoka's abhisheka; 259 + 118 = 377 for the Council of Vesâlî, and 377 + 100 = 477 for Buddha's death, instead of 543 B.C.[1]

These dates are, of course, approximate only, and they depend on one or two points on which people may differ. But, with that reservation, I see no ground whatever for modifying the chronological system which I put forward more than twenty years ago. Professor Westergaard and Professor Kern, who have since suggested different dates for the death of Buddha, do not really differ from me in principle, but only in their choice of one or the other alternative, which I readily admit as possible, but not as more certain than my own. Professor Westergaard[2], for instance, fixes Buddha's death at 368 (370), instead of 477. This seems a wide difference, but it is so in appearance only.

Following Justinus, who says that Sandrokyptos[3] had conquered the empire of India at the time when Seleucus laid the foundations of his own greatness, I had accepted 315[4], half-way between the murder of Porus and the taking of Babylon by Seleucus, as the probable beginning

[1] According to Bigandet, Life of Gaudama, p. 361, the era of Buddha's death was introduced by A*g*âta*s*atru, at the conclusion of the First Council, and began in the year 146 of the older Eetzana era (p. 12). See, however, Rhys Davids, Num. Orient. vi, p. 38. In the Kâra*nd*a-vyûha, p. 96, a date is given as 300 after the Nirvâ*n*a, 't*r*itîye varsha*s*ate gate mama parinirv*r*itasya.' In the A*s*oka-avadâna we read, mama nirv*r*itim ârabhya *s*atavarshagata Upagupto nâma bhikshur utpatsyati.

[2] Über Buddha's Todesjahr (1860), 1862.

[3] The Greek name Sandrokyptus shows that the Pâli corruption *K*andagutta was not yet the recognised name of the king.

[4] Mr. Rhys Davids accepts 315 B.C. as the date when, after the murder of king Nanda, *K*andragupta stept into the vacant throne, though he had begun to count his reign seven or eight years before. Buddhism, p. 220.

of *K*andragupta's reign. Westergaard prefers 320 as a more likely date for *K*andragupta, and therefore places the death of the last Nanda and the beginning of A*s*oka's royal pretensions 268. Here there is a difference between him and me of five years, which depends chiefly on the view we take as to the time when Seleucus really laid what Justinus calls the foundation of his future greatness. Secondly, Westergaard actually adopts the idea, at which I only hinted as possible, that the southern Buddhists made two A*s*okas out of one, and two Councils out of one. Trusting in the tradition that 118 years elapsed between Buddha's death and the Council under A*s*oka (at Pâ*t*aliputra), and that the Council took place in the king's tenth year (as was the case with the imaginary Kâlâ*s*oka's Council), he gets 268 – 10 = 258 as the date of the Council, and 368 or 370 as the date of Buddha's death[1].

The two points on which Westergaard differs from me, seem to me questions which should be kept before our mind in dealing with early Buddhist history, but which, for the present at least, admit of no definite solution.

The same remark seems to me to apply to the calculations of another eminent Sa*n*skrit scholar, Professor Kern[2]. He lays great stress on the general untrustworthiness of Indian chronology, and I am the last to differ from him on that point. He then places the beginning of *K*andragupta's reign in 322 B.C. Allowing twenty-four years to him and twenty-eight to his son Bindusâra, he places the beginning of A*s*oka's reign in 270. A*s*oka's inscriptions would fall about 258. As A*s*oka reigned thirty-six or thirty-seven years, his death would fall in 234 or 233 B.C. Like Westergaard, Professor Kern too eliminates Kâlâ*s*oka, as a kind of chronological A*s*oka, and the Council of Vai*s*âlî, and therefore places Buddha's death, according to the northern tradition, 100 or 110 years before Dharmâ*s*oka, i. e. 270 + 100 or + 110 = 370 or 380[3]; while, according to the southern

[1] Westergaard, loc. cit. p. 128.
[2] Jaartelling der Zuidelijke Buddhisten, 1873.
[3] See Professor Kern's remark in Indian Antiquary, 1874, p. 79.

tradition, that 118 years elapsed between Asoka's accession and Buddha's death, the Ceylonese monks would seem originally to have retained 270 + 118[1] = 388 B.C. as Buddha's Nirvâna, a date which, as Professor Kern holds, happens to coincide with the date assigned to the death of Mahâvîra, the founder of the *G*aina religion.

Here we see again that the moot point is the beginning of *K*andragupta's reign in accordance with the information supplied by Greek historians. Professor Kern places it in 322, Westergaard in 320, I myself in 315. That difference once granted, Dr. Kern's reasoning is the same as my own. According to the traditions which we follow, Buddha's death took place 100, 110, 118, or 228 years before Asoka. Hence Professor Westergaard arrives at 368 or 370 B.C. Professor Kern at 370 (380) or 388 B.C., I myself at 477 B.C. Every one of these dates is liable to certain objections, and if I prefer my own date, 477 B.C., it is simply because it seems to me liable to neither more nor less reservations than those of Professor Westergaard and Professor Kern, and because, so long as we always remember the grounds of our differences, namely, the beginning of *K*andragupta's reign, and the additional century, every one of these dates furnishes a good hypothesis to work on, until we can arrive at greater certainty in the ancient chronology of India.

To my mind all dates beyond *K*andragupta are as yet purely tentative, resting far more on a chronological theory than on actual tradition; and though I do not doubt the historical character of the Council of Vaisâlî, I look upon the date assigned to it, on the authority of the Dîpavamsa and Mahâvamsa, as, for the present, hypothetical only.

[1] When Professor Kern states that the Mahâvamsa (p. 22) places the Third Council 218 years after Buddha's death, this is not so. Asoka's abhisheka takes place in that year. The prophecy that a calamity would befall their religion, 118 years after the Second Council (Mahâvamsa, p. 28), does not refer to the Council, but to *K*andâsoka's accession, 477 − 218 = 259 B.C.

B.C.

557. Buddha born.

552. Bimbisâra born.

537–485. Bimbisâra, founder of Râgagriha, 5 years younger than Buddha, was 15 when crowned, 30 or 31 when he met Buddha in 522.

485–453. Agâtasatru (4 × 8 years).

477. Buddha's death (485 – 8 = 477).

477. COUNCIL AT RÂGAGRIHA, under Kâsyapa, Ânanda, and Upâli.

453–437. Udâyibhadra, founder of Pâtaliputra (2 × 8 years).

437–429. { Anuruddhaka (8 years). Munda (at Pâtaliputra).

429–405. Nâgadâsaka (3 × 8 years).

405–387. Sisunâga (at Vaisâlî).

387–359. Kâlâsoka.

377. COUNCIL AT VAISÂLÎ, under Yasas and Revata, a disciple of Ânanda (259 + 118 = 377).

359–337. Ten sons of Kâlâsoka (22 years).

337–315. Nine Nandas (22 years); the last, Dhanananda, killed by Kânakya.

315–291. Kandragupta (477 – 162 = 315; 3 × 8 years)[1]; Megasthenes, ambass. of Seleucus.

291–263. Bindusâra (Amitrochates).

263–259. Asoka, sub-king at Uggayinî, as pretender—his brothers killed; Daimachus, ambass. of Antiochus, son of Seleucus; Dionysius, ambass. of Ptolemy II.

259. Asoka anointed at Pâtaliputra, H. Ths. I, 160 (477 – 218 = 259).

256. Asoka converted by Nigrodha (D.V. VI, 18).

256–253. Building of Vihâras, Sthûpas, &c.

255. Conversion of Tishya (M.V. p. 34).

253. Ordination of Mahendra (born 477—204 = 273).

251. Tishya and Sumitra die (D.V. VII, 32).

242. COUNCIL AT PÂTALIPUTRA (259 – 17 = 242; 477 – 236 = 241), under Tishya Maudgalîputra (477 – 236 = 241; D.V. VII, 37).

241. Mahendra to Ceylon.

222. Asoka died (259 – 37 = 222).

193. Mahendra died (D.V. XVII, 93).

161. Dutthagâmani.

88–76. Vattagâmani, canon reduced to writing.

[1] Westergaard, 320 – 296; Kern, 322 – 298.

A. D.
400. Dîpavamsa.

420. Buddhaghosha, Pâli commentaries, 30 years later Devardhiganina, Jacobi, p. 16.

459-477. Mahâvamsa.

Though the preceding table, embodying in the main the results at which I arrived in my History of Ancient Sanskrit Literature, still represents what I hold to be true or most probable with respect to Indian chronology, previous to the beginning of our era, yet I suppose I may be expected to say here a few words on the two latest attempts to fix the date of Buddha's death; the one by Mr. Rhys Davids in the Numismata Orientalia, Part VI, 1877, the other by Dr. Bühler in the Indian Antiquary, 1877 and 1878 [1]. Mr. Rhys Davids, to whom we owe so much for the elucidation of the history of Buddha's religion, accepts Westergaard's date for the beginning of *K*andragupta's reign, 320 B.C., instead of 322 (Kern), 315 (myself); and as he assigns (p. 41) to Bindusâra 25 years instead of 28 (Mahâvamsa, p. 21), he arrives at 268 as the year of Asoka's coronation [2]. He admits that the argument derived from the mention of the five foreign kings in one of Asoka's inscriptions, dated the twelfth year of his reign, is too precarious to enable us to fix the date of Asoka's reign more definitely, and though, in a general way, that inscription confirms the date assigned by nearly all scholars to Asoka in the middle of the third century B.C., yet there is nothing in it that Asoka might not have written in 247 quite as well as in 258-261. What chiefly distinguishes Mr. Rhys Davids' chronology from that of his predecessors is the shortness of the period between Asoka's coronation and Buddha's death. On the strength of an examination of the list of kings and the list of the so-called patriarchs, he reduces the traditional 218 years to 140 or 150, and thus arrives at 412 B.C. as the probable beginning of the Buddhist era.

In this, however, I cannot follow him, but prefer to follow Dr. Bühler. As soon as I saw Dr. Bühler's first

[1] Three New Edicts of Asoka, Bombay, 1877; Second Notice, Bombay, 1878.

[2] Mr. Rhys Davids on p. 50 assigns the 25 years of Bindusâra rightly to the Purânas, the 28 years to the Ceylon Chronicles.

essay on the Three New Edicts of Asoka, I naturally felt delighted at the unexpected confirmation which he furnished of the date which I had assigned to Buddha's death, 477 B.C. And though I am quite aware of the danger of unexpected confirmations of one's own views, yet, after carefully weighing the objections raised by Mr. Rhys Davids and Professor Pischel against Dr. Bühler's arguments, I cannot think that they have shaken Dr. Bühler's position. I fully admit the difficulties in the phraseology of these inscriptions: but I ask, Who could have written these inscriptions, if not Asoka? And how, if written by Asoka, can the date which they contain mean anything but 256 years after Buddha's Nirvâna? These points, however, have been argued in so masterly a manner by Dr. Bühler in his 'Second Notice,' that I should be afraid of weakening his case by adding anything of my own, and must refer my readers to his 'Second Notice.' Allowing that latitude which, owing to the doubtful readings of MSS., and the constant neglect of odd months, we must allow in the interpretation of Buddhist chronology, Asoka is the only king we know of who could have spoken of a thirty-fourth year since the beginning of his reign and since his conversion to Buddhism. And if he calls that year, say the very last of his reign (222 B.C.), 256 after the departure of the Master, we have a right to say that as early as Asoka's time, Buddha was believed to have died about 477 B.C. Whether the inscriptions have been accurately copied and rightly read is, however, a more serious question, and the doubts raised by Dr. Oldenberg (Mahâvagga, p. xxxviii) make a new collation of the originals absolutely indispensable, before we can definitely accept Dr. Bühler's interpretation.

I cannot share Dr. Bühler's opinion[1] as to the entire worthlessness of the *G*aina chronology in confirming the date of Buddha's death. If the *S*vetâmbara *G*ainas place the death of Mahâvîra 470 before Vikramâditya, i.e. 56 B.C. + 470 = 526 B.C., and the Digambaras 605, i.e. 78 A.D. deducted

[1] Three Edicts, p. 21; Second Notice, pp. 9, 10.

from 605=527 B.C., this so far confirms Dr. Bühler's and Dr. Jacobi's brilliant discovery that Mahâvîra was the same as Nigantha Nâtaputta, who died at Pâvâ during Buddha's lifetime [1]. Most likely 527 is too early a date, while another tradition fixing Mahâvîra's death 155 years before *K*andragupta [2], 470 B.C., is too late. Yet they both show that the distance between A*s*oka (259–222 B.C.), the grandson of *K*andragupta (315–291 B.C.), and the contemporaries of Buddha was by the *G*ainas also believed to be one of two rather than one century.

When I saw that the date of Buddha's death, 477 B.C., which in my History of Ancient Sanskrit Literature (1859) I had myself tried to support by such arguments as were then accessible, had received so powerful a support by the discovery of the inscriptions of Sahasrâm, Rûpnâth, and Bairât, due to General Cunningham, who had himself always been an advocate of the date 477 B.C., and through their careful decipherment by Dr. Bühler, I lost no time in testing that date once more by the Dîpava*m*sa, that Ceylonese chronicle having lately become accessible through Dr. Oldenberg's edition and translation [3]. And here I am able to say that, before having read Dr. Bühler's Second Notice, I arrived, though by a somewhat different way, at nearly the same conclusions as those so wel worked out by Dr. Bühler in his restoration of the Episcopal Succession (therâvali) of the Buddhists, and therefore feel convinced that, making all such allowances as the case requires, we know now as much of early Bud hist chronology as could be known at the time of A*s*oka's ouncil, 242 B.C.

Taking the date of Buddha's death 477 B.C. for granted, I found that Upâli, who rehearsed the Vinaya at the First Council, 477 B.C., had been in orders sixty years in the twenty-fourth year of A*g*âta*s*atru, i.e. 461 B.C., which was the sixteenth year A.B. He must therefore [4] have been born

[1] See Jacobi, Kalpa-sûtra of Bhadrabâhu, and Oldenberg, Zeitschrift der D. M. G., XXXIV, p. 749.

[2] Oldenberg, loc. cit. p. 750.

[3] The Dîpava*m*sa, an ancient Buddhist historical record. London, 1879.

[4] Assuming twenty to be the minimum age at which a man could be ordained.

in 541 B.C., and he died 447 B.C., i.e. thirty years A.B., at the age of 94. This is said to have been the sixth year of Udâyi, and so it is, 453−6=447 B.C.

In the year 461 B.C. Dâsaka received orders from Upâli, who was then 80 years of age; and when Dâsaka had been in orders forty-five years (Dîpavamsa IV, 41), he ordained Saunaka. This would give us 461−45=416 B.C., while the tenth year of Nâgadâsa, 429−10, would give us 419 A.D. Later on the Dîpavamsa (V, 78) allows an interval of forty years between the ordinations of Dâsaka and Saunaka, which would bring the date of Saunaka's ordination to 421 B.C., instead of 419 or 416 B.C. Here there is a fault which must be noted. Dâsaka died 461−64=397 A.D., which is called the eighth year of Sisunâga, and so it is, 405−8=397 A.D.

When Saunaka had been in orders forty years, i.e. 416−40=376, Kâlâsoka is said to have reigned a little over ten years, i.e. 387−11=376 A.D., and in that year Saunaka ordained Siggava. He died 416−66=350 A.D., which is called the sixth year of the Ten, while in reality it is the ninth, 359−6=353 A.D. If, however, we take 419 as the year of Saunaka's ordination, his death would fall 419−66=353 B.C.

Siggava, when he had been in orders sixty-four years, ordained Tishya Maudgalîputra. This date 376−64=312 B.C. is called more than two years after Kandragupta's accession, and so it very nearly is, 315−2=313.

Siggava died when he had been in orders seventy-six years, i.e. 376−76=300 A.D. This year is called the fourteenth year of Kandragupta, which it very nearly is, 315−14=301.

When Tishya had been in orders sixty[1] years, he ordained Mahendra, 312−60=252 B.C. This is called six years after Asoka's coronation, 259−6=253, and so it very nearly is. He died 312−80=232 B.C., which is called the twenty-sixth year of Asoka, and so it very nearly is.

[1] I take 60 (80), as given in Dîpavamsa V, 95, 107, instead of 66 (86), as given in Dîpavamsa V, 94.

BUDDHIST PATRIARCHS.

	Birth.	Ordination.	Ordination of successor.	Death.	Age.	Patriarchate.
Upâli	(Generally 20 years before ordination)	527 (60)	461	447	94	30
Dâ*s*aka		461 45 42 40	416 419 421	397	84	50
*S*aunaka	„	416 419 421 (40)	376 379 381	350 353	86	44 (47)
Siggava	„	376½ (64)	312½	300½	96	50 (52)
Tishya	„	312½ (60)	253	233	100	68
Mahendra	273	253	„	193	80	40
						282 (284)

If we test the dates of this table by the length of time assigned to each patriarchate, we find that Upâli ruled thirty years, from Buddha's death, 477 to 447; Dâ*s*aka fifty years. To *S*aunaka forty-four years are assigned, instead of forty-seven, owing to a fault pointed out before; and to Siggava fifty-two years, or fifty-five[1] instead of fifty. Tishya's patriarchate is said to have lasted sixty-eight years, which agrees with previous statements.

Lastly, the years of the death of the six patriarchs, as fixed according to the reigns of the kings of Magadha, agree extremely well.

Upâli died in the sixth year of Udâyi, i.e. 453 − 6 = 447 B.C.

Dâ*s*aka died in the eighth year of *S*i*s*unâga, i.e. 405 − 8 = 397 B.C.

*S*aunaka died in the sixth year of the Ten, i.e. 359 − 6 = 353 B.C., showing again the difference of three years.

---

[1] The combined patriarchates of *S*aunaka and Siggava are given as 99 by the Dîpava*m*sa.

Siggava died in the fourteenth year of *K*andragupta, i.e. 315−14=301 B.C.

Tishya died in the twenty-sixth or twenty-seventh year of A*s*oka, i.e. 259−27=233 B.C.

This general and more than general agreement between dates taken from the history of the kings and the history of the patriarchs leaves on my mind a decided impression of a tradition which, though not strictly historical, in our sense of the word, represents at all events the result of such enquiries as could be made into the past ages of Buddhism at the time of A*s*oka. There are difficulties in that tradition which would certainly have been avoided, if the whole chronology had been simply made up: but there is no doubt a certain method perceptible throughout, which warns us that we must not mistake a smooth chronology for solid history.

The Title of Dhammapada.

The title of Dhammapada has been interpreted in various ways. It is an ambiguous word, and has been accepted as such by the Buddhists themselves. Dhamma has many meanings. Under one aspect it means religion, particularly the religion taught by Buddha, the law which every Buddhist should accept and observe. Under another aspect dhamma is virtue, or the realisation of the law.

Pada also has many meanings. In the Abhidhânapadîpikâ it is explained by place, protection, Nirvâ*n*a, cause, word, thing, portion, foot, footstep.

Hence dhammapada may mean 'footstep of religion,' and thus the title was first rendered by Gogerly, only that he used the plural instead of the singular, and called it 'The Footsteps of Religion,' while Spence Hardy still more freely called it 'The Paths of Religion.' It may be quite true, as pointed out by Childers, that pada by itself never means path. But it means footstep, and the footstep towards a thing is much the same as what we call the path to a thing. Thus we read, verse 21, 'appamâdo amatapadam,' earnestness is the step, i.e. the path that leads to immortality. Again, 'pamâdo ma*kk*uno padam' can hardly mean anything but that thoughtlessness is the path of death, is the path that leads to death. The commentator, too, rightly explains it here by amatasya adhigamupâya, the means of obtaining immortality, i.e. Nirvâ*n*a, or simply by upâyo, and even by maggo, the way. If we compare verses 92 and 93 of our text, and verses 254 and 255, we see that pada is used synonymously with gati, going. In the same manner dhammapada would mean the footstep or the footpath of virtue, i.e. the path that leads to virtue, and supply a very appropriate title for a collection of moral precepts. In verses 44 and 45 'path of virtue' seems to be the most appropriate meaning for dhammapada[1], and it is hardly possible to assign any other meaning to it in the following verse (*K*undasutta, v. 6):

Yo dhammapade sudesite
Magge *g*îvati sa*ññ*ato satimâ,
Anava*gg*a-padâni sevamâno
Tatîyam bhikkhum âhu magga*g*îvim,

He who lives restrained and attentive in the way that has been well pointed out, in the path of the law, cultivating blameless words, such a Bhikkhu they call a Magga*g*îvi (living in the way).'

I therefore think that 'Path of Virtue,' or 'Footstep of the Law,' was the idea most prominent in the mind of those who originally framed the title of this collection of verses. It seems to me that Buddhaghosa also took the same view, for the verse which D'Alwis[2] quotes from the introduction of Buddhaghosa's commentary,—

Sampatta-saddhammapado satthâ dhammapada*m* subha*m*
Desesi,

and which he translates, 'The Teacher who had reached the very depths (lit. bottom) of Saddhamma, preached this holy Dhammapada,'—lends itself far better to another translation, viz. 'The Teacher who had gained a firm

[1] Cf. Dhammapada, v. 285, nibbâna*m* sugatena desita*m*.
[2] Buddhist Nirvâ*n*a, p. 62.

footing in the Good Law, showed (preached) the holy Path of the Law.'

Gogerly, again, who may generally be taken as a faithful representative of the tradition of the Buddhists still preserved in Ceylon, translates the title by the 'Footsteps of Religion,' so that there can be little doubt that the priests of that island accept Dhammapada in the sense of 'Vestiges of Religion,' or, from a different point of view, 'The Path of Virtue.'

M. L. Feer[1] takes a slightly different view, and assigning to pada the meaning of foot or base, he translates Dhammapada by Loi fondamentale, or Base de la Religion.

But it cannot be denied that the title of Dhammapada was very soon understood in a different sense also, namely, as 'Sentences of Religion.' Pada means certainly a foot of a verse, a verse, or a line, and dhammapadam actually occurs in the sense of a 'religious sentence.' Thus we read in verse 102, 'Though a man recite a hundred Gâthâs made up of senseless words, one dhammapadam, i.e. one single word or line of the law, is better, which if a man hears, he becomes quiet.' But here we see at once the difficulty of translating the title of 'dhammapadam' by 'religious sentences.' Dhammapadam means one law verse, or wise saw, not many. Professor Fausböll, who in his excellent edition of the Dhammapada translated that title by 'a collection of verses on religion,' appeals to such passages as verses 44 and 102 in support of his interpretation. But in verse 42 dhammapada*m* sudesita*m*, even if it does not mean the path of the law, could never mean 'versus legis bene enarratos,' but only versum legis bene enarratum, as Dr. Fausboll himself renders eka*m* dhammapada*m*, in verse 102, by unus legis versus. Buddhaghosa, too, when he speaks of many law verses uses the plural, for instance[2], 'Be it known that the Gâthâ consists of the Dhammapadâni, Theragâthâ, Therîgâthâ, and those unmixed (detached) Gâthâ not comprehended in any of the above-named Suttânta.'

[1] Revue Critique, 1870, p. 378.

[2] D'Alwis, Pâli Grammar, p. 61.

The only way in which Dhammapada could be defended in the sense of 'Collection of Verses of the Law,' would be if we took it for an aggregate compound. But such aggregate compounds, in Sanskrit at least, are possible with numerals only; for instance, tribhuvanam, the three worlds; *k*aturyugam, the four ages[1]. It might therefore be possible in Pâli, too, to form such compounds as da*s*apadam, a collection of ten padas, a work consisting of ten padas, a decamerone, but it would in no wise follow that we could in that language attempt such a compound as Dhammapadam, in order to express a collection of law verses[2]. Mr. Beal[3] informs us that the Chinese seem to have taken Dhammapada in the sense of 'stanzas of law,' 'law texts,' or 'scripture texts.'

It should be remembered, also, that the idea of representing life, and particularly the life of the faithful, as a path of duty or virtue leading to deliverance, (in Sanskrit dharmapatha,) is very familiar to Buddhists. The four great truths of their religion[4] consist in the recognition of the following principles: 1. that there is suffering; 2. that there is a cause of that suffering; 3. that such cause can be removed; 4. that there is a way of deliverance, viz. the doctrine of Buddha. This way is the ash*t*âṅga-mârga, the eightfold way[5], taught by Buddha, and leading to Nirvâ*n*a[6]. The faithful advances on that road, padât padam,

[1] See M. M.'s Sanskrit Grammar, § 519.

[2] Mr. D'Alwis' arguments (Buddhist Nirvâ*n*a, pp. 63-67) in support of this view, viz. the dhammapada may be a collective term, do not seem to me to strengthen my own conjecture.

[3] Dhammapada from Chinese, p. 4.

[4] Spence Hardy, Manual, p. 496.

[5] Burnouf, Lotus, p. 520, 'Ajoutons, pour terminer ce que nous trouvons à dire sur le mot magga, quelque commentaire qu'on en donne d'ailleurs, que suivant une définition rapportée par Turnour, le magga renferme une sous-division que l'on nomme pa*t*ipadâ, en sanscrit pratipad. Le magga, dit Turnour, est la voie qui conduit au Nibbâna, la pa*t*ipadâ, littéralement "la marche pas à pas, ou le degré," est la vie de rectitude qu'on doit suivre, quand on marche dans la voie du magga.'

[6] See Spence Hardy, Manual, p. 496. Should not *k*aturvidha-dharmapada, mentioned on p. 497, be translated by 'the fourfold path of the Law?' It can hardly be the fourfold word of the Law.

step by step, and it is therefore called pa*t*ipadâ, lit. the step by step.

If we make allowance for these ambiguities, inherent in the name of Dhammapada, we may well understand how the Buddhists themselves play with the word pada (see v. 45). Thus we read in Mr. Beal's translation of a Chinese version of the Prâtimoksha[1]:

'Let all those who desire such birth,
Who now are living in the world,
Guard and preserve these Precepts, as feet.'

TRANSLATION.

In translating the verses of the Dhammapada, I have followed the edition of the Pâli text, published in 1855 by Dr. Fausböll, and I have derived great advantage from his Latin translation, his notes, and his copious extracts from Buddhaghosa's commentary. I have also consulted translations, either of the whole of the Dhammapada, or of portions of it, by Burnouf, Gogerly[2], Upham, Weber, and others. Though it will be seen that in many places my translation differs from those of my predecessors, I can only claim for myself the name of a very humble gleaner in this field of Pâli literature. The greatest credit is due to Dr. Fausböll; and though later critics have been able to point out some mistakes, both in his text and in his translation, the value of their labours is not to be compared with that of the work accomplished single-handed by that eminent Danish scholar.

In revising my translation, first published in 1870[3], for the Sacred Books of the East, I have been able to avail myself of 'Notes on Dhammapada,' published by Childers

[1] Catena, p. 207.

[2] 'Several of the chapters have been translated by Mr. Gogerly, and have appeared in The Friend, vol. iv, 1840.' (Spence Hardy, Eastern Monachism, p. 169.)

[3] Buddhaghosha's Parables, translated from Burmese by Captain T. Rogers, R. E. With an Introduction, containing Buddha's Dhammapada, translated from Pâli by F. Max Müller. London, 1870.

in the Journal of the Royal Asiatic Society (May, 1871), and of valuable hints as to the meaning of certain words and verses scattered about in the Pâli Dictionary of that much regretted scholar, 1875. I have carefully weighed the remarks of Mr. James D'Alwis in his 'Buddhist Nirvâ*n*a, a review of Max Müller's Dhammapada' (Colombo, 1871), and accepted some of his suggestions. Some very successful renderings of a number of verses by Mr. Rhys Davids in his 'Buddhism,' and a French translation, too, of the Dhammapada, published by Fernand Hû [1], have been consulted with advantage.

It was hoped for a time that much assistance for a more accurate understanding of this work might be derived from a Chinese translation of the Dhammapada [2], of which Mr. S. Beal published an English translation in 1878. But this hope has not been entirely fulfilled. It was, no doubt, a discovery of great interest, when Mr. Beal announced that the text of the Dhammapada was not restricted to the southern Buddhists, but that similar collections existed in the north, and had been translated into Chinese. It was equally important when Schiefner proved the existence of the same work in the sacred canon of the Tibetans. But as yet neither a Chinese nor a Tibetan translation of the Pâli Dhammapada has been rendered accessible to us by translations of these translations into English or German, and what we have received instead, cannot make up for what we had hoped for.

The state of the case is this. There are, as Mr. Beal informs us, four principal copies of what may be called Dhammapada in Chinese, the first dating from the Wu dynasty, about the beginning of the third century A.D. This translation, called Fa-kheu-king, is the work of a Shaman Wei-*k*i-lan and others. Its title means 'the Sûtra of Law verses,' kheu being explained by gâthâ, a verse,

---

[1] Le Dhammapada avec introduction et notes par Fernand Hû, suivi du Sutra en 42 articles, traduit du Tibetain, par Léon Feer. Paris, 1878.

[2] Texts from the Buddhist Canon, commonly known as Dhammapada, translated from the Chinese by Samuel Beal. London, 1878.

a word which we shall meet with again in the Tibetan title, Gâthâsaṅgraha. In the preface the Chinese translator states that the Shamans in after ages copied from the canonical scriptures various gâthâs, some of four lines and some of six, and attached to each set of verses a title, according to the subject therein explained. This work of extracting and collecting is ascribed to Tsun-*k*e-Fa-kieou, i.e. Ârya-Dharmatrâta, the author of the Sa*m*yuktâbhidharma-*s*âstra and other works, and the uncle of Vasumitra. If this Vasumitra was the patriarch who took a prominent part in the Council under Kanishka, Dharmatrâta's collection would belong to the first century B.C.; but this is, as yet, very doubtful.

In the preface to the Fa-kheu-king we are told that the original, which consisted of 500 verses, was brought from India by Wai-*k*i-lan in 223 A.D., and that it was translated into Chinese with the help of another Indian called Tsiang-sin. After the translation was finished, thirteen sections were added, making up the whole to 752 verses, 14,580 words, and 39 chapters [1].

If the Chinese translation is compared with the Pâli text, it appears that the two agree from the 9th to the 35th chapter (with the exception of the 33rd), so far as their subjects are concerned, though the Chinese has in these chapters 79 verses more than the Pâli. But the Chinese translation has eight additional chapters in the beginning (viz. On Intemperance, Inciting to Wisdom, The *S*râvaka, Simple Faith, Observance of Duty, Reflection, Loving-kindness, Conversation), and four at the end (viz. Nirvâ*n*a, Birth and Death, Profit of Religion, and Good Fortune), and one between the 24th and 25th chapter of the Pâli text (viz. Advantageous Service), all of which are absent in our Pâli texts. This, the most ancient Chinese translation of Dharmatrâta's work, has not been rendered into English by Mr. Beal, but he assures us that

[1] Beal, Dhammapada, p. 30. The real number of verses, however, is 760. In the Pâli text, too, there are five verses more than stated in the Index; see M. M., Buddhaghosha's Parables, p. ix, note; Beal, loc. cit. p. 11, note.

it is a faithful reproduction of the original. The book which he has chosen for translation is the Fa-kheu-pi-ü, i.e. parables connected with the Dhammapada, and translated into Chinese by two Shamans of the western Tsin dynasty (A.D. 265–313). These parables are meant to illustrate the teaching of the verses, like the parables of Buddhaghosa, but they are not the same parables, nor do they illustrate all the verses.

A third Chinese version is called *K*uh-yan-king, i.e. the Sûtra of the Dawn (avadâna?), consisting of seven volumes. Its author was Dharmatrâta, its translator *K*u-fo-nien (Buddhasm*ri*ti), about 410 A.D. The MS. of the work is said to have been brought from India by a Shaman Saṅghabhadaṅga of Kipin (Cabul), about 345 A.D. It is a much more extensive work in 33 chapters, the last being, as in the Pâli text, on the Brâhma*n*a.

A fourth translation dates from the Sung dynasty (800 or 900 A.D.), and in it, too, the authorship of the text is ascribed to Ârya-Dharmatrâta.

A Tibetan translation of a Dhammapada was discovered by Schiefner in the 28th volume of the Sûtras, in the collection called Udânavarga. It contains 33 chapters, and more than 1000 verses, of which about one-fourth only can be traced in the Pâli text. The same collection is found also in the Tan*g*ur, vol. 71 of the Sûtras, foll. 1–53, followed by a commentary, the Udânavarga-vivara*n*a by the Â*k*ârya Pra*gñ*âvarman. Unfortunately Schiefner's intention of publishing a translation of it (Mélanges Asiatiques, tom. viii, p. 560) has been frustrated by his death. All that he gives us in his last paper is the Tibetan text with translation of another shorter collection, the Gâthâsaṅgraha by Vasubandhu, equally published in the 72nd volume of the Sûtras in the Tan*g*ur, and accompanied by a commentary.

SPELLING OF BUDDHIST TERMS.

I had on a former occasion[1] pleaded so strongly in favour of retaining, as much as possible, the original Sanskrit forms of Pâli Buddhist terms, that I feel bound to confess openly that I hold this opinion no longer, or, at all events, that I see it is hopeless to expect that Pâlí scholars will accept my proposal. My arguments were these: 'Most of the technical terms employed by Buddhist writers come from Sanskrit; and in the eyes of the philologist the various forms which they have assumed in Pâli, in Burmese, in Tibetan, in Chinese, in Mongolian, are only so many corruptions of the same original form. Everything, therefore, would seem to be in favour of retaining the Sanskrit forms throughout, and of writing, for instance, Nirvâ*n*a instead of the Pâli Nibbâna, the Burmese Niban or Nepbhân, the Siamese Niruphan, the Chinese Nipan. The only hope, in fact, that writers on Buddhism will ever arrive at a uniform and generally intelligible phraseology seems to lie in their agreeing to use throughout the Sanskrit terms in their original form, instead of the various local disguises and disfigurements which they present in Ceylon, Burmah, Siam, Tibet, China, and Mongolia.'

I fully admitted that many Buddhist words have assumed such a strongly marked local or national character in the different countries and in the different languages in which the religion of Buddha has found a new home, that to translate them back into Sanskrit might seem as affected, nay, prove in certain cases as misleading, as if, in speaking of priests and kings, we were to speak of presbyters and cynings. The rule by which I meant mainly to be guided was to use the Sanskrit forms as much as possible; in fact, everywhere except where it seemed affected to do so. I therefore wrote Buddhaghosha instead of the Pâli Buddhaghosa, because the name of that famous theologian, 'the Voice of Buddha,' seemed to lose its significance if turned

[1] Introduction to Buddhaghosha's Parables, 1870, p. l.

into Buddhaghosa. But I was well aware what may be said on the other side. The name of Buddhaghosa, 'Voice of Buddha,' was given him after he had been converted from Brahmanism to Buddhism, and it was given to him by people to whom the Pâli word ghosa conveyed the same meaning as ghosha does to us. On the other hand, I retained the Pâli Dhammapada instead of Dharmapada, simply because, as the title of a Pâli book, it has become so familiar that to speak of it as Dharmapada seemed like speaking of another work. We are accustomed to speak of Samanas instead of *S*rama*n*as, for even in the days of Alexander's conquest, the Sanskrit word *S*rama*n*a had assumed the prakritized or vulgar form which we find in Pâli, and which alone could have been rendered by the later Greek writers (first by Alexander Polyhistor, 80-60 B.C.) by σαμαναῖοι[1]. As a Buddhist term, the Pâli form Samana has so entirely supplanted that of *S*rama*n*a that, even in the Dhammapada (v. 388), we find an etymology of Samana as derived from sam, 'to be quiet,' and not from *s*ram, 'to toil.' But if we speak of Samanas, we ought also to speak of Bâhma*n*as instead of Brâhma*n*as, for this word had been replaced by bâhma*n*a at so early a time, that in the Dhammapada it is derived from a root vah, 'to remove, to separate, to cleanse[2].'

I still believe that it would be best if writers on Buddhist literature and religion were to adopt Sanskrit throughout as the lingua franca. For an accurate understanding of the original meaning of most of the technical terms of Buddhism a knowledge of their Sanskrit form is indispensable; and nothing is lost, while much would be gained, if, even in the treating of southern Buddhism, we were to

---

[1] See Lassen, Indische Alterthumskunde, vol. ii, p. 700, note. That Lassen is right in taking the Σαρμᾶναι, mentioned by Megasthenes, for Brahmanic, not for Buddhist ascetics, might be proved also by their dress. Dresses made of the bark of trees are not strictly Buddhistic.

[2] See Dhammapada, v. 388; Bastian, Völker des östlichen Asien, vol. iii, p. 412: 'Ein buddhistischer Mönch erklärte mir, dass die Brahmanen ihren Namen führten, als Leute, die ihre Sünden abgespült hätten.' See also Lalitavistara, p. 551, line 1; p. 553, line 7.

speak of the town of *S*râvastî instead of Sâvatthi in Pâli, Sevet in Sinhalese; of Tripi*t*aka, 'the three baskets,' instead of Tipi*t*aka in Pâli, Tunpitaka in Sinhalese; of Arthakathâ, 'commentary,' instead of A*tth*akathâ in Pâli, Atuwâva in Sinhalese; and therefore also of Dharmapada, 'the path of virtue,' instead of Dhammapada.

But inclinations are stronger than arguments. Pâli scholars prefer their Pâli terms, and I cannot blame them for it. Mr. D'Alwis (Buddhist Nirvâ*n*a, p. 68) says: 'It will be seen how very difficult it is to follow the rule rigidly. We are, therefore, inclined to believe that in translating Pâli works, at least, much inconvenience may not be felt by the retention of the forms of the language in which the Buddhist doctrines were originally delivered.' For the sake of uniformity, therefore, I have given up my former plan. I use the Pâli forms when I quote from Pâli, but I still prefer the Sanskrit forms, not only when I quote from Sanskrit Buddhist books, but also when I have to speak of Buddhism in general. I speak of Nirvâ*n*a, dharma, and bhikshu, rather than of Nibbâna, dhamma, and bhikkhu, when discussing the meaning of these words without special reference to southern Buddhism; but when treating of the literature and religion of the Theravâda school I must so far yield to the arguments of Pâli scholars as to admit that it is but fair to use their language when speaking of their opinions.

DHAMMAPADA.

DHAMMAPADA.

CHAPTER I.

THE TWIN-VERSES.

1. All that we are is the result of what we have thought: it is founded on our thoughts, it is made up of our thoughts. If a man speaks or acts with an evil thought, pain follows him, as the wheel follows the foot of the ox that draws the carriage.

---

1. Dharma, though clear in its meaning, is difficult to translate. It has different meanings in different systems of philosophy, and its peculiar application in the phraseology of Buddhism has been fully elucidated by Burnouf, Introduction à l'Histoire du Buddhisme, p. 41 seq. He writes: 'Je traduis ordinairement ce terme par condition, d'autres fois par lois, mais aucune de ces traductions n'est parfaitement complète; il faut entendre par dharma ce qui fait qu'une chose est ce qu'elle est, ce qui constitue sa nature propre, comme l'a bien montré Lassen, à l'occasion de la célèbre formule, "Ye dharmâ hetuprabhavâ."' Etymologically the Latin for-ma expresses the same general idea which was expressed by dhar-ma. See also Burnouf, Lotus de la bonne Loi, p. 524. Fausböll translates: 'Naturae a mente principium ducunt,' which shows that he rightly understood dharma in the Buddhist sense. Gogerly (see Spence Hardy, Eastern Monachism, p. 28) translates: 'Mind precedes action,' which, if not wrong, is at all events wrongly expressed; while Professor Weber's rendering, 'Die Pflichten aus dem Herz folgern,' is not admissible. D'Alwis (Buddhist Nirwana, p. 70 seq.), following the commentary, proposes to give a more technical interpretation of this verse, viz. 'Mind is the leader of all its faculties. Mind is the chief (of all its faculties). The very mind is made up of those (faculties). If one speaks or acts with a polluted mind, then affliction follows him as the wheel follows the feet of the bearer (the bullock).' To me this technical acceptation

2. All that we are is the result of what we have thought: it is founded on our thoughts, it is made up of our thoughts. If a man speaks or acts with a pure thought, happiness follows him, like a shadow that never leaves him.

3. 'He abused me, he beat me, he defeated me, he robbed me,'—in those who harbour such thoughts hatred will never cease.

---

seems not applicable here, where we have to deal with the simplest moral precepts, and not with psychological niceties of Buddhist philosophy. It should be stated, however, that Childers, who first (s.v. dhamma) approved of my translation, seems afterwards to have changed his opinion. On p. 120 of his excellent Pâli Dictionary he said: 'Three of the five khandhas, viz. vedanâ, sa*ññ*â, and saṅkhâra, are collectively termed dhammâ (plur.), "mental faculties," and in the first verse of Dhammapada the commentator takes the word dhammâ to mean those three faculties. But this interpretation appears forced and unnatural, and I look upon Dr. Max Müller's translation, "All that we are is the result of what we have thought," as the best possible rendering of the spirit of the phrase mano pubbaṅgamâ dhammâ.' But on p. 577 the same scholar writes: 'Of the four mental khandhas the superiority of vi*ññ*â*n*a is strongly asserted in the first verse of Dhammapada, "The mental faculties (vedanâ, sa*ññ*â, and saṅkhâra) are dominated by Mind, they are governed by Mind, they are made up of Mind." That this is the true meaning of the passage I am now convinced; see D'Alwis, Nirwana, pp. 70–75.' I do not deny that this may have been the traditional interpretation, at all events since the days of Buddhaghosa, but the very legend quoted by Buddhaghosa in illustration of this verse shows that its simpler and purely moral interpretation was likewise supported by tradition, and I therefore adhere to my original translation. See also v. 109.

2. See Beal, Dhammapada, p. 169.

3. On akko*kkh*i, see Ka*kk*âyana VI, 4, 17. D'Alwis, Pâli Grammar, p. 38 note. 'When akko*kkh*i means "he abused," it is derived from kru*s*, not from krudh.' See Senart, Ka*kk*âyana, l. c.

On upanayhati = upanandhati, see J. P. T. S. 1887, p. 126; it would mean literally he who ties up such thoughts, that is he who holds fast to them.

4. 'He abused me, he beat me, he defeated me, he robbed me,'—in those who do not harbour such thoughts hatred will cease.

5. For hatred does not cease by hatred at any time: hatred ceases by love, this is an old rule.

6. The world does not know that we must all come to an end here;—but those who know it, their quarrels cease at once.

7. He who lives looking for pleasures only, his senses uncontrolled, immoderate in his food, idle, and weak, Mâra (the tempter) will certainly overthrow him, as the wind throws down a weak tree.

8. He who lives without looking for pleasures, his senses well controlled, moderate in his food, faithful and strong, him Mâra will certainly not overthrow, any more than the wind throws down a rocky mountain.

9. He who wishes to put on the yellow dress

---

5. Sanantana, translated by Childers by 'perpetual, ancient, primeval,' cf. Sk. sana, sanâ, sanât, sanâtana. Buddhaghosa explains it by porâ*n*aka.

6. Pare is explained by 'fools,' but it has that meaning by implication only. It is οἱ πολλοί, cf. Vinaya, ed. Oldenberg, vol. i, p. 5, l. 4. Yamâmase, a 1 pers. plur. imp. Âtm., but really a Le*t* in Pâli. See Fausböll, Five *G*âtakas, p. 38. Weber translates, 'Wir sollen uns bezähmen hier,' which may be right, but differs from Buddhaghosa.

7. Mâra must be taken in the Buddhist sense of 'tempter,' or 'evil spirit.' See Burnouf, Introduction, p. 76: 'Mâra est le démon de l'amour, du péché et de la mort; c'est le tentateur et l'ennemi de Buddha.' As to the definite meaning of vîrya, see Burnouf, Lotus, p. 548.

In the Buddhistical Sanskrit, kusîda, 'idle,' is the exact counterpart of the Pâli kusîta; see Burnouf, Lotus, p. 548. On the change of Sanskrit d into Pâli t, see Kuhn, Beiträge zur Pali Grammatik, p. 40; Weber, Ind. Studien, XIII, p. 135.

9. The dark yellow dress, the Kâsâva or Kâshâya, is the dis-

without having cleansed himself from sin, who disregards also temperance and truth, is unworthy of the yellow dress.

10. But he who has cleansed himself from sin, is well grounded in all virtues, and endowed also with temperance and truth, he is indeed worthy of the yellow dress.

11. They who imagine truth in untruth, and see untruth in truth, never arrive at truth, but follow vain desires.

12. They who know truth in truth, and untruth in untruth, arrive at truth, and follow true desires.

---

tinctive garment of the Buddhist priests. See Vish*n*u-sûtra LXIII, 36. The play on the words anikkasâvo kâsâvam, or in Sanskrit anishkashâya*h* kâshâyam, cannot be rendered in English. Kashâya means 'impurity,' nish-kashâya, 'free from impurity,' anish-kashâya, 'not free from impurity,' while kâshâya is the name of the yellowish Buddhist garment. The pun is evidently a favourite one, for, as Fausböll shows, it occurs also in the Mahâbhârata, XII, 568:

Anishkashâye kâshâyam îhârtham iti viddhi tam,
Dharmadhva*g*ânâ*m* mu*nd*ânâ*m* v*ri*ttyartham iti me mati*h*.

'Know that this yellow-coloured garment on a man who is not free from impurity, serves only for the purpose of cupidity; my opinion is, that it is meant to supply the means of living to those shavelings, who carry their virtue or the dharma like a flag.'

(I read v*ri*ttyartham, according to the Bombay edition, instead of k*ri*târtham, the reading of the Calcutta edition.)

On the exact colour of the dress, see Bishop Bigandet, The Life or Legend of Gaudama, the Budha of the Burmese, Rangoon, 1866, p. 504. Cf. *G*âtaka, vol. ii, p. 198.

10. With regard to sîla, 'virtue,' see Burnouf, Lotus, p. 547.

11, 12. Sâra, which I have translated by 'truth,' has many meanings in Sanskrit. It means the sap of a thing, then essence or reality; in a metaphysical sense, the highest reality; in a moral sense, truth. It is impossible in a translation to do more than indicate the meaning of such words, and in order to understand them fully, we must know not only their definition, but their history. See Beal, Dhammapada, p. 64.

13. As rain breaks through an ill-thatched house, passion will break through an unreflecting mind.

14. As rain does not break through a well-thatched house, passion will not break through a well-reflecting mind.

15. The evil-doer mourns in this world, and he mourns in the next; he mourns in both. He mourns and suffers when he sees the evil (result) of his own work.

16. The virtuous man delights in this world, and he delights in the next; he delights in both. He delights and rejoices, when he sees the purity of his own work.

17. The evil-doer suffers in this world, and he suffers in the next; he suffers in both. He suffers when he thinks of the evil he has done; he suffers more when going on the evil path.

18. The virtuous man is happy in this world, and he is happy in the next; he is happy in both. He is happy when he thinks of the good he has

---

13. See Beal, Dhammapada, p. 65.

15. Kili*tth*a is klish*t*a, a participle of kli*s*. It means literally, what is spoilt. The abstract noun kle*s*a, 'evil or sin,' is constantly employed in Buddhist works; see Burnouf, Lotus, p. 443.

16. Like klish*t*a in the preceding verse, vi*s*uddhi in the present has a technical meaning. One of Buddhaghosa's most famous works is called Visuddhi-magga. See Burnouf, Lotus, p. 844; Beal, Dhammapada, p. 67.

17, 18. 'The evil path and the good path' are technical expressions for the descending and ascending scale of worlds through which all beings have to travel upward or downward, according to their deeds; see Bigandet, Life of Gaudama, p. 5, note 4, and p. 449; Burnouf, Introduction, p. 599; Lotus, p. 865, l. 7; l. 11. Fausböll translates 'heaven and hell,' which comes to the same; cf. vv. 126, 306.

done; he is still more happy when going on the good path.

19. The thoughtless man, even if he can recite a large portion (of the law), but is not a doer of it, has no share in the priesthood, but is like a cowherd counting the cows of others.

20. The follower of the law, even if he can recite only a small portion (of the law), but, having forsaken passion and hatred and foolishness, possesses true knowledge and serenity of mind, he, caring for nothing in this world or that to come, has indeed a share in the priesthood.

---

19. In taking sahitam in the sense of sa*m*hitam or sa*m*hitâ, I follow the commentator who says, Tepi*t*akassa Buddhava*k*anass' eta*m* nâma*m*, but I cannot find another passage where the Tipi*t*aka, or any portion of it, is called Sahita. Sa*m*hita in vv. 100–102 has a different meaning. The fact that some followers of Buddha were allowed to learn short portions only of the sacred writings by heart, and to repeat them, while others had to learn a larger collection, is shown by the story of *K*akkhupâla, p. 3, of Mahâkâla, p. 26, &c. See Childers, s. v. sahita.

20. Sâma*ññ*a, which I have rendered by 'priesthood,' expresses all that belongs to, or constitutes a real Sama*n*a or *S*rama*n*a, this being the Buddhist name corresponding to the Brâhma*n*a, or priest, of the orthodox Hindus. Buddha himself is frequently called the Good Sama*n*a. Fausböll takes the abstract word sâma*ññ*a as corresponding to the Sanskrit sâmânya, 'community,' but Weber has well shown that it ought to be taken as representing *s*râma*n*ya. He might have quoted the Sâma*ññ*a-phala-sutta, of which Burnouf has given such interesting details in his Lotus, p. 449 seq. Fausböll also, in his notes on v. 332, rightly explains sâma*ññ*atâ by *s*râma*n*yatâ. See Childers, s. v. sâma*ññ*a.

Anupâdiyâno, which I have translated by 'caring for nothing,' has a technical meaning. It is the negative of the fourth Nidâna, the so-called Upâdâna, which Köppen has well explained by Anhänglichkeit, 'clinging to the world, loving the world.' Köppen, Die Religion des Buddha, p. 610. Cf. Suttanipâta, v. 470.

On huram, see J. P. T. S., 1884, p. 103 seq.

CHAPTER II.

ON EARNESTNESS[1].

21. Earnestness is the path of immortality (Nirvâ*n*a), thoughtlessness the path of death. Those who are in earnest do not die, those who are thoughtless are as if dead already.

22. Having understood this clearly, those who are advanced in earnestness delight in earnestness, and rejoice in the knowledge of the Ariyas (the elect).

23. These wise people, meditative, steady, always possessed of strong powers, attain to Nirvâ*n*a, the highest happiness.

---

[1] There is nothing in the tenth section of the Dhammapada, as translated by Beal, corresponding to the verses of this chapter.

21. Apramâda, which Fausböll translates by 'vigilantia,' Gogerly by 'religion,' Childers by 'diligence,' expresses literally the absence of that giddiness or thoughtlessness which characterizes the state of mind of worldly people. It is the first entering into oneself, and hence all virtues are said to have their root in apramâda. (Ye ke*k*i kusalâ dhammâ sabbe te appamâdamûlakâ.) I have translated it by 'earnestness,' sometimes by 'reflection.' 'Immortality,' amr*i*ta, is explained by Buddhaghosa as Nirvâ*n*a. Amr*i*ta is used, no doubt, as a synonym of Nirvâ*n*a, but this very fact shows how many different conceptions entered from the very first into the Nirvâ*n*a of the Buddhists. See Childers, s. v. nibbâna, p. 269.

This verse, as recited to A*s*oka, occurs in the Dîpava*m*sa VI, 53, and in the Mahâva*m*sa, p. 25. See also Sanatsu*g*âtîya, translated by Telang, Sacred Books of the East, vol. viii, p. 138.

22. The Ariyas, the noble or elect, are those who have entered on the path that leads to Nirvâ*n*a; see Köppen, p. 396. Their knowledge and general status is fully described; see Köppen, p. 436.

23. Childers, s. v. nibbâna, thinks that nibbâna here and in many other places means Arhatship.

24. If an earnest person has roused himself, if he is not forgetful, if his deeds are pure, if he acts with consideration, if he restrains himself, and lives according to law,—then his glory will increase.

25. By rousing himself, by earnestness, by restraint and control, the wise man may make for himself an island which no flood can overwhelm.

26. Fools follow after vanity, men of evil wisdom. The wise man keeps earnestness as his best jewel.

27. Follow not after vanity, nor after the enjoyment of love and lust! He who is earnest and meditative, obtains ample joy.

28. When the learned man drives away vanity by earnestness, he, the wise, climbing the terraced heights of wisdom, looks down upon the fools, free from sorrow he looks upon the sorrowing crowd, as one that stands on a mountain looks down upon them that stand upon the plain.

29. Earnest among the thoughtless, awake among the sleepers, the wise man advances like a racer, leaving behind the hack.

30. By earnestness did Maghavan (Indra) rise to the lordship of the gods. People praise earnestness; thoughtlessness is always blamed.

31. A Bhikshu (mendicant) who delights in earnestness, who looks with fear on thoughtless-

---

25. Childers explains this island again as the state of an Arhat (arahatta-phalam).

28. Cf. Childers, Dictionary, Preface, p. xiv. See Vinaya, ed. Oldenberg, vol. i, p. 5, s. f.

31. Instead of saha*m*, which Dr. Fausböll translates by 'vincens,' Dr. Weber by 'conquering,' I think we ought to read *d*ahan, 'burning,' which was evidently the reading adopted by Buddha-

ness, moves about like fire, burning all his fetters, small or large.

32. A Bhikshu (mendicant) who delights in reflection, who looks with fear on thoughtlessness, cannot fall away (from his perfect state)—he is close upon Nirvâ*n*a.

---

ghosa. Mr. R. C. Childers, whom I requested to see whether the MS. at the India Office gives saha*m* or *d*aha*m*, writes that the reading *d*aha*m* is as clear as possible in that MS. Prof. Fausböll also now writes that my conjecture is confirmed by his own MSS. also. Mr. Neumann, however, retains saha*m*. The fetters are meant for the senses. See verse 370.

32. See Childers, Notes, p. 5.

CHAPTER III.

THOUGHT.

33. As a fletcher makes straight his arrow, a wise man makes straight his trembling and unsteady thought, which is difficult to guard, difficult to hold back,

34. As a fish taken from his watery home and thrown on the dry ground, our thought trembles all over in order to escape the dominion of Mâra (the tempter).

35. It is good to tame the mind, which is difficult to hold in and flighty, rushing wherever it listeth; a tamed mind brings happiness.

36. Let the wise man guard his thoughts, for they are difficult to perceive, very artful, and they rush wherever they list: thoughts well guarded bring happiness.

37. Those who bridle their mind which travels far, moves about alone, is without a body, and hides in the chamber (of the heart), will be free from the bonds of Mâra (the tempter).

38. If a man's faith is unsteady, if he does not know the true law, if his peace of mind is troubled, his knowledge will never be perfect.

---

33. *K*itta, here translated by thought, may be rendered also by mind or heart. It is, however, incorporeal, dwells in the heart, and is opposed to the body, see Ab. 152, 338. Cf. *G*âtaka, vol. i, p. 400.

34. On Mâra, see verses 7 and 8.

35–39. Cf. *G*âtaka, vol. i, pp. 312, 400.

39. If a man's thoughts are not dissipated, if his mind is not perplexed, if he has ceased to think of good or evil, then there is no fear for him while he is watchful.

---

39. Fausböll traces anavassuta, 'dissipated,' back to the Sanskrit root *s*yai, 'to become rigid;' but the participle of that root would be *s*îta, not *s*yuta. Professor Weber suggests that anavassuta stands for the Sanskrit anavasruta, which he translates unbefleckt, 'unspotted.' If avasruta were the right word, it might be taken in the sense of 'not fallen off, not fallen away,' but it could not mean 'unspotted;' cf. dhairya*m* no*s*susruvat, 'our firmness ran away.' I have little doubt, however, that avassuta represents the Sanskrit ava*s*ruta, and is derived from the root *s*ru, here used in its technical sense, peculiar to the Buddhist literature, and so well explained by Burnouf in his Appendix XIV (Lotus, p. 820). He shows that, according to Hema*k*andra and the *G*ina-alaṅkâra, â*s*ravakshaya, Pâli âsavasa*m*khaya is counted as the sixth abhi*gñ*â, wherever six of these intellectual powers are mentioned, instead of five. The Chinese translate the term in their own Chinese fashion by 'stillationis finis,' but Burnouf claims for it the definite sense of destruction of faults or vices. He quotes from the Lalita-vistara (Adhyâya XXII, ed. Râjendra Lal Mittra, p. 448) the words uttered by Buddha when he arrived at his complete Buddhahood:—

*S*ushkâ â*s*ravâ na puna*h* *s*ravanti,

'The vices are dried up, they will not flow again;'

and he shows that the Pâli Dictionary, the Abhidhânappadîpikâ, explains âsava simply by kâma, 'love, pleasure of the senses.' In the Mahâparinibbâna-sutta, three classes of âsava are distinguished, the kâmâsavâ, the bhavâsavâ, and the avi*gg*âsavâ. See also Burnouf, Lotus, p. 665; Childers, s. v. âsavo.

That *s*ru means 'to run,' and is in fact a merely dialectic variety of sru, has been proved by Burnouf, while Boehtlingk thinks the substitution of *s* for s is a mistake. Â*s*rava therefore, or âsrava, meant originally 'the running out towards objects of the senses' (cf. saṅga, âlaya, &c.), and had nothing to do with âsrâva, 'a running, a sore,' Atharva-veda I, 2, 4. This conception of the original purport of â + *s*ru or ava-*s*ru is confirmed by a statement of Colebrooke's, who, when treating of the *G*ainas, writes (Miscellaneous Essays, I, 382): 'Âsrava is that which directs the embodied spirit (âsravayati purusham) towards external objects. It is the

40. Knowing that this body is (fragile) like a jar, and making his thought firm like a fortress, one should attack Mâra (the tempter) with the weapon of knowledge, one should watch him when conquered, and should never rest.

41. Before long, alas! this body will lie on the earth, despised, without understanding, like a useless log.

---

occupation and employment (v*ri*tti or prav*ri*tti) of the senses or organs on sensible objects. Through the means of the senses it affects the embodied spirit with the sentiment of taction, colour, smell, and taste. Or it is the association or connection of body with right and wrong deeds. It comprises all the karmas, for they (âsravayanti) pervade, influence, and attend the doer, following him or attaching to him. It is a misdirection (mithyâ-prav*ri*tti) of the organs, for it is vain, a cause of disappointment, rendering the organs of sense and sensible objects subservient to fruition. Sa*m*vara is that which stops (sa*m*v*ri*noti) the course of the foregoing, or closes up the door or passage to it, and consists in self-command or restraint of organs internal and external, embracing all means of self-control and subjection of the senses, calming and subduing them.'

For a full account of the â*s*ravas, see Lalita-vistara, ed. Calc. pp. 445 and 552, where Kshî*n*â*s*rava is given as a name of Buddha. Â*s*râva occurs in Âpastamba's Dharma-sûtras II, 5, 9, where the commentator explains it by objects of the senses, by which the soul is made to run out. It is better, however, to take â*s*râva here, too, as the act of running out, the affections, appetites, passions.

40. Anivesana has no doubt a technical meaning, and may signify, one who has left his house, his family and friends, to become a monk. A monk shall not return to his home, but travel about; he shall be anivesana, 'homeless,' anâgâra, 'houseless.' But I doubt whether this can be the meaning of anivesana here, as the sentence, let him be an anchorite, would come in too abruptly. I translate it therefore in a more general sense, let him not return or turn away from the battle, let him watch Mâra, even after he is vanquished, let him keep up a constant fight against the adversary, without being attached to anything or anybody.

42. Whatever a hater may do to a hater, or an enemy to an enemy, a wrongly-directed mind will do him greater mischief.

43. Not a mother, not a father will do so much, nor any other relatives; a well-directed mind will do us greater service.

43. See Beal, Dhammapada, p. 73.

CHAPTER IV.

FLOWERS [1].

44. Who shall overcome this earth, and the world of Yama (the lord of the departed), and the world of the gods? Who shall find out the plainly shown path of virtue, as a clever man finds the (right) flower?

45. The disciple will overcome the earth, and the world of Yama, and the world of the gods. The disciple will find out the plainly shown path of virtue, as a clever man finds the (right) flower.

---

[1] See Beal, Dhammapada, p. 75.

44, 45. If I differ from the translation of Fausböll and Weber, it is because the commentary takes the two verbs, vigessati and pa*k*essati, to mean in the end the same thing, i. e. sa*kkh*i-karissati, 'he will perceive.' I have not ventured to take vigessate for viganissati, though it should be remembered that the overcoming of the earth and of the worlds below and above, as here alluded to, is meant to be achieved by means of knowledge. Pa*k*essati, 'he will gather' (of. vi-*k*i, Indische Sprüche, 4560), means also, like 'to gather' in English, 'he will perceive or understand,' and the dhammapada, or 'path of virtue,' is distinctly explained by Buddhaghosa as consisting of the thirty-seven states or stations which lead to Bodhi. (See Burnouf, Lotus, p. 430; Hardy, Manual, p. 497.) Dhammapada might, no doubt, mean also 'a law-verse,' and sudesita, 'well taught,' and this double meaning may be intentional here as elsewhere. Buddha himself is called Mârga-dar*s*aka and Mârga-de*s*ika (cf. Lal. Vist. p. 551). There is a curious similarity between these verses and verses 6540–41, and 9939 of the *S*ântiparva :

Pushpâ*n*îva vi*k*invantam anyatragatamanasam,
Anavâpteshu kâmeshu m*ri*tyur abhyeti mânavam.

'Death approaches man like one who is gathering flowers, and

46. He who knows that this body is like froth, and has learnt that it is as unsubstantial as a mirage, will break the flower-pointed arrow of Mâra, and never see the king of death.

47. Death carries off a man who is gathering flowers, and whose mind is distracted, as a flood carries off a sleeping village.

48. Death subdues a man who is gathering flowers, and whose mind is distracted, before he is satiated in his pleasures.

49. As the bee collects nectar and departs without injuring the flower, or its colour or scent, so let a sage dwell in his village.

---

whose mind is turned elsewhere, before his desires have been fulfilled.'

Supta*m* vyâghra*m* mahaugho vâ m*ri*tyur âdâya ga*kkh*ati,
Sa*ñk*invânakam evaina*m* kâmânâm avit*ri*ptikam.

'As a stream (carries off) a sleeping tiger, death carries off this man who is gathering flowers, and who is not satiated in his pleasures.'

This last verse, particularly, seems to me clearly a translation from Pâli, and the kam of sa*ñk*invânakam looks as if put in metri causâ. See also verse 12063.

46. The flower-arrows of Mâra, the tempter, are borrowed from Kâma, the Hindu god of love. For a similar expression see Lalita-vistara, ed. Calc. p. 40, l. 20, mâyâmarî*k*isad*ri*s*â vidyutphenopamâ*s k*apalâ*h*. It is on account of this parallel passage that I prefer to translate marî*k*i by 'mirage,' and not by 'sunbeam,' as Fausböll, or by 'solar atom,' as Weber proposes. The expression, 'he will never see the king of death,' is supposed to mean Arhatship by Childers, s. v. nibbâna, p. 270.

47. See Thiessen, Die Legende von Kisâgotamî, p. 9.

48. Antaka, 'death,' is given as an explanation of Mâra in the Amarakosha and Abhidhânappadîpika (cf. Fausböll, p. 210).

49. See Beal, Catena, p. 159, where vv. 49 and 50 are ascribed to Wessabhu, i.e. Vi*s*vabhû. See also Der Weise und der Thor, p. 134.

See Fausböll, Nogle Bemerkninger. Buddhaghosa renders ahe-

50. Not the perversities of others, not their sins of commission or omission, but his own misdeeds and negligences should a sage take notice of.

51. Like a beautiful flower, full of colour, but without scent, are the fine but fruitless words of him who does not act accordingly.

52. But, like a beautiful flower, full of colour and full of scent, are the fine and fruitful words of him who acts accordingly.

53. As many kinds of wreaths can be made from a heap of flowers, so many good things may be achieved by a mortal when once he is born.

54. The scent of flowers does not travel against the wind, nor (that of) sandal-wood, or (of) Tagara and Mallikâ flowers; but the odour of good people travels even against the wind; a good man pervades every place.

55. Sandal-wood or Tagara, a lotus-flower, or a Vassikî, among these sorts of perfumes, the perfume of virtue is unsurpassed.

56. Mean is the scent that comes from Tagara and sandal-wood;—the perfume of those who possess virtue rises up to the gods as the highest.

---

*th*ayam by avinâsento; and Kern, Verhandelingen der Koninkligke Akademie, Amsterdam, 1888, p. 19.

51. St. Matthew xxiii. 3, 'For they say, and do not.'

54. Tagara, a plant from which a scented powder is made. Mallaka or mallikâ, according to Benfey, is an oil vessel. Hence tagaramallikâ was supposed to mean a bottle holding aromatic powder, or oil made of the Tagara. Mallikâ, however, is given by Dr. Eitel (Handbook of Chinese Buddhism) as the name of a flower now called Casturi (musk) on account of its rich odour, and Dr. Morris informs me that he has found mallikâ in Pâli as a name of jasmine. See also Childers, s.v.; Notes, p. 6; and Beal, Dhammapada, p. 76.

57. Of the people who possess these virtues, who live without thoughtlessness, and who are emancipated through true knowledge, Mâra, the tempter, never finds the way.

58, 59. As on a heap of rubbish cast upon the highway the lily will grow full of sweet perfume and delight, thus among those who are mere rubbish the disciple of the truly enlightened Buddha shines forth by his knowledge above the blinded worldling.

58, 59. Cf. Beal, Dhammapada, p. 76.

CHAPTER V.

THE FOOL.

60. Long is the night to him who is awake; long is a mile to him who is tired; long is life to the foolish who do not know the true law.

61. If a traveller does not meet with one who is his better, or his equal, let him firmly keep to his solitary journey; there is no companionship with a fool.

62. 'These sons belong to me, and this wealth belongs to me,' with such thoughts a fool is tormented. He himself does not belong to himself; how much less sons and wealth?

63. The fool who knows his foolishness, is wise at least so far. But a fool who thinks himself wise, he is called a fool indeed.

64. If a fool be associated with a wise man even all his life, he will perceive the truth as little as a spoon perceives the taste of soup.

65. If an intelligent man be associated for one minute only with a wise man, he will soon perceive the truth, as the tongue perceives the taste of soup.

66. Fools of poor understanding have themselves

---

60. 'Life,' sa*m*sâra, is the constant revolution of birth and death which goes on for ever until the knowledge of the true law or the true doctrine of Buddha enables a man to free himself from sa*m*sâra, and to enter into Nirvâ*n*a. See Buddhaghosha's Parables, Parable XIX, p. 134.

61. Cf. Suttanipâta, v. 46.

63. Cf. Beal, Dhammapada, p. 77.

64. The same verses occur in the Mahâbh. Sauptikap. v. 178; see also Sabhâp. v. 1945.

65. Cf. Beal, Dhammapada, p. 78.

for their greatest enemies, for they do evil deeds which bear bitter fruits.

67. That deed is not well done of which a man must repent, and the reward of which he receives crying and with a tearful face.

68. No, that deed is well done of which a man does not repent, and the reward of which he receives gladly and cheerfully.

69. As long as the evil deed done does not bear fruit, the fool thinks it is like honey; but when it ripens, then the fool suffers grief.

70. Let a fool month after month eat his food (like an ascetic) with the tip of a blade of Ku*s*a grass, yet is he not worth the sixteenth particle of those who have well weighed the law.

71. An evil deed, like newly-drawn milk, does not turn (suddenly); smouldering, like fire covered by ashes, it follows the fool.

---

67. See Beal, l. c. p. 78.

69. Taken from the Sa*m*yutta-nikâya, where, however, we read thânanhi instead of madhuvâ; see Feer, Comptes Rendus, 1871, p. 64.

70. The commentator clearly takes sankhâta in the sense of sankhyâta, 'reckoned,' for he explains it by *ñ*âtadhammâ, tulitadhammâ. The eating with the tip of Ku*s*a grass has reference to the fastings performed by the Brâhmans, but disapproved of, except as a moderate discipline, by the followers of Buddha. This verse seems to interrupt the continuity of the other verses which treat of the reward of evil deeds, or of the slow but sure ripening of every sinful act. See Childers, s. v. sankhâto.

71. I am not at all certain of the simile, unless mu*kk*ati, as applied to milk, can be used in the sense of changing or turning sour. In Manu IV, 172, where a similar sentence occurs, the commentators are equally doubtful: Nâdharma*s* *k*arito loke sadya*h* phalati gaur iva, 'for an evil act committed in the world does not bear fruit at once, like a cow;' or 'like the earth (in due season);' or 'like milk.' See Childers, Notes, p. 6.

72. And when the evil deed, after it has become known, turns to sorrow for the fool, then it destroys his bright lot, nay, it cleaves his head.

73. Let the fool wish for a false reputation, for precedence among the Bhikshus, for lordship in the convents, for worship among other people!

74. 'May both the layman and he who has left the world think that this is done by me; may they be subject to me in everything which is to be done or is not to be done,' thus is the mind of the fool, and his desire and pride increase.

75. 'One is the road that leads to wealth, another the road that leads to Nirvâ*n*a;' if the Bhikshu, the disciple of Buddha, has learnt this, he will not yearn for honour, he will strive after separation from the world.

---

72. I take *ñ*attam for *gñ*apitam, the causative of *gñ*âtam, for which in Sanskrit, too, we have the form without i, *gñ*aptam. This *gñ*aptam, 'made known, revealed,' stands in opposition to the *kh*anna, 'covered, hid,' of the preceding verse. Sukka*m*sa, which Fausböll explains by *s*uklâ*m*sa, has probably a more technical and special meaning. Childers traces *ñ*attam to the Vedic *gñ*âtram, 'knowledge.' Fausböll refers to *G*âtaka, vol. i, p. 445, v. 118.

75. Viveka, which in Sanskrit means chiefly understanding, has several meanings with the Buddhists, and among them the more technical meaning of separation, whether separation from the world and retirement to the solitude of the forest (kâya-viveka), or separation from idle thoughts (*k*itta-viveka), or the highest separation and freedom (Nirvâ*n*a). As true knowledge cannot be said to be a road to wealth, I have taken a*ññ*a, not for â*gñ*â, but for anyâ.

CHAPTER VI.

THE WISE MAN (PANDITA).

76. If you see a man who shows you what is to be avoided, who administers reproofs, and is intelligent, follow that wise man as you would one who tells of hidden treasures; it will be better, not worse, for him who follows him.

77. Let him admonish, let him teach, let him forbid what is improper!—he will be beloved of the good, by the bad he will be hated.

78. Do not have evil-doers for friends, do not have low people for friends: have virtuous people for friends, have for friends the best of men.

79. He who drinks in the law lives happily with a serene mind: the sage rejoices always in the law, as preached by the elect (Ariyas).

80. Well-makers lead the water (wherever they like); fletchers bend the arrow; carpenters bend a log of wood; wise people fashion themselves.

---

78. It is hardly possible to take mitte kalyâne in the technical sense of kalyâna-mitra, 'ein geistlicher Rath,' a spiritual guide. Burnouf (Introd. p. 284) shows that in the technical sense kalyâna-mitra was widely spread in the Buddhist world.

79. Ariya, 'elect, venerable,' is explained by the commentator as referring to Buddha and other teachers.

80. See verses 33 and 145, the latter being a mere repetition of our verse. The nettikâs, to judge from the commentary and from the general purport of the verse, are not simply water-carriers, but builders of canals and aqueducts, who force the water to go over the fields where it would not go by itself. The Chinese translator says, 'the pilot manages his ship.' See Beal, l. c. p. 79.

81. As a solid rock is not shaken by the wind, wise people falter not amidst blame and praise.

82. Wise people, after they have listened to the laws, become serene, like a deep, smooth, and still lake.

83. Good men indeed walk (warily) under all circumstances; good men speak not out of a desire for sensual gratification; whether touched by happiness or sorrow wise people never appear elated or depressed.

84. If, whether for his own sake, or for the sake of others, a man wishes neither for a son, nor for wealth, nor for lordship, and if he does not wish for his own success by unfair means, then he is good, wise, and virtuous.

85. Few are there among men who arrive at the

---

83. The first line is very doubtful. Mr. Childers writes, 'I think it will be necessary to take sabbattha in the sense of "everywhere," or "under all circumstances;" pa*ñk*akhandâdibhedesu, sabbadhammesu, says Buddhaghosa. I do not think we need assume that B. means the word vi*g*ahanti to be a synonym of va*g*anti. I would rather take the whole sentence together as a gloss upon the word va*g*anti:—va*g*antîti arahattañânena apaka*ddh*antâ *kh*andarâ*gam* vi*g*ahanti; va*g*anti means that, ridding themselves of lust by the wisdom which Arhatship confers, they cast it away.' The line means 'the righteous walk on (unmoved) in all the conditions of life.' Nindâ, pasa*m*sâ, sukha, dukkha are four of the eight lokadhammas, or earthly conditions; the remaining lokadhammas are lâbha, alâbha, yasa, ayasa. I have adopted the translation of W. Morris, see Journal of P. T. S., 1891-93, p. 41.

In v. 245, passatâ, 'by a man who sees,' means 'by a man who sees clearly or truly.' In the same manner vra*g* may mean, not simply 'to walk,' but 'to walk properly,' or may be used synonymously with pravra*g*.

84. That the last line forms the apodosis is shown by the demonstrative pronoun sa.

85. 'The other shore' is meant for Nirvâ*n*a, 'this shore' for

other shore (become Arhats); the other people here run up and down the shore.

86. But those who, when the law has been well preached to them, follow the law, will pass over the dominion of death, however difficult to cross.

87, 88. A wise man should leave the dark state (of ordinary life), and follow the bright state (of the Bhikshu). After going from his home to a homeless state, he should in his retirement look for enjoyment where enjoyment seemed difficult. Leaving all pleasures behind, and calling nothing his own, the wise man should purge himself from all the troubles of the mind.

89. Those whose mind is well grounded in the (seven) elements of knowledge, who without cling-

---

common life. On reaching Nirvâ*n*a, the dominion of death is overcome. The commentator supplies târitvâ, 'having crossed,' in order to explain the accusative ma*kk*udheyyam, but possibly pâram essanti should here be taken as one word, in the sense of overcoming.

87, 88. Dark and bright are meant for bad and good; cf. Suttanipâta, v. 526, and Dhp. v. 167. Leaving one's home is the same as becoming a mendicant, without a home or family, an anâgâra, or anchorite. A man in that state of viveka, or retirement (see v. 75, note), sees, that where before there seemed to be no pleasure there real pleasure is to be found, or vice versâ. A similar idea is expressed in verse 99. See Burnouf, Lotus, p. 474, where he speaks of 'Le plaisir de la satisfaction, né de la distinction.' On pariyodapeyya, see Childers, s. v.

The five troubles or evils of the mind are passion, anger, ignorance, arrogance, pride; see Burnouf, Lotus, pp. 360, 443. As to pariyodapeyya, see verse 183, and Lotus, pp. 523, 528; as to aki*ñk*ano, see Mahâbh. XII, 6568, 1240.

89. The elements of knowledge are the seven Sambodhyaṅgas, on which see Burnouf, Lotus, p. 796. D'Alwis explains them as the thirty-seven Bodhipakkhiya-dhammâ. Khî*n*âsavâ, which I have translated by 'they whose frailties have been conquered,' may also

ing to anything, rejoice in freedom from attachment, whose appetites have been conquered, and who are full of light, they are free (even) in this world.

---

be taken in a more metaphysical sense, as explained in the note to v. 39. The same applies to the other terms occurring in this verse, such as âdâna, anupâdâya, &c. Dr. Fausböll seems inclined to take âsava in this passage, and in the other passages where it occurs, as the Pâli representative of âsraya. But âsraya, in Buddhist phraseology, means rather the five organs of sense with manas, 'the soul,' and these are kept distinct from the âsavas, 'the inclinations, the appetites, passions, or vices.' The commentary on the Abhidharma, when speaking of the Yogâkâras, says, 'En réunissant ensemble les réceptacles (âsraya), les choses reçues (âsrita) et les supports (âlambana), qui sont chacun composés de six termes, on a dix-huit termes qu'on appelle "Dhâtus" ou contenants. La collection des six réceptacles, ce sont les organes de la vue, de l'ouïe, de l'odorat, du goût, du toucher, et le "manas" (ou l'organe du cœur), qui est le dernier. La collection des six choses reçues, c'est la connaissance produite par la vue et par les autres sens jusqu'au "manas" inclusivement. La collection des six supports, ce sont la forme et les autres attributs sensibles jusqu'au "Dharma" (la loi ou l'être) inclusivement.' See Burnouf, Introduction, p. 449.

Parinibbuta is again a technical term, the Sanskrit parinivrita meaning 'freed from all worldly fetters,' like vimukta. See Burnouf, Introduction, p. 590. See Childers, s.v. nibbâna, p. 270, and Notes on Dhammapada, p. 3; and D'Alwis, Buddhist Nirvâna, p. 75.

CHAPTER VII.

THE VENERABLE (ARHAṬ).

90. There is no suffering for him who has finished his journey, and abandoned grief, who has freed himself on all sides, and thrown off all fetters.

91. They exert themselves with their thoughts well-collected, they do not tarry in their abode; like swans who have left their lake, they leave their house and home.

92. Men who have no riches, who live on recognised food, who have perceived void and unconditioned freedom (Nirvâ*n*a), their path is difficult to understand, like that of birds in the air.

---

91. Satîmanto, Sanskrit sm*ri*timanta*h*, 'possessed of memory, but here used in the technical sense of sati, the first of the Bodhyaṅgas. See Burnouf, Introduction, p. 797. Clough translates it by 'intense thought,' and this is the original meaning of smar, even in Sanskrit. See Lectures on the Science of Language, vol. ii, p. 332.

Uyyu*ñg*anti, which Buddhaghosa explains by 'they exert themselves,' may possibly signify 'they depart,' i. e. they leave their family, and embrace an ascetic life. See note to verse 235. See also Rhys Davids, Mahâparinibbâna-sutta, Sacred Books of the East, vol. xi, p. 22.

92. Su*ññ*ato and animitto are adjectives belonging to vimokho, one of the many names of Nirvâ*n*a, or, according to Childers, s. v. nibbâna, p. 270, Arhatship; see Burnouf, Introduction, pp. 442, 462, on *s*ûnya. The Sanskrit expression *s*ûnyatânimittâpra*n*ihitam occurs in L'enfant egare, 5 a, l. 4. Nimitta is cause in the most general sense, i. e. what causes existence. The commentator explains it chiefly in a moral sense: Râgâdinimittâbhâvena animitta*m*, tehi *k*a vimuttan ti animitto vimokho, i. e. owing to the absence of passion and other causes, without causation; because freed from

93. He whose appetites are stilled, who is not absorbed in enjoyment, who has perceived void and unconditioned freedom (Nirvâ*n*a), his path is difficult to understand, like that of birds in the air.

94. The gods even envy him whose senses, like horses well broken in by the driver, have been subdued, who is free from pride, and free from appetites;

95. Such a one who does his duty is tolerant like the earth, or like a threshold; he is like a lake without mud; no new births are in store for him.

96. His thought is quiet, quiet are his word and deed, when he has obtained freedom by true knowledge, when he has thus become a quiet man.

---

these causes, therefore it is called freedom without causation. See Childers, Pâli Dictionary, p. 270, col. 2, line 1.

The simile is intended to compare the ways of those who have obtained spiritual freedom to the flight of birds, it being difficult to understand how the birds move on without putting their feet on anything. This, at least, is the explanation of the commentator. The same metaphor occurs Mahâbh. XII, 6763. Childers translates, 'leaving no more trace of existence than a bird in the air.'

95. Without the hints given by the commentator, we should probably take the three similes of this verse in their natural sense, as illustrating the imperturbable state of an Arahanta, or venerable person. The earth is always represented as an emblem of patience; the bolt of Indra, if taken in its technical sense, as the bolt of a gate, might likewise suggest the idea of firmness; while the lake is a constant representative of serenity and purity. The commentator, however, suggests that what is meant is, that the earth, though flowers are cast on it, does not feel pleasure, nor a door-step displeasure, although less savoury things are thrown upon it; and that in like manner a wise person is indifferent to honour and dishonour.

96. That this very natural threefold division, thought, word, and deed, the trividha-dvâra or the three doors of the Buddhists (Hardy, Manual. p. 494), was not peculiar to the Buddhists or unknown to

97. The man who is free from credulity, but knows the uncreated, who has cut all ties, removed all temptations, renounced all desires, he is the greatest of men.

---

the Brâhmans, has been proved against Dr. Weber by Professor Köppen in his 'Religion des Buddha,' I, p. 445. He particularly called attention to Manu XII, 4–8; and he might have added Mahâbh. XII, 4059, 6512, 6549, 6554; XIII, 5677, &c. Dr. Weber has himself afterwards brought forward a passage from the Atharva-veda, VI, 96, 3 (ya*k* *k*akshushâ manasâ ya*k* *k*a vâ*k*â upârima), which, however, has a different meaning. A better one was quoted by him from the Taitt. Âr. X, 1, 12 (yan me manasâ, vâ*k*â, karma*n*â vâ dushk*ri*ta*m* k*ri*tam). Similar expressions have been shown to exist in the Zend-avesta, and among the Manichæans (Lassen, Indische Alterthumskunde, III, p. 414; see also Boehtlingk's Dictionary, s. v. kâya, and Childers, s. v. kâyo). There was no ground, therefore, for supposing that this formula had found its way into the Christian liturgy from Persia, for, as Professor Cowell remarks (Journal of Philology, vol. iii, p. 215), Greek writers, such as Plato, employ very similar expressions, e. g. Protag. p. 348, 30, πρὸς ἅπαν ἔργον καὶ λόγον καὶ διανόημα. In fact, the opposition between words and deeds occurs in almost every writer, from Homer downwards; and the further distinction between thoughts and words is clearly implied even in such expressions as, 'they say in their heart.' That the idea of sin being committed by thought was not a new idea, even to the Jews, may be seen from Prov. xxiv. 9, 'the thought of foolishness is sin.' In the Âpastamba-sûtras, lately edited by Professor Bühler, we find the expression, atho yatki*ñk*a manasâ vâ*k*â *k*akshushâ vâ sankalpayan dhyâyaty âhâbhivipa*s*yati vâ tathaiva tad bhavatîtyupadi*s*anti, 'they say that whatever a Brahman intending with his mind, voice, or eye, thinks, says, or looks, that will be.' This is clearly a very different division, and it is the same which is intended in the passage from the Atharva-veda, quoted above. In the mischief done by the eye, we have, perhaps, the first indication of the evil eye. (Mahâbh. XII, 3417. See Dhammapada, vv. 231–234, and Nâgârguna's Suh*ri*llekha.)

On the technical meaning of tâdi, see Childers, s.v. D'Alwis (p. 78) has evidently received the right interpretation, but has not understood it. Mâd*ri*s*a also is used very much like tâd*ri*s*a, and from it mâriso, a venerable person, in Sanskrit mârsha.

98. In a hamlet or in a forest, on sea or on dry land, wherever venerable persons (Arahanta) dwell, that place is delightful.

99. Forests are delightful; where the world finds no delight, there the passionless will find delight, for they look not for pleasures.

---

98. See Childers, s. v. ninna*m*.

CHAPTER VIII.

THE THOUSANDS.

100. Even though a speech be a thousand (of words), but made up of senseless words, one word of sense is better, which if a man hears, he becomes quiet.

101. Even though a Gâthâ (poem) be a thousand (of words), but made up of senseless words, one word of a Gâthâ is better, which if a man hears, he becomes quiet.

102. Though a man recite a hundred Gâthâs made up of senseless words, one word of the law is better, which if a man hears, he becomes quiet.

103. If one man conquer in battle a thousand times thousand men, and if another conquer himself, he is the greatest of conquerors.

104, 105. One's own self conquered is better than all other people; not even a god, a Gandharva, not Mâra with Brahman could change into defeat the

---

100. This Sahasravarga, or Chapter of the Thousands, is quoted by that name in the Mahâvastu (Minayeff, Mélanges Asiatiques, VI, p. 583): Teshâm Bhagavâñ *g*a*t*ilânâ*m* Dharmapadeshu sahasravargam bhâshati: 'Sahasram api vâ*k*ânâm anarthapadasa*m*hitânâm, ekârthavatî *s*reyâ yâ*m* *s*rutvâ upa*s*âmyati. Sahasram api gâthânâm anarthapadasa*m*hitânâm, ekârthavatî *s*reyâ yâ*m* *s*rutvâ upa*s*âmyati' (MS. R. A. S. Lond.) Here the Pâli text seems decidedly more original and perfect.

104. *G*ita*m*, according to the commentator, stands for *g*ito (liṅgavipallâso, i. e. viparyâsa); see also Senart in Journal Asiatique, 1880, p. 500.

The Devas (gods), Gandharvas (fairies), and other fanciful beings of the Brahmanic religion, such as the Nâgas, Sarpas, Garu*d*as, &c.,

victory of a man who has vanquished himself, and always lives under restraint.

106. If a man for a hundred years sacrifice month by month with a thousand, and if he but for one moment pay homage to a man whose soul is grounded (in true knowledge), better is that homage than a sacrifice for a hundred years.

107. If a man for a hundred years worship Agni (fire) in the forest, and if he but for one moment pay homage to a man whose soul is grounded (in true knowledge), better is that homage than sacrifice for a hundred years.

108. Whatever a man sacrifice in this world as an offering or as an oblation for a whole year in order to gain merit, the whole of it is not worth a quarter (a farthing); reverence shown to the righteous is better.

---

were allowed to continue in the traditional language of the people who had embraced Buddhism. See the pertinent remarks of Burnouf, Introduction, pp. 134 seq., 184. On Mâra, the tempter, see v. 7. Sâstram Aiyar, On the *G*aina Religion, p. xx, says: 'Moreover "as it is declared in the *G*aina Vedas that all the gods worshipped by the various Hindu sects, viz. *S*iva, Brahma, Vish*n*u, Ga*n*apati, Subramaniyan, and others, were devoted adherents of the above-mentioned Tîrthaṅkaras, the *G*ainas therefore do not consider them as unworthy of their worship; but as they are servants of Arugan, they consider them to be deities of their system, and accordingly perform certain pû*g*âs in honour of them, and worship them also.' The case is more doubtful with orthodox Buddhists.

Orthodox Buddhists,' as Mr. D'Alwis writes (Attanagalu-vansa, p. 55), 'do not consider the worship of the Devas as being sanctioned by him who disclaimed for himself and all the Devas any power over man's soul. Yet the Buddhists are everywhere idol-worshippers. Buddhism, however, acknowledges the existence of some of the Hindu deities, and from the various friendly offices which those Devas are said to have rendered to Gotama, Buddhists evince a respect for their idols.' See also Buddhaghosha's Parables, p. 162.

109. He who always greets and constantly reveres the aged, four things will increase to him, viz. life, beauty, happiness, power.

110. But he who lives a hundred years, vicious and unrestrained, a life of one day is better if a man is virtuous and reflecting.

111. And he who lives a hundred years, ignorant and unrestrained, a life of one day is better if a man is wise and reflecting.

112. And he who lives a hundred years, idle and weak, a life of one day is better if a man has attained firm strength.

113. And he who lives a hundred years, not seeing beginning and end, a life of one day is better if a man sees beginning and end.

114. And he who lives a hundred years, not seeing the immortal place, a life of one day is better if a man sees the immortal place.

115. And he who lives a hundred years, not seeing the highest law, a life of one day is better if a man sees the highest law.

---

109. Dr. Fausböll, in a most important note, called attention to the fact that the same verse, with slight variations, occurs in Manu. We there read, II, 121:

Abhivâdana*s*îlasya nitya*m* v*ri*ddhopasevina*h*,
*K*atvâri sampravardhante âyur vidyâ ya*s*o balam.

Here the four things are, life, knowledge, glory, power.

In the Âpastamba-sûtras, I, 2, 5, 15, the reward promised for the same virtue is svargam âyus *k*a, 'heaven and long life.' It seems, therefore, as if the original idea of this verse came from the Brahmans, and was afterwards adopted by the Buddhists. See Mahâbh. V, 1398; Weber, Ind. Stud. XIII, p. 405. How largely it spread is shown by Dr. Fausböll from the Asiatic Researches, XX, p. 259, where the same verse of the Dhammapada is mentioned as being widely in use among the Buddhists of Siam.

112. On kusîto, see note to verse 7.

CHAPTER IX.

EVIL.

116. A man should hasten towards the good, and should keep his thought away from evil; if a man does what is good slothfully, his mind delights in evil.

117. If a man commits a sin, let him not do it again; let him not delight in sin: the accumulation of evil is painful.

118. If a man does what is good, let him do it again; let him delight in it: the accumulation of good is delightful.

119. Even an evil-doer sees happiness so long as his evil deed does not ripen; but when his evil deed ripens, then does the evil-doer see evil.

120. Even a good man sees evil days so long as his good deed does not ripen; but when his good deed ripens, then does the good man see good things.

121. Let no man think lightly of evil, saying in his heart, It will not come nigh unto me. Even by the falling of water-drops a water-pot is filled; the fool becomes full of evil, even if he gather it little by little.

122. Let no man think lightly of good, saying in his heart, It will not come nigh unto me. Even by the falling of water-drops a water-pot is filled; the wise man becomes full of good, even if he gather it little by little.

123. Let a man avoid evil deeds, as a merchant, if he has few companions and carries much wealth,

avoids a dangerous road; as a man who loves life avoids poison.

124. He who has no wound on his hand, may touch poison with his hand; poison does not affect one who has no wound; nor is there evil for one who does not commit evil.

125. If a man offend a harmless, pure, and innocent person, the evil falls back upon that fool, like light dust thrown up against the wind.

126. Some people are born again; evil-doers go to hell; righteous people go to heaven; those who are free from all worldly desires attain Nirvâ*n*a.

127. Not in the sky, not in the midst of the sea, not if we enter into the clefts of the mountains, is there known a spot in the whole world where a man might be freed from an evil deed.

128. Not in the sky, not in the midst of the sea, not if we enter into the clefts of the mountains, is there known a spot in the whole world where death could not overcome (the mortal).

---

125. Cf. Suttanipâta, v. 661; Indische Sprüche, 1582; Kathâsaritsâgara, 49, 222.

126. For a description of hell and its long, yet not endless sufferings, see Buddhaghosha's Parables, p. 132. The pleasures of heaven, too, are frequently described in these Parables and elsewhere. Buddha himself enjoyed these pleasures of heaven, before he was born for the last time. It is probably when good and evil deeds are equally balanced, that men are born again as human beings; this, at least, is the opinion of the *G*ainas. Cf. Chintâma*n*i, ed. H. Bower, Introd. p. xv.

127. Cf. St. Luke xii. 2, 'For there is nothing covered that shall not be revealed;' and Psalm cxxxix. 8–12.

CHAPTER X.

PUNISHMENT.

129. All men tremble at punishment, all men fear death; remember that you are like unto them, and do not kill, nor cause slaughter.

130. All men tremble at punishment, all men love life; remember that thou art like unto them, and do not kill, nor cause slaughter.

131. He who, seeking his own happiness, punishes or kills beings who also long for happiness, will not find happiness after death.

---

129. One feels tempted, no doubt, to take upama in the sense of 'the nearest (der Nächste), the neighbour,' and to translate, 'having made oneself one's neighbour,' i. e. loving one's neighbour as oneself. But as upamăm, with a short a, is the correct accusative of upamâ, we must translate, 'having made oneself the likeness, the image of others, having placed oneself in the place of others.' This is an expression which occurs frequently in Sanskrit; cf. Hitopadesa I, 11:

Prâ*n*â yathâtmano*bhîsh*t*â bhûtânâm api te tathâ,
Âtmaupamyena bhûteshu dayâ*m* kurvanti sâdhava*h*.

'As life is dear to oneself, it is dear also to other living beings: by comparing oneself with others, good people bestow pity on all beings.'

See also Hit. I, 12; Râm. V, 23, 5, âtmânam upamâ*m* k*ri*tvâ sveshu dâreshu ramyatâm, 'making oneself a likeness, i.e. putting oneself in the position of other people, it is right to love none but one's own wife.' Dr. Fausböll has called attention to similar passages in the Mahâbhârata, XIII, 5569 seq.

130. Cf. St. Luke vi. 31.

131. Dr. Fausböll points out the striking similarity between this verse and two verses occurring in Manu and the Mahâbhârata:—

132. He who seeking his own happiness does not punish or kill beings who also long for happiness, will find happiness after death.

133. Do not speak harshly to anybody; those who are spoken to will answer thee in the same way. Angry speech is painful, blows for blows will touch thee.

134. If, like a shattered metal plate (gong), thou utter nothing, then thou hast reached Nirvâ*n*a; anger is not known to thee.

135. As a cowherd with his staff drives his cows into the stable, so do Age and Death drive the life of men.

136. A fool does not know when he commits his evil deeds: but the wicked man burns by his own deeds, as if burnt by fire.

137. He who inflicts pain on innocent and harmless persons, will soon come to one of these ten states:

Manu V, 45:

Yo*hi*m*sakâni bhûtâni hinasty âtmasukhe*kkh*ayâ,

Sa *g*îva*ms* *k*a m*ri*ta*s* *k*aiva na kva*k*it sukham edhate.

Mahâbhârata XIII, 5568:

Ahi*m*sakâni bhûtâni da*nd*ena vinihanti ya*h*,

Âtmana*h* sukham i*kkh*an sa pretya naiva sukhî bhavet.

If it were not for ahi*m*sakâni, in which Manu and the Mahâbhârata agree, I should say that the verses in both were Sanskrit modifications of the Pâli original. The verse in the Mahâbhârata presupposes the verse of the Dhammapada.

133. See Mahâbhârata XII, 4056.

134. See Childers, s.v. nibbâna, p. 270, and s.v. kâ*m*so; D'Alwis, Buddhist Nirvâ*n*a, p. 35.

136. The metaphor of 'burning' for 'suffering' is very common in Buddhist literature. Everything burns, i. e. everything suffers, was one of the first experiences of Buddha himself. See v. 146.

138. He will have cruel suffering, loss, injury of the body, heavy affliction, or loss of mind,

139. Or a misfortune coming from the king, or a fearful accusation, or loss of relations, or destruction of treasures,

140. Or lightning-fire will burn his houses; and when his body is destroyed, the fool will go to hell.

141. Not nakedness, not platted hair, not dirt, not fasting, or lying on the earth, not rubbing with dust,

138. 'Cruel suffering' is explained by sîsaroga, 'headache,' &c. 'Loss' is taken for loss of money. 'Injury of the body' is held to be the cutting off of the arm, and other limbs. 'Heavy afflictions' are, again, various kinds of diseases.

139. Upasarga means 'accident, misfortune.' Dr. Fausböll translates râ*g*ato va upassaggam by 'fulgentis (lunae) defectionem;' Dr. Weber by 'Bestrafung vom König;' Beal by 'some governmental difficulty.' Abbhakkhânam, Sanskrit abhyâkhyânam, is a heavy accusation for high treason, or similar offences. Beal translates, 'some false accusation.' The 'destruction of pleasures or treasures' is explained by gold being changed to coals (see Buddhaghosha's Parables, p. 98; Thiessen, Kisâgotamî, p. 6), pearls to cotton seed, corn to potsherds, and by men and cattle becoming blind, lame, &c.

141. Cf. Hibbert Lectures, p. 355. Dr. Fausböll has pointed out that the same or a very similar verse occurs in a legend taken from the Divyâvadâna, and translated by Burnouf (Introduction, p. 313 seq.) Burnouf translates the verse: 'Ce n'est ni la coutume de marcher nu, ni les cheveux nattés, ni l'usage d'argile, ni le choix des diverses especes d'aliments, ni l'habitude de coucher sur la terre nue, ni la poussière, ni la malpropreté, ni l'attention à fuir l'abri d'un toit, qui sont capables de dissiper le trouble dans lequel nous jettent les désirs non-satisfaits; mais qu'un homme, maître de ses sens, calme, recueilli, chaste, évitant de faire du mal à aucune créature, accomplisse la Loi, et il sera, quoique paré d'ornements, un Brâhmane, un Cramana, un Religieux.' See also Suttanipâta, v. 248.

Walking naked and the other things mentioned in our verse are outward signs of a saintly life, and these Buddha rejects because they do not calm the passions. Nakedness he seems to have

not sitting motionless, can purify a mortal who has not overcome desires.

142. He who, though dressed in fine apparel, exercises tranquillity, is quiet, subdued, restrained, chaste, and has ceased to find fault with all other beings, he indeed is a Brâhma*n*a, an ascetic (*s*rama*n*a), a friar (bhikshu).

143. Is there in this world any man so restrained by shame that he does not provoke reproof, as a noble horse the whip?

144. Like a noble horse when touched by the

---

rejected on other grounds too, if we may judge from the Sumâgadhâ-avadâna: 'A number of naked friars were assembled in the house of the daughter of Anâtha-pi*nd*ika. She called her daughter-in-law, Sumâgadhâ, and said, "Go and see those highly respectable persons." Sumâgadhâ, expecting to see some of the saints, like *S*âriputra, Maudgalyâyana, and others, ran out full of joy. But when she saw these friars with their hair like pigeon wings, covered by nothing but dirt, offensive, and looking like demons, she became sad. "Why are you sad?" said her mother-in-law. Sumâgadhâ replied, "O mother, if these are saints, what must sinners be like?"'

Burnouf (Introduction, p. 312) supposed that the *G*ainas only, and not the Buddhists, allowed nakedness. But the *G*ainas, too, do not allow it universally. They are divided into two parties, the *S*vetambaras and Digambaras. The *S*vetambaras, clad in white, are the followers of Par*s*vanâtha, and wear clothes. The Digambaras, i. e. sky-clad, disrobed, are followers of Mahâvîra, resident chiefly in Southern India. At present they, too, wear clothing, but not when eating. See Sâstram Aiyar, p. xxi.

The *ga*t*â*, or the hair platted and gathered up in a knot, was a sign of a *S*aiva ascetic. The sitting motionless is one of the postures assumed by ascetics. Clough explains ukku*t*ika as 'the act of sitting on the heels;' Wilson gives for utka*t*ukâsana, 'sitting on the hams.' See Fausböll, note on verse 140.

142. This verse has to be taken in connection with the preceding verse, to show that though a man cares about his outward appearance and is well dressed, he may be a true disciple for all that, if only he practises virtue. As to da*nd*anidhâna, see Mahâbh. XII, 6559, and Suttanipâta, v. 34.

whip, be ye strenuous and eager, and by faith, by virtue, by energy, by meditation, by discernment of the law you will overcome this great pain, perfect in knowledge and in behaviour, and never forgetful.

145. Well-makers lead the water (wherever they like); fletchers bend the arrow; carpenters bend a log of wood; good people fashion themselves.

---

145. The same as verse 80. According to Fausböll and Subhûti we ought to render the verses by, 'What man is there found on earth so restrained by shame that he never provokes reproof, as a good horse the whip?' See, however, Childers, s.v. appabodhati. Fausböll maintains his view.

CHAPTER XI.

OLD AGE.

146. How is there laughter, how is there joy, as this world is always burning? Do you not seek a light, ye who are surrounded by darkness?

147. Look at this dressed-up lump, covered with wounds, joined together, sickly, full of many schemes, but which has no strength, no hold!

148. This body is wasted, full of sickness, and frail; this heap of corruption breaks to pieces, life indeed ends in death.

---

148. Dr. Fausböll informs me that Childers proposed the emendation mara*n*anta*m* hi *g*îvita*m*. The following extract from a letter, addressed by Childers to Dr. Fausböll, will be read with interest:—'As regards Dhp. v. 148, I have no doubt whatever. I quite agree with you that the idea (mors est vita ejus) is a profound and noble one, but the question is, Is the idea there? I think not. Mara*n*a*m* tamhi *g*îvita*m* is not Pâli, I mean not a Pâli construction, and years ago even it grated on my ear as a harsh phrase. The reading of your MSS. of the texts is nothing; your MSS. of Dhammapada are very bad ones, and it is merely the vicious Sinhalese spelling of bad MSS., like kamma*m*ta*m* for kammanta*m*. But the comment sets the question at rest at once, for it explains mara*n*anta*m* by mara*n*a-pariyosâna*m*, which is exactly the same. I see there is one serious difficulty left, that all your MSS. seem to have tamhi, and not ta*m* hi; but are you sure it is so? There was a Dhammapada in the India Office Library, and I had a great hunt for it a few days ago, but to my deep disappointment it is missing. I do not agree with you that the sentence "All Life is bounded by Death," is trivial: it is a truism, but half the noblest passages in poetry are truisms, and unless I greatly mistake, this very passage will be found in many other literatures.'

Dr. Fausböll adds:—

'I have still the same doubt as before, because of all my

149. After one has looked at those grey bones, thrown away like gourds in the autumn, what pleasure is there (left in life)!

150. After a stronghold has been made of the bones, it is covered with flesh and blood, and there dwell in it old age and death, pride and deceit.

151. The brilliant chariots of kings are destroyed, the body also approaches destruction, but the virtue of good people never approaches destruction,—thus do the good say to the good.

152. A man who has learnt little, grows old like an ox; his flesh grows, but his knowledge does not grow.

153, 154. Looking for the maker of this tabernacle, I have run through a course of many births,

---

MSS. reading mara*n*a*m* tamhi. I do not know the readings of the London MSS. The explanation of the commentary does not settle the question, as it may as well be considered an explanation of my reading as of the reading which Childers proposed.—V. Fausböll.'

Fausböll has now surrendered his doubts, and he produces himself a number of passages where this phrase mara*n*ânta*m* hi *g*îvanam occurs, e.g. Mahâbh. (ed. Calcutta), XI, 48; 207; XII, 829; Râmây. (ed. Bombay), Ayodhyâk., p. 197; Divyâvadâna, p. 27; 100.

149. In the Rudrâya*n*âvadâna of the Divyâvadâna this verse appears as,

Yânîmâny apariddhâni vikshiptâni di*s*o di*s*a*h*,
Kapotavar*n*âny asthîni tâni d*ri*sh*t*vaiha kâ rati*h*.

See Schiefner, Mél. Asiat. VIII, p. 589; *G*âtaka, vol. i, p. 322.

150. The expression ma*m*salohitalepanam is curiously like the expression used in Manu VI, 76, mâ*m*sa*s*o*n*italepanam, and in several passages of the Mahâbhârata, XII, 12462, 12053, as pointed out by Dr. Fausböll.

153, 154. These two verses are famous among Buddhists, for they are the words which the founder of Buddhism is supposed to have uttered at the moment he attained to Buddhahood. (See Spence Hardy, Manual, p. 180.) According to the Lalita-vistara,

not finding him; and painful is birth again and again. But now, maker of the tabernacle, thou hast been seen; thou shalt not make up this tabernacle again. All thy rafters are broken, thy ridge-pole is sundered; the mind, approaching the Eternal

---

however, the words uttered on that solemn occasion were those quoted in the note to verse 39. In the commentary on the Brahma*g*âla this verse is called the first speech of Buddha, his last speech being the words in the Mahâparinibbâna-sutta, 'Life is subject to age; strive in earnest, &c.' The words used in the Mahâparinibbâna-sutta, Chap. IV, 2, *K*atunna*m* dhammânam ananubodhâ appa*t*ivedhâ evam ida*m* dîgham addhâna*m* sandhâvita*m* sa*m*sârita*m* mama*ñ* *k*' eva tumhâka*ñ* *k*a, answer to the anticipation expressed in our verse.

The exact rendering of this verse has been much discussed, chiefly by Mr. D'Alwis in the Attanugaluvansa, p. cxxviii, and again in his Buddhist Nirvâ*n*a, p. 78; also by Childers, Notes on Dhammapada, p. 4, and in his Dictionary. Gogerly translated: 'Through various transmigrations I must travel, if I do not discover the builder whom I seek.' Spence Hardy: 'Through many different births I have run (to me not having found), seeking the architect of the desire-resembling house.' Fausböll: 'Multiplices generationis revolutiones percurreram, non inveniens, domus (corporis) fabricatorem quaerens.' And again (p. 322): 'Multarum generationum revolutio mihi subeunda esset, nisi invenissem domus fabricatorem.' Childers: 'I have run through the revolution of countless births, seeking the architect of this dwelling and finding him not.' D'Alwis: 'Through transmigrations of numerous births have I run, not discovering, (though) seeking the house-builder.' All depends on how we take sandhavissam, which Fausböll takes as a conditional, Childers, following Trenckner, as an aorist, because the sense imperatively requires an aorist. I had formerly translated it as a future, though qualifying it by the participle present anibbisan, i.e. not finding, and taking it in the sense of, if or so long as I do not find the true cause of existence. Anibbisan I had translated by not resting (anirvi*s*an), but the commentator seems to authorise the meaning of not finding (avindanto, alabhanto), and in that case all the material difficulties of the verse seem to me to disappear.

'The maker of the tabernacle' is explained as a poetical expression for the cause of new births, at least according to the views of

(visaṅkhâra, nirvâ*n*a), has attained to the extinction of all desires.

155. Men who have not observed proper discipline, and have not gained wealth in their youth, perish like old herons in a lake without fish.

156. Men who have not observed proper discipline, and have not gained wealth in their youth, lie, like broken bows, sighing after the past.

Buddha's followers, whatever his own views may have been. Buddha had conquered Mâra, the representative of worldly temptations, the father of worldly desires, and as desires (ta*m*hâ) are, by means of upâdâna and bhava, the cause of *g*âti, or 'birth,' the destruction of desires and the conquest of Mâra are nearly the same thing, though expressed differently in the philosophical and legendary language of the Buddhists. Ta*m*hâ, 'thirst' or 'craving,' is mentioned as serving in the army of Mâra. (Lotus, p. 443.)

155. On *gh*âyanti, i.e. kshâyanti, see Dr. Bollensen's learned remarks, Zeitschrift der Deutschen Morgenl. Gesellschaft, XVIII, 834, and Boehtlingk-Roth, s.v. kshâ.

CHAPTER XII.

SELF.

157. If a man hold himself dear, let him watch himself carefully; during one at least out of the three watches a wise man should be watchful.

158. Let each man direct himself first to what is proper, then let him teach others; thus a wise man will not suffer.

159. If a man make himself as he teaches others to be, then, being himself well subdued, he may subdue (others); for one's own self is difficult to subdue.

160. Self is the lord of self, who else could be the lord? With self well subdued, a man finds a lord such as few can find.

161. The evil done by oneself, self-begotten, self-bred, crushes the foolish, as a diamond breaks even a precious stone.

162. He whose wickedness is very great brings himself down to that state where his enemy wishes him to be, as a creeper does with the tree which it surrounds.

163. Bad deeds, and deeds hurtful to ourselves, are easy to do; what is beneficial and good, that is very difficult to do.

---

157. The three watches of the night are meant for the three stages of life. Cf. St. Mark xiii. 37, 'And what I say unto you, I say unto all, Watch.'

158. Cf. *G*âtaka, vol. ii, p. 441.

161. The Chinese translation renders vagiram by 'steel drill.'

164. The foolish man who scorns the rule of the venerable (Arahat), of the elect (Ariya), of the virtuous, and follows a false doctrine, he bears fruit to his own destruction, like the fruits of the Ka*tth*aka reed.

165. By oneself the evil is done, by oneself one suffers; by oneself evil is left undone, by oneself one is purified. The pure and the impure (stand and fall) by themselves, no one can purify another.

166. Let no one forget his own duty for the sake of another's, however great; let a man, after he has discerned his own duty, be always attentive to his duty.

---

164. The reed either dies after it has borne fruit, or is cut down for the sake of its fruit.

Di*tth*i, literally 'view,' is used even by itself, like the Greek 'hairesis,' in the sense of heresy (see Burnouf, Lotus, p. 444). In other places a distinction is made between mi*kkh*âdi*tth*i (vv. 167, 316) and sammâdi*tth*i (v. 319). If arahata*m* ariyâna*m* are used in their technical sense, we should translate 'the reverend Arhats,'—Arhat being the highest degree of the four orders of Ariyas, viz. *S*rotaâpanna, Sakadâgâmin, Anâgâmin, and Arhat. See note to verse 178.

166. Attha, lit. 'object,' must here be taken in a moral sense, as 'duty' rather than as 'advantage.' Childers rendered it by 'spiritual good.' The story which Buddhaghosa tells of the Thera Attadattha gives a clue to the origin of some of his parables, which seem to have been invented to suit the text of the Dhammapada rather than vice versâ. A similar case occurs in the commentary to verse 227.

CHAPTER XIII.

THE WORLD.

167. Do not follow the evil law! Do not live on in thoughtlessness! Do not follow false doctrine! Be not a friend of the world.

168. Rouse thyself! do not be idle! Follow the law of virtue! The virtuous rests in bliss in this world and in the next.

169. Follow the law of virtue; do not follow that of sin. The virtuous rests in bliss in this world and in the next.

170. Look upon the world as you would on a bubble, look upon it as you would on a mirage: the king of death does not see him who thus looks down upon the world.

171. Come, look at this world, glittering like a royal chariot; the foolish are immersed in it, but the wise do not touch it.

172. He who formerly was reckless and afterwards became sober, brightens up this world, like the moon when freed from clouds.

173. He whose evil deeds are covered by good deeds, brightens up this world, like the moon when freed from clouds.

---

167. Childers says, I have not the slightest notion of the meaning of lokavaddhano. Could it mean, Do not swell the number of worldlings?

168, 169. See Rhys Davids, Buddhism, p. 65.

170. See Suttanipâta, v. 1118.

174. This world is dark, few only can see here; a few only go to heaven, like birds escaped from the net.

175. The swans go on the path of the sun, they go miraculously through the ether; the wise are led out of this world, when they have conquered Mâra and his train.

176. If a man has transgressed the one law, and speaks lies, and scoffs at another world, there is no evil he will not do.

177. The uncharitable do not go to the world of the gods; fools only do not praise liberality; a wise man rejoices in liberality, and through it becomes blessed in the other world.

178. Better than sovereignty over the earth, better

175. Ha*m*sa may be meant for the bird, whether flamingo, or swan, or ibis (see Hardy, Manual, p. 17), but it may also, I believe, be taken in the sense of saint. As to iddhi, 'magical power,' i.e. *ri*ddhi, see Burnouf, Lotus, p. 310; Spence Hardy, Manual, pp. 498, 504; Legends, pp. 55, 177; and note to verse 254.

178. Sotâpatti, the technical term for the first step in the path that leads to Nirvâ*n*a. There are four such steps, or stages, and on entering each, a man receives a new title:—

(1) The *S*rotaâpanna, lit. he who has got into the stream. A man may have seven more births before he reaches the other shore, i.e. Nirvâ*n*a.

(2) Sak*ri*dâgâmin, lit. he who comes back once, so called because, after having entered this stage, a man is born only once more among men or gods. Childers shows that this involves really two more births, one in the deva world, the other in the world of men. Burnouf says the same, Introduction, p. 293.

(3) Anâgâmin, lit. he who does not come back, so called because, after this stage, a man cannot be born again in a lower world, but can only be born into a Brahman world, before he reaches Nirvâ*n*a.

(4) Arhat, the venerable, the perfect, who has reached the highest stage that can be reached, and from which Nirvâ*n*a is perceived

than going to heaven, better than lordship over all worlds, is the reward of Sotâpatti, the first step in holiness.

(sukkhavipassanâ, Lotus, p. 849). See Hardy, Eastern Monachism, p. 280; Burnouf, Introduction, p. 209; Köppen, p. 398; D'Alwis, Attanugaluvansa, p. cxxiv; Feer, Sutra en 42 articles, p. 6.

CHAPTER XIV.

THE BUDDHA (THE AWAKENED).

179. He whose conquest cannot be conquered again, into whose conquest no one in this world enters, by what track can you lead him, the Awakened, the Omniscient, the trackless?

180. He whom no desire with its snares and poisons can lead astray, by what track can you lead him, the Awakened, the Omniscient, the trackless?

181. Even the gods envy those who are awakened and not forgetful, who are given to meditation, who are wise, and who delight in the repose of retirement (from the world).

182. Difficult (to obtain) is the conception of men, difficult is the life of mortals, difficult is the hearing of the True Law, difficult is the birth of the Awakened (the attainment of Buddhahood).

179, 180. Buddha, the Awakened, is to be taken as an appellative rather than as the proper name of the Buddha (see v. 183). It means, anybody who has arrived at complete knowledge. Anantago*k*aram I take in the sense of, possessed of unlimited knowledge. Apadam, which Dr. Fausböll takes as an epithet of Buddha and translates by 'non investigabilis,' is translated 'trackless,' in order to show the play on the word pada; see Childers, s. v. The commentator says: 'The man who is possessed of even a single one of such conditions as râga, &c., him ye may lead forward; but the Buddha has not even one condition or basis of renewed existence, and therefore by what track will you lead this unconditioned Buddha?' Cf. Dhp. vv. 92, 420; and *G*âtaka, vol. i, pp. 79, 313.

182. Mr. Beal (Dhammapada, p. 110) states that this verse occurs also in the Sûtra of the forty-two sections.

183. Not to commit any sin, to do good, and to purify one's mind, that is the teaching of (all) the Awakened.

184. The Awakened call patience the highest penance, long-suffering the highest Nirvâ*n*a; for he is not an anchorite (pravra*g*ita) who strikes others, he is not an ascetic (*s*rama*n*a) who insults others.

185. Not to blame, not to strike, to live restrained under the law, to be moderate in eating, to sleep and sit alone, and to dwell on the highest thoughts,—this is the teaching of the Awakened.

---

183. This verse is again one of the most solemn verses among the Buddhists. According to Csoma Körösi, it ought to follow the famous Âryâ stanza, 'Ye dhammâ' (Lotus, p. 522), and serve as its complement. But though this may be the case in Tibet, it was not so originally. The same verse (ascribed to Kanakamuni) occurs at the end of the Chinese translation of the Prâtimoksha (Beal, J. R. A. S. XIX, p. 473; Catena, p. 159); in the Tibetan translation of the Gâthâsaṅgraha, v. 14 (Schiefner, Mél. Asiat. VIII, pp. 568, 586; and Csoma Körösi, As. Res. XX, p. 79). Burnouf has fully discussed the metre and meaning of our verse on pp. 527, 528 of his 'Lotus.' He prefers sa*k*ittaparidamanam, which Csoma translated by 'the mind must be brought under entire subjection' (sva*k*ittaparidamanam), and the late Dr. Mill by 'proprii intellectus subjugatio.' But his own MS. of the Mahâpadhâna-sutta gave likewise sa*k*ittapariyodapanam, and this is no doubt the correct reading. (See D'Alwis, Attanugaluvansa, p. cxxix.) We found pariyodapeyya in verse 88, in the sense of purging oneself from the troubles of the mind. From the same verb, (pari) ava + dai, we may derive the name Avadâna, a legend, originally a pure and virtuous act, an ἀρίστεια, afterwards a sacred story, and possibly a story the hearing of which purifies the mind. See Boehtlingk-Roth, s. v. avadâna.

184. Childers, following the commentator, translates, 'Patience, which is long-suffering, is the best devotion, the Buddhas declare that Nirvâ*n*a is the best (of things).'

185. Pâtimokkhe, 'under the law,' i. e. according to the law, the law which leads to Moksha, or 'freedom.' Prâtimoksha is the title of the oldest collection of the moral laws of the Buddhists (Burnouf,

186. There is no satisfying lusts, even by a shower of gold pieces; he who knows that lusts have a short taste and cause pain, he is wise;

187. Even in heavenly pleasures he finds no satisfaction, the disciple who is fully awakened delights only in the destruction of all desires.

188. Men, driven by fear, go to many a refuge, to mountains and forests, to groves and sacred trees.

189. But that is not a safe refuge, that is not the best refuge; a man is not delivered from all pains after having gone to that refuge.

190. He who takes refuge with Buddha, the Law,

Introduction, p. 300; Bigandet, The Life of Gaudama, p. 439; Rhys Davids, Buddhism, p. 162), and as it was common both to the Southern and the Northern Buddhists, pâtimokkhe in our passage may possibly be meant, as Professor Weber suggests, as the title of that very collection. The commentator explains it by *gettha*kasîla and pâtimokkhasîla. Sayanâsam might stand for *s*ayanâ*s*anam, see Mahâbh. XII, 6684; but in Buddhist literature it is intended for *s*ayanâsanam; see also Mahâbh. XII, 9978, *s*ayyâsane.' Fausböll now reads pânta*m* instead of patthañ, as in Suttanipâta, 337.

187. There is a curious similarity between this verse and verse 6503 (9919) of the *S*ântiparva:

Ya*kk*a kâmasukha*m* loke, ya*k k*a divyam mahat sukham,
T*ri*sh*n*âkshayasukhasyaite nârhata*h* sho*d*a*s*î*m* kalâm.

'And whatever delight of love there is on earth, and whatever is the great delight in heaven, they are not worth the sixteenth part of the pleasure which springs from the destruction of all desires.' The two verses 186, 187 are ascribed to king Mandhât*ri*, shortly before his death (Mél. Asiat. VIII, p. 471; see also *G*âtaka, vol. ii, p. 113).

188–192. These verses occur in Sanskrit in the Prâtihâryasûtra, translated by Burnouf, Introduction, pp. 162–189; see p. 186. Burnouf translates rukkha*k*etyâni by 'arbres consacrés;' properly, sacred shrines under or near a tree. See also *G*âtaka, vol. i, p. 97.

190. Buddha, Dharma, and Sangha are called the Tri*s*ara*n*a (cf. Burnouf, Introd. p. 630). The four holy truths are the four statements that there is pain in this world, that the source of

and the Church; he who, with clear understanding, sees the four holy truths:—

191. Viz. pain, the origin of pain, the destruction of pain, and the eightfold holy way that leads to the quieting of pain;—

192. That is the safe refuge, that is the best refuge; having gone to that refuge, a man is delivered from all pain.

193. A supernatural person (a Buddha) is not easily found, he is not born everywhere. Wherever such a sage is born, that race prospers.

194. Happy is the arising of the awakened, happy is the teaching of the True Law, happy is peace in the church, happy is the devotion of those who are at peace.

195, 196. He who pays homage to those who deserve homage, whether the awakened (Buddha) or their disciples, those who have overcome the host (of evils), and crossed the flood of sorrow, he who pays homage to such as have found deliverance and know no fear, his merit can never be measured by anybody.

---

pain is desire, that desire can be annihilated, that there is a way (shown by Buddha) by which the annihilation of all desires can be achieved, and freedom be obtained. That way consists of eight parts. (See Burnouf, Introduction, p. 630.) The eightfold way forms the subject of Chapter XVIII. (See also Feer, Journal As. 1870, p. 418, and Chips from a German Workshop, 2nd ed. vol. i, p. 251 seq.)

CHAPTER XV.

HAPPINESS.

197. We live happily indeed, not hating those who hate us! among men who hate us we dwell free from hatred!

198. We live happily indeed, free from ailments among the ailing! among men who are ailing let us dwell free from ailments!

199. We live happily indeed, free from greed among the greedy! among men who are greedy let us dwell free from greed!

200. We live happily indeed, though we call nothing our own! We shall be like the bright gods, feeding on happiness!

201. Victory breeds hatred, for the conquered is unhappy. He who has given up both victory and defeat, he, the contented, is happy.

---

198. The ailment here meant is moral rather than physical. Cf. Mahâbh. XII, 9924, sa*m*pra*s*ânto nirâmaya*h*; 9925, yo*sau prâ*n*ântiko rogas tâ*m* t*r*ish*n*â*m* tya*g*ata*h* sukham.

200. The words placed in the mouth of the king of Videha, while his residence Mithilâ was in flames, are curiously like our verse; cf. Mahâbh. XII, 9917,

Susukha*m* vata *g*îvâmi yasya me nâsti ki*ñk*ana,
Mithilâyâm pradîptâyâ*m* na me dahyati ki*ñk*ana.

'I live happily, indeed, for I have nothing; while Mithilâ is in flames, nothing of mine is burning.' Cf. Muir, Religious Sentiments, p. 106.

The âbhassara, i.e. âbhâsvara, 'the bright gods,' are frequently mentioned. Cf. Burnouf, Introd. p. 611.

201. This verse is ascribed to Buddha, when he heard of the defeat of A*g*âta*s*atru by Prasena*g*it. It exists in the Northern or

202. There is no fire like passion; there is no losing throw like hatred; there is no pain like this body; there is no happiness higher than rest.

203. Hunger is the worst of diseases, the elements of the body the greatest evil; if one knows this truly, that is Nirvâ*n*a, the highest happiness.

Sanskrit and in the Southern or Pâli texts, i.e. in the Avadâna-*s*ataka, in the Sa*m*yutta-nikâya. See Feer, Comptes Rendus, 1871, p. 44, and Journal As. 1880, p. 509. In the Avadâna-*s*ataka, the Sanskrit version is—

*G*ayo vairam prasavati, du*h*kha*m* *s*ete parâ*g*ita*h*,
Upa*s*ânta*h* sukha*m* *s*ete hitvâ *g*ayaparâ*g*ayam.

202. I take kali in the sense of an unlucky die which makes a player lose his game. A real simile seems wanted here, as in verse 251, where, for the same reason, I translate graha by 'shark,' not by 'captivitas,' as Dr. Fausböll proposes. The same scholar translates kali in our verse by 'peccatum.' If there is any objection to translating kali in Pâli by 'unlucky die,' I should still prefer to take it in the sense of the age of depravity, or the demon of depravity. To judge from Abhidhânappadîpikâ, 1106, kali was used for parâ*g*aya, i. e. loss at game, a losing throw, and occurs in that sense again in verse 252. The Chinese translation has, 'there is no distress (poison) worse than hate.' A similar verse occurs Mahâbh. *S*ântip. 175, v. 35.

'Body' for khandha is a free translation, but it is difficult to find any better rendering. The Chinese translation also has 'body.' According to the Buddhists each sentient being consists of five khandhas (skandha), or aggregates, the organized body (rûpa-khandha) with its four internal capacities of sensation (vedanâ), perception (sa*ñg**ñ*â), conception (sa*m*skâra), knowledge (vi*g**ñ*âna). See Burnouf, Introd. pp. 589, 634; Lotus, p. 335.

203. Sa*m*skâra is the fourth of the five khandhas, but the commentator takes it here, as well as in verse 255, for the five khandhas together, in which case we can only translate it by 'body,' or 'elements of the body.' See also verse 278. Childers proposes 'organic life' (Notes on Dhammapada, p. 1). There are, however, other sa*m*skâras, which follow immediately upon avidyâ, 'ignorance,' as second in the series of the nidânas, or 'causes of existence,' and these too might be called the greatest pain, considering that they are the cause of birth, which is the cause of all pain. Sometimes,

204. Health is the greatest of gifts, contentedness the best riches; trust is the best of relationships, Nirvâ*n*a the highest happiness.

205. He who has tasted the sweetness of solitude and tranquillity, is free from fear and free from sin, while he tastes the sweetness of drinking in the law.

206. The sight of the elect (Arya) is good, to live with them is always happiness; if a man does not see fools, he will be truly happy.

207. He who walks in the company of fools suffers a long way; company with fools, as with an enemy, is always painful; company with the wise is pleasure, like meeting with kinsfolk.

208. Therefore, one ought to follow the wise, the intelligent, the learned, the much enduring, the dutiful, the elect; one ought to follow such a good and wise man, as the moon follows the path of the stars.

---

again, sa*m*skâra seems to have a different and less technical meaning, being used in the sense of conceptions, plans, desires, as, for instance, in verse 368, where saṅkhârâna*m* khayam is used much like ta*n*hâkhaya. Again, in his comment on verse 75, Buddhaghosa says, upadhiviveko saṅkhârasaṅga*n*ika*m* vinodeti; and again, upadhiviveko *k*a nirupadhînâ*m* puggalâna*m* visaṅkhâra gatânâm.

For a similar sentiment, see Stanislas Julien, Les Avadânas, vol. i, p. 40, 'Le corps est la plus grande source de souffrance,' &c. I should say that the khandhas in verse 202 and the saṅkhâras in verse 203 are nearly, if not quite, synonymous. I should prefer to read *g*iga*kkh*â-paramâ as a compound. *G*iga*kkh*â, or as it is written in one MS., diga*kkh*â (Sk. *g*ighatsâ), means not only 'hunger,' but 'appetite, desire.'

204. Childers translates, 'the best kinsman is a man you can trust.'

205. Cf. Suttanipâta, v. 256.

207. I should like to read sukho *k*a dhîrasa*m*vâso.

CHAPTER XVI.

PLEASURE.

209. He who gives himself to vanity, and does not give himself to meditation, forgetting the real aim (of life) and grasping at pleasure, will in time envy him who has exerted himself in meditation.

210. Let no man ever cling to what is pleasant, or to what is unpleasant. Not to see what is pleasant is pain, and it is pain to see what is unpleasant.

211. Let, therefore, no man love anything; loss of the beloved is evil. Those who love nothing, and hate nothing, have no fetters.

212. From pleasure comes grief, from pleasure comes fear; he who is free from pleasure knows neither grief nor fear.

213. From affection comes grief, from affection comes fear; he who is free from affection knows neither grief nor fear.

214. From lust comes grief, from lust comes fear; he who is free from lust knows neither grief nor fear.

215. From love comes grief, from love comes fear; he who is free from love knows neither grief nor fear.

216. From greed comes grief, from greed comes fear; he who is free from greed knows neither grief nor fear.

217. He who possesses virtue and intelligence,

---

214. See Beal Catena, p. 200.

who is just, speaks the truth, and does what is his own business, him the world will hold dear.

218. He in whom a desire for the Ineffable (Nirvâ*n*a) has sprung up, who in his mind is satisfied, and whose thoughts are not bewildered by love, he is called ûrdhva*m*srotas (carried upwards by the stream).

219. Kinsmen, friends, and lovers salute a man who has been long away, and returns safe from afar.

220. In like manner his good works receive him who has done good, and has gone from this world to the other;—as kinsmen receive a friend on his return.

---

218. Ûrdhva*m*srotas or uddha*m*soto is the technical name for one who has reached the world of the Av*ri*has (Aviha), and is proceeding to that of the Akanish*th*as (Akani*tth*a). This is the last stage before he reaches the formless world, the Arûpadhâtu. (See Buddhaghosha's Parables, p. 123; Burnouf, Introduction, p. 599.) Originally ûrdhva*m*srotas may have been used in a less technical sense, meaning one who swims against the stream, and is not carried away by the vulgar passions of the world.

CHAPTER XVII.

ANGER.

221. Let a man leave anger, let him forsake pride, let him overcome all bondage! No sufferings befall the man who is not attached to name and form, and who calls nothing his own.

222. He who holds back rising anger like a rolling chariot, him I call a real driver; other people are but holding the reins.

223. Let a man overcome anger by love, let him overcome evil by good; let him overcome the greedy by liberality, the liar by truth!

224. Speak the truth, do not yield to anger; give, if thou art asked for little; by these three steps thou wilt go near the gods.

225. The sages who injure nobody, and who always control their body, they will go to the unchangeable place (Nirvâ*n*a), where, if they have gone, they will suffer no more.

226. Those who are ever watchful, who study day and night, and who strive after Nirvâ*n*a, their passions will come to an end.

227. This is an old saying, O Atula, this is not as if of to-day: 'They blame him who sits silent,

---

221. 'Name and form' is the translation of nâma-rûpa, the ninth of the Buddhist Nidânas. It comprises everything in the phenomenal world. Cf. Burnouf, Introduction, p. 501; see also Gogerly, Lecture on Buddhism, and Bigandet, The Life of Gaudama, p. 454.

223. Mahâbh. XII, 3550, asâdhu*m* sadhunâ *g*ayet. Cf. Ten *G*âtakas, ed. Fausböll, p. 5.

227. It appears from the commentary that porâ*n*am and a*gg*ata-

they blame him who speaks much, they also blame him who says little; there is no one on earth who is not blamed.'

228. There never was, there never will be, nor is there now, a man who is always blamed, or a man who is always praised.

229, 230. But he whom those who discriminate praise continually day after day, as without blemish, wise, rich in knowledge and virtue, who would dare to blame him, like a coin made of gold from the *G*ambû river? Even the gods praise him, he is praised even by Brahman.

231. Beware of bodily anger, and control thy body! Leave the sins of the body, and with thy body practise virtue!

232. Beware of the anger of the tongue, and control thy tongue! Leave the sins of the tongue, and practise virtue with thy tongue!

233. Beware of the anger of the mind, and control thy mind! Leave the sins of the mind, and practise virtue with thy mind!

234. The wise who control their body, who control their tongue, the wise who control their mind, are indeed well controlled.

---

nam are neuters, referring to what happened formerly and what happens to-day, and that they are not to be taken as adjectives referring to âsînam, &c. The commentator must have read atula instead of atulam, and he explains it as the name of a pupil whom Gautama addressed by that name (see note to verse 166). Others take atula in the sense of incomparable (Mahâbh. XIII, 1937), and in that case we ought to supply, with Professor Weber, some such word as 'saw' or 'saying.'

230. The Brahman worlds are higher than the Deva worlds as the Brahman is higher than a Deva; see Hardy, Manual, p. 25; Burnouf, Introduction, pp. 134, 184.

CHAPTER XVIII.

IMPURITY.

235. Thou art now like a sear leaf, the messengers of death (Yama) have come near to thee; thou standest at the door of thy departure, and thou hast no provision for thy journey.

236. Make thyself an island, work hard, be wise! When thy impurities are blown away, and thou art free from guilt, thou wilt enter into the heavenly world of the elect (Ariya).

237. Thy life has come to an end, thou art come near to death (Yama), there is no resting-place for thee on the road, and thou hast no provision for thy journey.

238. Make thyself an island, work hard, be wise! When thy impurities are blown away, and thou art free from guilt, thou wilt not enter again into birth and decay.

239. Let a wise man blow off the impurities of himself, as a smith blows off the impurities of silver, one by one, little by little, and from time to time.

---

235. Uyyoga seems to mean departure. See Buddhaghosa's commentary on verse 152, p. 319, l. 1; Fausböll, Five *G*âtakas, p. 35.

236. 'An island,' for a drowning man to save himself; (see verse 25.) It is well known that Dîpańkara is the name of one of the former Buddhas, and it is also used as an appellative of the Buddha, but this name is derived from dîpo, 'a lamp,' and has nothing to do with dîpa, used metaphorically here and elsewhere in the sense of resting-place, shelter, or even Nirvâ*n*a; see Childers, s. v. dîpo.

239. This verse is the foundation of the thirty-fourth section of the Sûtra of the forty-two sections; see Beal, Catena, p. 201; Suttanipâta, v. 962.

240. As the impurity which springs from the iron, when it springs from it, destroys it; thus do a transgressor's own works lead him to the evil path.

241. The taint of prayers is non-repetition; the taint of houses, non-repair; the taint of complexion is sloth; the taint of a watchman, thoughtlessness.

242. Bad conduct is the taint of woman, niggardliness the taint of a benefactor; tainted are all evil ways, in this world and in the next.

243. But there is a taint worse than all taints,—ignorance is the greatest taint. O mendicants! throw off that taint, and become taintless!

244. Life is easy to live for a man who is without shame, a crow hero, a mischief-maker, an insulting, bold, and wretched fellow.

245. But life is hard to live for a modest man, who always looks for what is pure, who is disinterested, quiet, spotless, and intelligent.

246. He who destroys life, who speaks untruth, who in the world takes what is not given him, who goes to another man's wife;

247. And the man who gives himself to drinking intoxicating liquors, he, even in this world, digs up his own root.

248. O man, know this, that the unrestrained are

---

241. On atidhona*k*ârin, see Morris, J. P. T. S. 1887, p. 100.

244. Pakkhandin is identified by Dr. Fausböll with praskandin, one who jumps forward, insults, or, as Buddhaghosa explains it, one who meddles with other people's business, an interloper. At all events, it is a term of reproach, and, as it would seem, of theological reproach.

246. On the five principal commandments which are recapitulated in verses 246 and 247, see Buddhaghosha's Parables, p. 153.

248. Cf. Mahâbhârata XII, 4055, yeshâ*m* v*ri*tti*s* *k*a sa*m*yatâ. See also verse 307.

in a bad state; take care that greediness and vice do not bring thee to grief for a long time!

249. The world gives according to their faith or according to their pleasure: if a man frets about the food and the drink given to others, he will find no rest either by day or by night.

250. He in whom that feeling is destroyed, and taken out with the very root, finds rest by day and by night.

251. There is no fire like passion, there is no shark like hatred, there is no snare like folly, there is no torrent like greed.

252. The fault of others is easily perceived, but that of oneself is difficult to perceive; a man winnows his neighbour's faults like chaff, but his own fault he hides, as a cheat hides the bad die from the player.

253. If a man looks after the faults of others, and is always inclined to be offended, his own passions will grow, and he is far from the destruction of passions.

254. There is no path through the air, a man

---

249. This verse has evidently regard to the feelings of the Bhikshus or mendicants who receive either much or little, and who are exhorted not to be envious if others receive more than they themselves. Several of the Parables illustrate this feeling.

251. Dr. Fausböll translates gaho by 'captivitas,' Dr. Weber by 'fetter.' I take it in the same sense as grâha in Manu VI, 78; and Buddhaghosa does the same, though he assigns to grâha a more general meaning, viz. anything that seizes, whether an evil spirit (yakkha), a serpent (a*g*agara), or a crocodile (kumbhîla).

Greed or thirst is represented as a river in Lalita-vistara, ed. Calc. p. 482, trish*n*â-nadî tivegâ pra*s*oshitâ me *gñ*ânasûrye*n*a, 'the wild river of thirst is dried up by the sun of my knowledge.'

252. See Childers, Notes, p. 7; St. Matthew vii. 3.

253. As to âsava, 'appetite, passion,' see note to verse 39.

254. I have translated this verse very freely, and not in accord-

is not a Sama*n*a outwardly. The world delights in vanity, the Tathâgatas (the Buddhas) are free from vanity.

255. There is no path through the air, a man is not a Sama*n*a outwardly. No creatures are eternal; but the awakened (Buddha) are never shaken.

---

ance with Buddhaghosa's commentary. Dr. Fausböll proposed to translate, 'No one who is outside the Buddhist community can walk through the air, but only a Sama*n*a;' and the same view is taken by Professor Weber, though he arrives at it by a different construction. Now it is perfectly true that the idea of magical powers (*ri*ddhi) which enable saints to walk through the air, &c., occurs in the Dhammapada, see v. 175, note. But the Dhammapada may contain earlier and later verses, and in that case our verse might be an early protest on the part of Buddha against the belief in such miraculous powers. We know how Buddha himself protested against his disciples being called upon to perform vulgar miracles. 'I command my disciples not to work miracles,' he said, 'but to hide their good deeds, and to show their sins' (Burnouf, Introd. p. 170). It would be in harmony with this sentiment if we translated our verse as I have done. As to bahira, I should take it in the sense of 'external,' as opposed to adhyâtmika, or 'internal;' and the meaning would be, 'a Sama*n*a is not a Sama*n*a by outward acts, but by his heart.' D'Alwis translates (p. 85): 'There is no footprint in the air; there is not a Sama*n*a out of the pale of the Buddhist community.'

Prapa*ñk*a, which I have here translated by 'vanity,' seems to include the whole host of human weaknesses; cf. v. 196, where it is explained by ta*m*hâdi*tth*imânapapa*ñk*a; in our verse by ta*m*hâdisu papa*ñk*esu: cf. Lalita-vistara, p. 564, anâlaya*m* nishprapa*ñk*am anutpâdam asambhavam (dharma*k*akram). As to Tathâgata, a name of Buddha, cf. Burnouf, Introd. p. 75.

255. Sankhâra for sa*m*skâra; cf. note to verse 203. Creature does not, as Mr. D'Alwis (p. 69) supposes, involve the Christian conception of creation. Buddhaghosa takes sankhârâ as the five skandhas.

CHAPTER XIX.

THE JUST.

256, 257. A man is not just if he carries a matter by violence; no, he who distinguishes both right and wrŏng, who is learned and guides others, not by violence, but by the same law, being a guardian of the law and intelligent, he is called just.

258. A man is not learned because he talks much; he who is patient, free from hatred and fear, he is called learned.

259. A man is not a supporter of the law because he talks much; even if a man has learnt little, but sees the law bodily, he is a supporter of the law, a man who never neglects the law.

260. A man is not an elder because his head is grey; his age may be ripe, but he is called 'Old-in-vain.'

261. He in whom there is truth, virtue, pity, restraint, moderation, he who is free from impurity and is wise, he is called an elder.

262. An envious, stingy, dishonest man does not become respectable by means of much talking only, or by the beauty of his complexion.

263. He in whom all this is destroyed, and taken out with the very root, he, when freed from hatred and wise, is called respectable.

---

259. Buddhaghosa here takes law (dhamma) in the sense of the four great truths, see note to verse 190. Could dhamma*m* kâyena passati mean, 'he observes the law in his acts, or sees the law with his bodily eyes?' Hardly, if we compare expressions like dhamma*m* vipassato, v. 373.

264. Not by tonsure does an undisciplined man who speaks falsehood become a Sama*n*a; can a man be a Sama*n*a who is still held captive by desire and greediness?

265. He who always quiets the evil, whether small or large, he is called a Sama*n*a (a quiet man), because he has quieted all evil.

266. A man is not a mendicant (Bhikshu) simply because he asks others for alms; he who adopts the whole law is a Bhikshu, not he who only begs.

267. He who is above good and evil, who is chaste, who with care passes through the world, he indeed is called a Bhikshu.

268, 269. A man is not a Muni because he observes silence (mona, i. e. mauna), if he is foolish

---

265. This is a curious etymology, because it shows that at the time when this verse was written, the original meaning of *s*rama*n*a had been forgotten. *S*rama*n*a meant originally, in the language of the Brahmans, a man who performed hard penances, from *s*ram, 'to work hard,' &c. When it became the name of the Buddhist ascetics, the language had changed, and *s*rama*n*a was pronounced sama*n*a. Now there is another Sanskrit root, *s*am, 'to quiet,' which in Pâli becomes likewise sam, and from this root sam, 'to quiet,' and not from *s*ram, 'to tire,' did the popular etymology of the day and the writer of our verse derive the title of the Buddhist priests. The original form *s*rama*n*a became known to the Greeks as Σαρμᾶναι, that of sama*n*a as Σαμαναῖοι; the former through Megasthenes, the latter through Bardesanės, 80–60 B.C. (See Lassen, Indische Alterthumskunde, II, 700.) The Chinese Shamen and the Tungusian Shamen do not come from the same source, though this has sometimes been doubted. See Schott, Über die doppelte Bedeutung des Wortes Schamane, in the Philosophical Transactions of the Berlin Academy, 1842, p. 463 seq.

266–270. The etymologies here given of the ordinary titles of the followers of Buddha are entirely fanciful, and are curious only as showing how the people who spoke Pâli had lost the etymological consciousness of their language. A Bhikshu is a beggar, i. e. a Buddhist friar who has left his family and lives entirely on

and ignorant; but the wise who, as with the balance, chooses the good and avoids evil, he is a Muni, and is a Muni thereby; he who in this world weighs both sides is called a Muni.

270. A man is not an elect (Ariya) because he injures living creatures; because he has pity on all living creatures, therefore is a man called Ariya.

271, 272. Not only by discipline and vows, not only by much learning, not by entering into a trance, not by sleeping alone, do I earn the happiness of release which no worldling can know. O Bhikshu, he who has obtained the extinction of desires, has obtained confidence.

---

alms. Muni is a sage, hence *S*âkya-muni, a name of Gautama. Muni comes from man, 'to think,' and from muni comes mauna, 'silence.' Ariya, again, is the general name of those who embrace a religious life. It meant originally 'respectable, noble.' In verse 270 it seems as if the writer wished to guard against deriving ariya from ari, 'enemy.' See note to verse 22.

272. See Childers, Notes, p. 7. Nekkhamana-sukham is explained by the commentator as anâgami-sukham, the happiness of one who can be born again once only in the world of Brahma. The same commentator takes Bhikkhu as a vocative. The last line is obscure, and Fausböll with his usual modesty adds, num recte alterum hemistichium intellexerim docti videant. The text of the commentary is so imperfect that in its present state it cannot help us much. Following its indications, however, Childers proposed an emendation, Bhikkhu vissâsa*m* mâ âpâdi, lit. priest, enter not into confidence. Bhikkhu may, of course, be vocative or nominative. I formerly followed Fausböll's conjecture, but I should now prefer to take Bhikkhu as a nominative, referring it to the person who is speaking, i.e. I or the Bhikshu in general, has obtained confidence or peace of mind, as soon as he has obtained the extinction of passions. Âpâdi is here not a first, but a third person. Kuhn, Pâli Grammatik, p. 109. Appatto stands for âpatto, Sk. âpanno. See Kuhn, Pâli Grammatik, p. 119. Athavâ, in v. 270, means or, and corresponds to vâ; it can mean nothing else here but what it means everywhere, whether in Sanskrit or in Pâli.

CHAPTER XX.

THE WAY.

273. The best of ways is the eightfold; the best of truths the four words; the best of virtues passionlessness; the best of men he who has eyes to see.

274. This is the way, there is no other that leads to the purifying of intelligence. Go on this path! This is the confusion of Mâra (the tempter).

275. If you go on this way, you will make an end of pain! The way was preached by me, when I had understood the removal of the thorns (in the flesh).

276. You yourself must make an effort. The Tathâgatas (Buddhas) are only preachers. The thoughtful who enter the way are freed from the bondage of Mâra.

277. 'All created things perish,' he who knows and sees this becomes passive in pain; this is the way to purity.

---

273. The eightfold or eight-membered way is the technical term for the way by which Nirvâ*n*a is attained. (See Burnouf, Lotus, p. 519.) This very way constitutes the fourth of the Four Truths, or the four words of truth, viz. Du*h*kha, 'pain;' Samudaya, 'origin;' Nirodha, 'destruction;' Mârga, 'road.' (Lotus, p. 517.) See note to verse 178. For another explanation of the Mârga, or 'way,' see Hardy, Eastern Monachism, p. 280.

274. The last line means, 'this following the true path is to confound Mâra,' i. e. the discomfiture of Mâra.

275. The *s*alyas, 'arrows or thorns,' are the *s*oka*s*alya, 'the arrows of grief.' Buddha himself is called mahâ*s*alya-hartâ, 'the great remover of thorns.' (Lalita-vistara, p. 550; Mahâbh. XII, 5616.)

277. See v. 255. Nibbeda is sthâyibhâva.

278. 'All created things are grief and pain,' he who knows and sees this becomes passive in pain; this is the way that leads to purity.

279. 'All forms are unreal,' he who knows and sees this becomes passive in pain; this is the way that leads to purity.

280. He who does not rouse himself when it is time to rise, who, though young and strong, is full of sloth, whose will and thought are weak, that lazy and idle man never finds the way to knowledge.

281. Watching his speech, well restrained in mind, let a man never commit any wrong with his body! Let a man but keep these three roads of action clear, and he will achieve the way which is taught by the wise.

282. Through zeal knowledge is gotten, through lack of zeal knowledge is lost; let a man who knows this double path of gain and loss thus place himself that knowledge may grow.

283. Cut down the whole forest (of desires), not a tree only! Danger comes out of the forest (of desires). When you have cut down both the forest (of desires) and its undergrowth, then, Bhikshus, you will be rid of the forest and of desires!

---

278. See v. 203.

279. Dhamma stands evidently for saṅkhâra, and means the five khandha, i. e. what constitutes a living body.

281. Cf. Beal, Catena, p. 159.

282. Bhûri was rightly translated 'intelligentia' by Dr. Fausböll. Dr. Weber renders it by 'Gedeihen,' but the commentator distinctly explains it as 'vast knowledge,' and in the technical sense the word occurs after vidyâ and before medhâ, in the Lalita-vistara, p. 541.

283. A pun, vana meaning both 'lust' and 'forest.' See some mistaken remarks on this verse in D'Alwis, Nirvâ*n*a, p. 86, and some good remarks in Childers, Notes, p. 7.

284. So long as the desire of man towards women, even the smallest, is not destroyed, so long is his mind in bondage, as the calf that drinks milk is to its mother.

285. Cut out the love of self, like an autumn lotus, with thy hand! Cherish the road of peace. Nirvâ*n*a has been shown by Sugata (Buddha).

286. 'Here I shall dwell in the rain, here in winter and summer,' thus the fool meditates, and does not think of death.

287. Death comes and carries off that man, honoured for his children and flocks, his mind distracted, as a flood carries off a sleeping village.

288. Sons are no help, nor a father, nor relations; there is no help from kinsfolk for one whom death has seized.

289. A wise and well-behaved man who knows the meaning of this, should quickly clear the way that leads to Nirvâ*n*a.

---

285. Cf. *G*âtaka, vol. i, p. 183.

286. Antarâya, according to the commentator, *g*îvitântarâya, means interitus, death, it does not mean here an obstacle only.

287. See notes to verse 47, Thiessen, Kisâgotamî, p. 11, and Mahâbh. XII, 9944, 6540. To clear is used in the sense of making clear or easy to enter, like our own to clear the way.

CHAPTER XXI.

MISCELLANEOUS.

290. If by leaving a small pleasure one sees a great pleasure, let a wise man leave the small pleasure, and look to the great.

291. He who, by causing pain to others, wishes to obtain pleasure for himself, he, entangled in the bonds of hatred, will never be free from hatred.

292. What ought to be done is neglected, what ought not to be done is done; the desires of unruly, thoughtless people are always increasing.

293. But they whose whole watchfulness is always directed to their body, who do not follow what ought not to be done, and who steadfastly do what ought to be done, the desires of such watchful and wise people will come to an end.

294. A true Brâhma*n*a goes scatheless, though he have killed father and mother, and two valiant kings, though he has destroyed a kingdom with all its subjects.

295. A true Brâhma*n*a goes scatheless, though he have killed father and mother, and two holy kings, and an eminent man besides.

---

292. Cf. Beal, Catena, p. 264.

294, 295. These two verses are either meant to show that a truly holy man who, by accident, commits all these crimes is guiltless, or they refer to some particular event in Buddha's history. The commentator is so startled that he explains them allegorically. Mr. D'Alwis is very indignant that I should have supposed Buddha capable of pardoning parricide. 'Can it be believed,' he writes, 'that a Teacher, who held life, even the life of the minutest insect,

296. The disciples of Gotama (Buddha) are always well awake, and their thoughts day and night are always set on Buddha.

297. The disciples of Gotama are always well awake, and their thoughts day and night are always set on the law.

298. The disciples of Gotama are always well awake, and their thoughts day and night are always set on the church.

299. The disciples of Gotama are always well awake, and their thoughts day and night are always set on their body.

---

nay, even a living tree, in such high estimation as to prevent its wanton destruction, has declared that the murder of a Brâhma*n*a, to whom he accorded reverence, along with his own Sangha, was blameless?' D'Alwis, Nirvâ*n*a, p. 88. Though something might be said in reply, considering the antecedents of king A*g*âta*s*atru, the patron of Buddha, and stories such as that quoted by the commentator on the Dhammapada (Beal, l. c. p. 150), or in Der Weise und der Thor, p. 306, still these two verses are startling, and I am not aware that Buddha has himself drawn the conclusion, which has been drawn by others, viz. that those who have reached the highest Sambodhi, and are in fact no longer themselves, are outside the domain of good and bad, and beyond the reach of guilt. Verses like 39 and 412 admit of a different explanation. Still our verses being miscellaneous extracts, might possibly have been taken from a work in which such an opinion was advanced, and I find that Mr. Childers, no mean admirer of Buddha, was not shocked by my explanation. 'In my judgment,' he says, 'this verse is intended to express in a forcible manner the Buddhist doctrine that the Arhat cannot commit a serious sin,' 'na hanti, na *k*a hanyate.' However, we have met before with far-fetched puns in these verses, and it is not impossible that the native commentators were right after all in seeing some puns or riddles in this verse. D'Alwis, following the commentary, explains mother as lust, father as pride, the two valiant kings as heretical systems, and the realm as sensual pleasure, while veyyaggha is taken by him for a place infested with the tigers of obstruction against final beatitude. Some confirmation of this

300. The disciples of Gotama are always well awake, and their mind day and night always delights in compassion.

301. The disciples of Gotama are always well awake, and their mind day and night always delights in meditation.

302. It is hard to leave the world (to become a friar), it is hard to enjoy the world; hard is the monastery, painful are the houses; painful it is to dwell with equals (to share everything in common), and the itinerant mendicant is beset with pain. Therefore let no man be an itinerant mendicant, and he will not be beset with pain.

303. A man full of faith, if endowed with virtue and glory, is respected, whatever place he may choose.

304. Good people shine from afar, like the snowy

---

interpretation is supplied by a passage in the third book of the Lankâvatâra-sûtra, as quoted by Mr. Beal in his translation of the Dhammapada, Introduction, p. 5. Here a stanza is quoted as having been recited by Buddha, in explanation of a similar startling utterance which he had made to Mahâmati:

> 'Lust, or carnal desire, this is the Mother,
> Ignorance, this is the Father,
> The highest point of knowledge, this is Buddha,
> All the klesas, these are the Rahats,
> The five skandhas, these are the Priests;
> To commit the five unpardonable sins
> Is to destroy these five
> And yet not suffer the pains of hell.'

The Lankâvatâra-sûtra was translated into Chinese by Bodhiruki (508–511); when it was written is doubtful. See also *G*âtaka, vol. ii, p. 263.

302. This verse is difficult, and I give my translation as tentative only. Childers (Notes, p. 11) has removed some, not all difficulties, and I have been chiefly guided by the interpretation put on the verse by the Chinese translator; see Beal, Dhammapada, p. 137.

mountains; bad people are not seen, like arrows shot by night.

305. Sitting alone, lying down alone, walking alone without ceasing, and alone subduing himself, let a man be happy near the edge of a forest.

---

305. Vanânte, within the forest, according to a pun pointed out before (v. 283), means both 'at the end of a forest,' and 'at the end of desires.'

CHAPTER XXII.

THE DOWNWARD COURSE.

306. He who says what is not, goes to hell; he also who, having done a thing, says I have not done it. After death both are equal, they are men with evil deeds in the next world.

307. Many men whose shoulders are covered with the yellow gown are ill-conditioned and unrestrained; such evil-doers by their evil deeds go to hell.

308. Better it would be to swallow a heated iron ball, like flaring fire, than that a bad unrestrained fellow should live on the charity of the land.

309. Four things does a reckless man gain who covets his neighbour's wife,—demerit, an uncomfortable bed, thirdly, punishment, and lastly, hell.

---

306. I translate niraya, 'the exit, the downward course, the evil path,' by 'hell,' because the meaning assigned to that ancient mythological name by Christian writers comes so near to the Buddhist idea of niraya, that it is difficult not to believe in some actual contact between these two streams of thought. See also Mahâbh. XII, 7176. Cf. *G*âtaka, vol. ii, p. 416; Suttanipâta, v. 660.

307, 308. These two verses are said to be taken from the Vinaya-pi*t*aka I, 4, 1; D'Alwis, Nirvâ*n*a, p. 29.

308. The charity of the land, i.e. the alms given, from a sense of religious duty, to every mendicant that asks for it.

309, 310. The four things mentioned in verse 309 seem to be repeated in verse 310. Therefore, apu*ññ*alâbha, 'demerit,' is the same in both: gatî pâpikâ must be niraya; da*nd*a corresponds to nindâ, and ratî thokikâ explains the anikâmaseyya*m*. Buddhaghosa

310. There is demerit, and the evil way (to hell), there is the short pleasure of the frightened in the arms of the frightened, and the king imposes heavy punishment; therefore let no man think of his neighbour's wife.

311. As a grass-blade, if badly grasped, cuts the arm, badly-practised asceticism leads to hell.

312. An act carelessly performed, a broken vow, and hesitating obedience to discipline (Brahma-*k*ariyam), all this brings no great reward.

313. If anything is to be done, let a man do it, let him attack it vigorously! A careless pilgrim only scatters the dust of his passions more widely.

314. An evil deed is better left undone, for a man repents of it afterwards; a good deed is better done, for having done it, one does not repent.

315. Like a well-guarded frontier fort, with defences within and without, so let a man guard himself. Not a moment should escape, for they who allow the right moment to pass, suffer pain when they are in hell.

316. They who are ashamed of what they ought not to be ashamed of, and are not ashamed of what they ought to be ashamed of, such men, embracing false doctrines, enter the evil path.

317. They who fear when they ought not to fear, and fear not when they ought to fear, such men, embracing false doctrines, enter the evil path.

---

takes the same view of the meaning of anikâmaseyya, i.e. yathâ i*kkh*ati eva*m* seyyam alabhitvâ, ani*kkh*ita*m* parittakam eva kâla*m* seyya*m* labhati, 'not obtaining the rest as he wishes it, he obtains it, as he does not wish it, for a short time only.'

313. As to raga meaning 'dust' and 'passion,' see Buddhaghosha's Parables, pp. 65, 66.

318. They who see sin where there is no sin, and see no sin where there is sin, such men, embracing false doctrines, enter the evil path.

319. They who see sin where there is sin, and no sin where there is no sin, such men, embracing the true doctrine, enter the good path.

CHAPTER XXIII.

THE ELEPHANT.

320. Silently I endured abuse as the elephant in battle endures the arrow sent from the bow: for the world is ill-natured.

321. They lead a tamed elephant to battle, the king mounts a tamed elephant; the tamed is the best among men, he who silently endures abuse.

322. Mules are good, if tamed, and noble Sindhu horses, and elephants with large tusks; but he who tames himself is better still.

323. For with these animals does no man reach the untrodden country (Nirvâ*n*a), where a tamed man goes on a tamed animal, viz. on his own well-tamed self.

324. The elephant called Dhanapâlaka, his temples running with pungent sap, and who is difficult to hold, does not eat a morsel when bound; the elephant longs for the elephant grove.

---

320. The elephant is with the Buddhists the emblem of endurance and self-restraint. Thus Buddha himself is called Nâga, 'the Elephant' (Lal. Vist. p. 553), or Mahânâga, 'the great Elephant' (Lal. Vist. p. 553), and in one passage (Lal. Vist. p. 554) the reason of this name is given, by stating that Buddha was sudânta, 'well-tamed,' like an elephant. He descended from heaven in the form of an elephant to be born on earth. On titikkhisam, see Childers, s.v. titikkhati.

See also Manu VI, 47, ativâdâ*m*s titiksheta.

323. I read, as suggested by Dr. Fausböll, yath' attanâ sudantena danto dantena ga*kkh*ati (cf. verse 160). The India Office MS. reads na hi etehi *th*ânehi ga*kkh*eya agata*m* disam, yath' attâna*m* sudantena danto dantena ga*kkh*ati. As to *th*ânehi instead of yânehi, see verse 224.

325. If a man becomes fat and a great eater, if he is sleepy and rolls himself about, that fool, like a hog fed on grains, is born again and again.

326. This mind of mine went formerly wandering about as it liked, as it listed, as it pleased; but I shall now hold it in thoroughly, as the rider who holds the hook holds in the furious elephant.

327. Be not thoughtless, watch your thoughts! Draw yourself out of the evil way, like an elephant sunk in mud.

328. If a man find a prudent companion who walks with him, is wise, and lives soberly, he may walk with him, overcoming all dangers, happy, but considerate.

329. If a man find no prudent companion who walks with him, is wise, and lives soberly, let him walk alone, like a king who has left his conquered country behind,—like an elephant in the forest.

330. It is better to live alone, there is no companionship with a fool; let a man walk alone, let

---

325. On nivâpa, see B.-R. Petersburg Dict. s. v.

326. Yoniso, i. e. yoni*s*a*h*, is rendered by Dr. Fausböll 'sapientiâ,' and this is the meaning ascribed to yoni by many Buddhist authorities. But the reference to Hema*k*andra (ed. Boehtlingk and Rieu, p. 281) shows clearly that it meant 'origin,' or 'cause.' Yoniso occurs frequently as a mere adverb, meaning 'thoroughly, radically' (Dhammapada, p. 359), and yoniso manasikâra (Dhammapada, p. 110) means 'taking to heart' or 'minding thoroughly,' or, what is nearly the same, 'wisely.' In the Lalita-vistara, p. 41, the commentator has clearly mistaken yoni*s*a*h*, changing it to ye*ni*s*o, and explaining it by yamani*s*am, whereas M. Foucaux has rightly translated it by 'depuis l'origine.' Professor Weber suspected in yoni*s*a*h* a double entendre, but even grammar would show that our author is innocent of it. In Lalita-vistara, p. 544, l. 4, ayoni*s*a occurs in the sense of error.

327. Appamâdarata, not delighting in pamâda.

328, 329. Cf. Suttanipâta, vv. 44, 45.

him commit no sin, with few wishes, like an elephant in the forest.

331. If the occasion arises, friends are pleasant; enjoyment is pleasant, whatever be the cause; a good work is pleasant in the hour of death; the giving up of all grief is pleasant.

332. Pleasant in the world is the state of a mother, pleasant the state of a father, pleasant the state of a Samana, pleasant the state of a Brâhmana.

333. Pleasant is virtue lasting to old age, pleasant is a faith firmly rooted; pleasant is attainment of intelligence, pleasant is avoiding of sins.

332. The commentator throughout takes these words, like matteyyatâ, &c., to signify, not the status of a mother, or maternity, but reverence shown to a mother.

CHAPTER XXIV.

THIRST.

334. The thirst of a thoughtless man grows like a creeper; he runs from life to life, like a monkey seeking fruit in the forest.

335. Whomsoever this fierce poisonous thirst overcomes, in this world, his sufferings increase like the abounding Bîra*n*a grass.

336. But from him who overcomes this fierce thirst, difficult to be conquered in this world, sufferings fall off, like water-drops from a lotus leaf.

337. This salutary word I tell you, 'Do ye, as many as are here assembled, dig up the root of thirst, as he who wants the sweet-scented U*s*îra root must dig up the Bîra*n*a grass, that Mâra (the tempter) may not crush you again and again, as the stream crushes the reeds.'

338. As a tree, even though it has been cut down, is firm so long as its root is safe, and grows again, thus, unless the feeders of thirst are destroyed, this pain (of life) will return again and again.

339. He whose thirty-six streams are strongly flowing in the channels of pleasure, the waves will

---

334. This is explained by a story in the Chinese translation. Beal, Dhammapada, p. 148.

335. Bîra*n*a grass is the Andropogon muricatum, and the scented root of it is called U*s*îra (cf. verse 337).

338. On Anusaya, i. e. Anu*s*aya (Anlage), see Wassiljew, Der Buddhismus, p. 240 seq.

339. The thirty-six channels, which are divided by the commentator into eighteen external and eighteen internal, are explained

carry away that misguided man, viz. his desires which are set on passion.

340. The channels run everywhere, the creeper (of passion) stands sprouting; if you see the creeper springing up, cut its root by means of knowledge.

341. A creature's pleasures are extravagant and luxurious; given up to pleasure and deriving happiness, men undergo (again and again) birth and decay.

342. Beset with lust, men run about like a snared hare; held in fetters and bonds, they undergo pain for a long time, again and again.

343. Beset with lust, men run about like a snared hare; let therefore the mendicant drive out thirst, by striving after passionlessness for himself.

344. He who having got rid of the forest (of lust) (i.e. after having reached Nirvâ*n*a) gives himself over to forest-life (i.e. to lust), and who, when free from the forest (i.e. from lust), runs to the forest (i.e. to lust), look at that man! though free, he runs into bondage.

---

by Burnouf (Lotus, p. 649), from a gloss of the *G*inaalaṅkâra: 'L'indication précise des affections dont un Buddha acte indépendant, affections qui sont au nombre de dix-huit, nous est fourni par la glose d'un livre appartenant aux Buddhistes de Ceylan,' &c. Gray, however, takes them as the six organs of sense, the six objects of sense, in relation (1) to a desire for sensual pleasure, (2) to a desire for existence, and (3) to a desire for non-existence. Subhûti gives the right reading as manâpassavanâ; cf. Childers, Notes, p. 12.

Vâhâ, which Dr. Fausböll translates by 'equi, should be vahâ, 'undae.' Cf. Suttanipâta, v. 1034.

344. This verse seems again full of puns, all connected with the twofold meaning of vana, 'forest and lust.' By replacing 'forest' by 'lust,' we may translate: 'He who, when free from lust, gives himself up to lust, who, when removed from lust runs into lust,

345. Wise people do not call that a strong fetter which is made of iron, wood, or hemp; passionately strong is the care for precious stones and rings, for sons and a wife.

346. That fetter wise people call strong which drags down, yields, but is difficult to undo; after having cut this at last, people leave the world, free from cares, and leaving the pleasures of love behind.

347. Those who are slaves to passions, run down the stream (of desires), as a spider runs down the web which he has made himself; when they have cut this, at last, wise people go onwards, free from cares, leaving all pain behind.

348. Give up what is before, give up what is behind, give up what is between, when thou goest to the other shore of existence; if thy mind is altogether free, thou wilt not again enter into birth and decay.

349. If a man is tossed about by doubts, full of strong passions, and yearning only for what is delightful, his thirst will grow more and more, and he will indeed make his fetters strong.

---

look at that man,' &c. Nibbana, though with a short a, may be intended to remind the hearer of Nibbâna. The right reading, according to Childers, Notes, p. 8, is nibbanatho.

345. Apekhâ, apekshâ, 'care;' see Manu VI, 41, 49; Suttanipâta, v. 37; and *G*âtaka, vol. ii, p. 140.

346. Paribbag, i.e. parivrag; see Manu VI, 41.

347. The commentator explains the simile of the spider as follows: 'As a spider, after having made its thread-web, sits in the middle, and after killing with a violent rush a butterfly or a fly which has fallen in its circle, drinks its juice, returns, and sits again in the same place, in the same manner creatures who are given to passions, depraved by hatred, and maddened by wrath, run along the stream of thirst which they have made themselves, and cannot cross it,' &c.

350. If a man delights in quieting doubts, and, always reflecting, dwells on what is not delightful (the impurity of the body, &c.), he certainly will remove, nay, he will cut the fetter of Mâra.

351. He who has reached the consummation, who does not tremble, who is without thirst and without sin, he has broken all the thorns of life: this will be his last body.

352. He who is without thirst and without affection, who understands the words and their interpretation, who knows the order of letters (those which are before and which are after), he has received his last body, he is called the great sage, the great man.

353. 'I have conquered all, I know all, in all conditions of life I am free from taint; I have left all, and through the destruction of thirst I am free; having learnt myself, whom should I indicate (as my teacher)?'

354. The gift of the law exceeds all gifts; the sweetness of the law exceeds all sweetness; the delight in the law exceeds all delights; the extinction of thirst overcomes all pain.

---

352. As to nirutti, and its technical meaning among the Buddhists, see Burnouf, Lotus, p. 841. Fausböll translates 'niruttis vocabulorum peritus,' which may be right, if we take nirutti in the sense of the language of the Scriptures. See note to verse 363. Could not sannipâta mean sa*m*hitâ or sannikarsha? Sannipâta occurs in the *S*âkala-prâti*s*âkhya, but with a different meaning.

353. Cf. Suttanipâta, v. 210. The commentator explains that this verse was spoken by Buddha on his way to Bârâ*n*asî, in answer to **Upaka**, who had asked him who his teacher was, when Buddha asserted that he had no teacher. Childers accepts this explanation, s. v. uddigati. See also Lalita-vistara XXVI, ed. Calc. p. 526 seq., and read tenopaka *g*ino hy aham.

354. The dhammadâna, or 'gift of the law,' is the technical

355. Riches destroy the foolish, if they look not for the other shore; the foolish by his thirst for riches destroys himself, as if he were (destroying) others.

356. The fields are damaged by weeds, mankind is damaged by passion: therefore a gift bestowed on the passionless brings great reward.

357. The fields are damaged by weeds, mankind is damaged by hatred: therefore a gift bestowed on those who do not hate brings great reward.

358. The fields are damaged by weeds, mankind is damaged by vanity: therefore a gift bestowed on those who are free from vanity brings great reward.

359. The fields are damaged by weeds, mankind is damaged by lust: therefore a gift bestowed on those who are free from lust brings great reward.

---

term for instruction in the Buddhist religion. See Buddhaghosha's Parables, p. 160, where the story of the Sakkadevarâ*g*a is told, and where a free rendering of our verse is given.

358. 'Vanity and vexation of spirit,' Ecclesiastes.

CHAPTER XXV.

THE BHIKSHU (MENDICANT).

360. Restraint in the eye is good, good is restraint in the ear, in the nose restraint is good, good is restraint in the tongue.

361. In the body restraint is good, good is restraint in speech, in thought restraint is good, good is restraint in all things. A Bhikshu, restrained in all things, is freed from all pain.

362. He who controls his hand, he who controls his feet, he who controls his speech, he who is well controlled, he who delights inwardly, who is collected, who is solitary and content, him they call Bhikshu.

363. The Bhikshu who controls his mouth, who speaks wisely and calmly, who teaches the meaning and the law, his word is sweet.

364. He who dwells in the law, delights in the law, meditates on the law, recollects the law, that Bhikshu will never fall away from the true law.

365. Let him not despise what he has received, nor ever envy others: a mendicant who envies others does not obtain peace of mind.

---

363. On artha and dharma, see Stanislas Julien, Les Avadânas, I, 217, note: 'Les quatre connaissances sont; 1° la connaissance du sens (artha); 2° la connaissance de la Loi (dharma); 3° la connaissance des explications (niroukti); 4° la connaissance de l'intelligence (prâtibhâna).'

364. The expression dhammârâmo, 'having his garden or delight (Lustgarten) in the law,' is well matched by the Brahmanic expression ekârâma, i. e. nirdvandva (Mahâbh. XIII, 1930). Cf. Suttanipâta, v. 326; Dhammapada, v. 32.

366. A Bhikshu who, though he receives little, does not despise what he has received, even the gods will praise him, if his life is pure, and if he is not slothful.

367. He who never identifies himself with name and form, and does not grieve over what is no more, he indeed is called a Bhikshu.

368. The Bhikshu who behaves with kindness, who is happy in the doctrine of Buddha, will reach the quiet place (Nirvâ*n*a), happiness arising from the cessation of natural inclinations.

369. O Bhikshu, empty this boat! if emptied, it will go quickly; having cut off passion and hatred, thou wilt go to Nirvâ*n*a.

370. Cut off the five (fetters), leave the five, rise above the five. A Bhikshu, who has escaped from the five fetters, he is called Oghati*nn*a, 'saved from the flood.'

371. Meditate, O Bhikshu, and be not heedless! Do not direct thy thought to what gives pleasure,

---

367. Nâmarûpa is here used again in its technical sense of mind and body, neither of which, however, is with the Buddhists âtman, or 'self.' Asat, 'what is not,' may therefore mean the same as nâmarûpa, or we may take it in the sense of what is no more, as, for instance, the beauty or youth of the body, the vigour of the mind, &c.

368. See Childers, Notes, p. 11, who translates, 'where existence is no more;' but if we take saṅkhâra in the plural, it may mean states of the mind, or predispositions, inclinations, good, bad, or indifferent. Verse 383 supports Childers' version.

370. Morris, J. P. T. S. 1887, p. 116, takes uttaribhâvaye in the sense of to cultivate especially. Fausböll translates removeat. The five are differently explained by the commentator. See also Childers, s. v. sa*m*yo*g*ana.

371. The swallowing of hot iron balls is considered as a punishment in hell; see verse 308. Professor Weber has perceived the

that thou mayest not for thy heedlessness have to swallow the iron ball (in hell), and that thou mayest not cry out when burning, 'This is pain.'

372. Without knowledge there is no meditation, without meditation there is no knowledge: he who has knowledge and meditation is near unto Nirvâ*n*a.

373. A Bhikshu who has entered his empty house, and whose mind is tranquil, feels a more than human delight when he sees the law clearly.

374. As soon as he has considered the origin and destruction of the elements (khandha) of the body, he finds happiness and joy which belong to those who know the immortal (Nirvâ*n*a).

375. And this is the beginning here for a wise Bhikshu: watchfulness over the senses, contentedness, restraint under the law; keep noble friends whose life is pure, and who are not slothful.

376. Let him live in charity, let him be perfect in his duties; then in the fulness of delight he will make an end of suffering.

377. As the Vassikâ plant sheds its withered flowers, men should shed passion and hatred, O ye Bhikshus!

378. The Bhikshu whose body and tongue and mind are quieted, who is collected, and has rejected the baits of the world, he is called quiet.

379. Rouse thyself by thyself, examine thyself by thyself, thus self-protected and attentive wilt thou live happily, O Bhikshu!

---

right meaning of bhavassu, which can only be bhâvayasva, but I doubt whether the rest of his rendering is right, for who would swallow an iron ball by accident?

372. Cf. Beal, Catena, p. 247.

375. Cf. Suttanipâta, v. 337.

380. For self is the lord of self, self is the refuge of self; therefore curb thyself as the merchant curbs a noble horse.

381. The Bhikshu, full of delight, who is happy in the doctrine of Buddha will reach the quiet place (Nirvâ*n*a), happiness consisting in the cessation of natural inclinations.

382. He who, even as a young Bhikshu, applies himself to the doctrine of Buddha, brightens up this world, like the moon when free from clouds.

---

381. See verse 368. D'Alwis translates, 'dissolution of the sankhâras (elements of existence).'

CHAPTER XXVI.

THE BRÂHMA*N*A (ARHAT).

383. Stop the stream valiantly, drive away the desires, O Brâhma*n*a! When you have understood the destruction of all that was made, you will understand that which was not made.

384. If the Brâhma*n*a has reached the other shore in both laws (in restraint and contemplation), all bonds vanish from him who has obtained knowledge.

385. He for whom there is neither the hither nor the further shore, nor both, him, the fearless and unshackled, I call indeed a Brâhma*n*a.

386. He who is thoughtful, blameless, settled, dutiful, without passions, and who has attained the highest end, him I call indeed a Brâhma*n*a.

387. The sun is bright by day, the moon shines by night, the warrior is bright in his armour, the Brâhma*n*a is bright in his meditation; but Buddha, the Awakened, is bright with splendour day and night.

388. Because a man is rid of evil, therefore he is called Brâhma*n*a; because he walks quietly, therefore he is called Sama*n*a; because he has sent away his own impurities, therefore he is called Pravra*g*ita (Pabba*g*ita, a pilgrim).

---

385. The exact meaning of the two shores is not quite clear, and the commentator who takes them in the sense of internal and external organs of sense, can hardly be right. See verse 86.

388. These would-be etymologies are again interesting as showing the decline of the etymological consciousness of the spoken

389. No one should attack a Brâhma*n*a, but no Brâhma*n*a (if attacked) should let himself fly at his aggressor! Woe to him who strikes a Brâhma*n*a, more woe to him who flies at his aggressor!

390. It advantages a Brâhma*n*a not a little if he holds his mind back from the pleasures of life; the more all wish to injure has vanished, the more all pain will cease.

391. Him I call indeed a Brâhma*n*a who does not offend by body, word, or thought, and is controlled on these three points.

392. He from whom he may learn the law, as taught by the Well-awakened (Buddha), him let him worship assiduously, as the Brâhma*n*a worships the sacrificial fire.

393. A man does not become a Brâhma*n*a by his platted hair, by his family, or by birth; in whom there is truth and righteousness, he is blessed, he is a Brâhma*n*a.

394. What is the use of platted hair, O fool! what of the raiment of goat-skins? Within thee there is ravening, but the outside thou makest clean.

---

language of India at the time when such etymologies became possible. But in order to derive Brâhma*n*a from vâh, it must have been pronounced bâhma*n*o; vâh, 'to remove,' occurs frequently in the Buddhistical Sanskrit. Cf. Lal. Vist. p. 551, l. 1; 553, l. 7. See note to verse 265.

390. I am afraid I have taken too much liberty with this verse. Dr. Fausböll translates, 'Non Brâhma*n*ae hoc paulo melius, quando retentio fit mentis a jucundis.'

392. I have followed Childers, s. v. yo, in the translation of this verse.

393. Fausböll proposes to read *gakk*â (*g*âtyâ). 'Both' in the first edition of my translation was a misprint for 'birth.'

394. I have not copied the language of the Bible more than

395. The man who wears dirty raiments, who is emaciated and covered with veins, who meditates alone in the forest, him I call indeed a Brâhma*n*a.

396. I do not call a man a Brâhma*n*a because of his origin or of his mother. He is indeed arrogant, and he is wealthy: but the poor, who is free from all attachments, him I call indeed a Brâhma*n*a.

397. Him I call indeed a Brâhma*n*a who after cutting all fetters never trembles, is free from bonds and unshackled.

398. Him I call indeed a Brâhma*n*a who after cutting the strap and the thong, the rope with all that pertains to it, has destroyed all obstacles, and is awakened.

399. Him I call indeed a Brâhma*n*a who, though he has committed no offence, endures reproach, stripes, and bonds, who has endurance for his force, and strength for his army.

I was justified in. The words are abbhantaran te gahana*m*, bâhira*m* parima*gg*asi, 'interna est abyssus, externum mundas.' Cf. *G*âtaka, vol. i, p. 481.

395. The expression Kisan dhamanisanthatam is the Sanskrit k*ri*s*am* dhamanîsantatam, the frequent occurrence of which in the Mahâbhârata has been pointed out by Boehtlingk, s. v. dhamani. It looks more like a Brâhmanic than like a Buddhist phrase.

396. From verse 396 to the first half of verse 423, the text of the Dhammapada agrees with the text of the Vasish*th*a-Bharadvâ*g*a-sûtra. These verses are translated by D'Alwis in his Nirvâ*n*a, pp. 113–118, and again by Fausböll, Suttanipâta, v. 620 seq.

The text contains puns on ki*ñk*ana, which means 'wealth,' but also 'attachment;' cf. Childers, s. v.

398. D'Alwis points out a double entendre in these words. Nandhi may be either the strap that goes round a drum, or enmity; varatta may be either a thong or attachment; sandâna either chain or scepticism; sahanakkamam either due order or all its concomitants; paligha either obstacle or ignorance.

399. The exact meaning of balânîka is difficult to find. Does

400. Him I call indeed a Brâhma*n*a who is free from anger, dutiful, virtuous, without appetites, who is subdued, and has received his last body.

401. Him I call indeed a Brâhma*n*a who does not cling to sensual pleasures, like water on a lotus leaf, like a mustard seed on the point of a needle.

402. Him I call indeed a Brâhma*n*a who, even here, knows the end of his own suffering, has put down his burden, and is unshackled.

403. Him I call indeed a Brâhma*n*a whose knowledge is deep, who possesses wisdom, who knows the right way and the wrong, and has attained the highest end.

404. Him I call indeed a Brâhma*n*a who keeps aloof both from laymen and from mendicants, who frequents no houses, and has but few desires.

405. Him I call indeed a Brâhma*n*a who without hurting any creatures, whether feeble or strong, does not kill nor cause slaughter.

406. Him I call indeed a Brâhma*n*a who is tolerant with the intolerant, mild with the violent, and free from greed among the greedy.

407. Him I call indeed a Brâhma*n*a from whom anger and hatred, pride and hypocrisy have dropt like a mustard seed from the point of a needle.

408. Him I call indeed a Brâhma*n*a who utters true speech, instructive and free from harshness, so that he offend no one.

409. Him I call indeed a Brâhma*n*a who takes

---

it mean, possessed of a strong army, or facing a force, or leading a force?

405. On tasa and thâvara, see Childers, s. v., and D'Alwis, Nirvâ*n*a, p. 115. On da*nd*a, 'the rod,' see Hibbert Lectures, p. 355, note.

nothing in the world that is not given him, be it long or short, small or large, good or bad.

410. Him I call indeed a Brâhma*n*a who fosters no desires for this world or for the next, has no inclinations, and is unshackled.

411. Him I call indeed a Brâhma*n*a who has no interests, and when he has understood (the truth), does not say How, how? and who has reached the depth of the Immortal.

412. Him I call indeed a Brâhma*n*a who in this world has risen above both ties, good and evil, who is free from grief, from sin, and from impurity.

413. Him I call indeed a Brâhma*n*a who is bright like the moon, pure, serene, undisturbed, and in whom all gaiety is extinct.

414. Him I call indeed a Brâhma*n*a who has traversed this miry road, the impassable world, difficult to pass, and its vanity, who has gone through, and reached the other shore, is thoughtful, steadfast, free from doubts, free from attachment, and content.

415. Him I call indeed a Brâhma*n*a who in this world, having abandoned all desires, travels about

---

411. Akathankathi is explained by Buddhaghosa as meaning, 'free from doubt or hesitation.' He also uses kathankathâ in the sense of 'doubt' (verse 414). In the Kâvyâdar*s*a, III, 17, the commentator explains akatham by kathârahitam, nirvivâdam, which would mean, 'without a kathâ, a speech, a story without contradiction, unconditionally.' From our passage, however, it seems as if kathankathâ was a noun derived from kathankathayati, 'to say How, how?' so that neither the first nor the second element had anything to do with kath, 'to relate;' and in that case akatham, too, ought to be taken in the sense of 'without a Why.'

412. See verse 39. The distinction between good and evil vanishes when a man has retired from the world, and has ceased to act, longing only for deliverance.

without a home, and in whom all concupiscence is extinct.

416. Him I call indeed a Brâhmana who, having abandoned all longings, travels about without a home, and in whom all covetousness is extinct.

417. Him I call indeed a Brâhmana who, after leaving all bondage to men, has risen above all bondage to the gods, and is free from all and every bondage.

418. Him I call indeed a Brâhmana who has left what gives pleasure and what gives pain, who is cold, and free from all germs (of renewed life), the hero who has conquered all the worlds.

419. Him I call indeed a Brâhmana who knows the destruction and the return of beings everywhere, who is free from bondage, welfaring (Sugata), and awakened (Buddha).

---

418. Upadhi, if not used in a technical sense, is best translated by 'passions or affections.' Technically there are four upadhis or substrata, viz. the kandhas, kâma, 'desire,' kilesa, 'sin,' and kamma, 'work.' The Brâhmana may be called nirupadhi, as being free from desire, misery, and work and its consequences, but not yet of the kandhas, which end through death only. The commentator explains nirupadhi by nirupakkilesa, 'free from sin.' See Childers, s. v. nibbâna, p. 268 a.

419. Sugata is one of those many words in Buddhist literature which it is almost impossible to translate, because they have been taken in so many acceptations by the Buddhists themselves. Sugata etymologically means 'one who has fared well,' sugati means 'happiness and blessedness.' It is wrong to translate it literally by 'welcome,' for that in Sanskrit is svâgata; and we can hardly accept Dr. Eitel's statement (Handbook, p. 138) that sugata stands incorrectly for svâgata. Sugata is one of the not very numerous technical terms in Buddhism for which hitherto we know of no antecedents in earlier Brahmanism. It may have been used in the sense of 'happy and blessed,' but it never became a title, while in Buddhism it has become, not only a title, but

420. Him I call indeed a Brâhma*n*a whose path the gods do not know, nor spirits (Gandharvas), nor men, whose passions are extinct, and who is an Arhat (venerable).

421. Him I call indeed a Brâhma*n*a who calls nothing his own, whether it be before, behind, or between, who is poor, and free from the love of the world.

422. Him I call indeed a Brâhma*n*a, the manly, the noble, the hero, the great sage, the conqueror, the indifferent, the accomplished, the awakened.

423. Him I call indeed a Brâhma*n*a who knows his former abodes, who sees heaven and hell, has reached the end of births, is perfect in knowledge, a sage, and whose perfections are all perfect.

---

almost a proper name of Buddha. The same applies to tathâgata, lit. 'thus come,' but used in Sanskrit very much like tathâvidha, in the sense of talis, while in Buddhism it means a Buddha. There are of course many interpretations of the word, and many reasons are given why Buddhas should be called Tathâgata (Burnouf, Introduction, p. 75, &c.). Boehtlingk s. v. supposed that, because Buddha had so many predicates, he was, for the sake of brevity, called 'such a one as he really is.' I think we may go a step further. Another word, tâd*ri*s*a, meaning talis, becomes in Pâli, under the form of tâdi, a name of Buddha's disciples, and afterwards of Buddha himself. If applied to Buddha's disciples, it may have meant originally 'such as he,' i. e. his fellows; but when applied to Buddha himself, it can only mean 'such a one,' i. e. 'so great a man.' The Sanskrit mârsha is probably the Pâli mâriso, which stands for mâdiso, Sk. mâd*ri*s*a, 'like me,' used in Pâli when a superior addresses others as his equals, and afterwards changed into a mere title of respect.

INDEX.

The figures of this Index refer to the numbers of the verses.

THE

SACRED BOOKS OF THE EAST

SUTTA-NIPÂTA

THE

SACRED BOOKS OF THE EAST

TRANSLATED

BY VARIOUS ORIENTAL SCHOLARS

AND EDITED BY

F. MAX MÜLLER

VOLUME X

PART II

SECOND EDITION

THE SUTTA-NIPÂTA

A COLLECTION OF DISCOURSES

BEING ONE OF THE CANONICAL BOOKS OF THE BUDDHISTS

TRANSLATED FROM PÂLI

BY

V. FAUSBÖLL

SECOND EDITION, REVISED

CONTENTS.

EXPLANATION OF WORDS

the meaning of which is not always given in the translation.

Â*g*îvika, one belonging to a sect of naked ascetics.

Arahat, a holy man, a saint.

Ariya, noble.

Bhagavat, worshipful, blessed, a name of a Buddha.

Bhikkhu, a mendicant.

Brahman, the supreme god of the Hindus.

Brâhma*n*a, a sage.

Buddha, enlightened, a name of certain holy men who have freed themselves from existence, particularly of Sama*n*a Gotama.

Dhamma, tenet, doctrine, custom, law, religion, virtue, thing.

Gaha*tth*a, Gihin, a householder.

Gotama, a name of the last Buddha.

*G*a*t*ila, an ascetic wearing clotted hair.

*G*ina, a conqueror, a name of a Buddha.

Isi, a sage.

Khattiya, a warrior, a prince.

*K*a*nd*âla, an outcast.

Mâra, a name of the king of death, the devil.

Muni, a thinker, a sage.

Nâga, an eminent man.

Namu*k*i = Mâra.

Nibbâna, extinction, the state of bliss of the Buddhist.

Niga*nth*a, a naked ascetic.

Pabba*gg*â, leaving the world, embracing ascetic life, taking the robe.

Pabba*g*ita, an ascetic, having taken the robe.

Paribbâ*g*a, Paribbâ*g*aka, a wandering mendicant.

Sakka = Sakya, belonging to the Sakya tribe.

Sakyamuni, the Sakya sage, a name of Buddha.

Sama*n*a, an ascetic.

Sa*m*khârâ, all compound things, the material world, the elements of existence.

Sa*m*sâra, revolution, transmigration.

Sâvaka, a hearer, a follower, a disciple of Buddha, including both laity and clergy.

Sekha, a novice, student.

Sudda, a man of the servile caste.

Sugata, happy, a name of a Buddha

Thera, an elder, a senior priest.

Titthiya, an ascetic adhering to a certain system of philosophy.

Upadhi, the elements of the world.

Upâsaka, a follower, a lay devotee.

Upasampadâ, priest's orders.

Vessa, Vessika, a man of the third caste.

Yakkha, a giant, a malignant spirit.

INTRODUCTION

TO

THE SUTTA-NIPÂTA.

THE Collection of Discourses, Sutta-Nipâta, which I have here translated[1], is very remarkable, as there can be no doubt that it contains some remnants of Primitive Buddhism. I consider the greater part of the Mahâvagga, and nearly the whole of the A*tth*akavagga as very old. I have arrived at this conclusion from two reasons, first from the language, and secondly from the contents.

1. We not only find here what we meet with in other Pâli poetry, the fuller Vedic forms of nouns and verbs in the plural, as avîtata*m*hâse, pa*nd*itâse, dhammâse, sitâse, upa*tth*itâse, pavâdiyâse, &c., and *k*arâmase, asmase, sikkhissâmase; the shorter Vedic plurals and the instrumental singular of nouns, as vini*kkh*ayâ, lakkha*n*â for vini*kkh*ayâni, lakkha*n*âni, mantâ, pari*ññ*â, vinayâ, lâbhakamyâ for mantâya, &c.; Vedic infinitives, as vippahâtave, sampayâtave, u*nn*ametave; contracted (or sometimes old) forms, as santyâ, *g*a*kk*â, dugga*kk*â, sammu*kk*â, titthyâ, thiyo, parihîrati for santiyâ, *g*âtiyâ, sammutiyâ, titthiyâ, itthiyo, parihariyati, by the side of protracted forms, such as âtumâna*m*; but also some unusual (sometimes old) forms and words, as apu*kkh*asi, sagghasi[2] = sakkhissasi, sussa*m* = su*n*issâmi (Sansk. *s*roshyâmi), pâva and pâvâ = vadati, pave*kkh*e = paveseyya, parikissati = parikilissati, vineyya, vi*k*eyya, ni*kkh*eyya, pappuyya, = vinayitvâ, &c., da*tth*u = disvâ (S. d*ri*sh*t*vâ), atisitvâ = atikkamitvâ, anuvi*kk*a = anuviditvâ, paribbasâna = vasamâna, garuna*m*, bhikkhuna*m*, munina*m*, vedaguna*m* (accus.), amhanâ (S. a*s*manâ) = pâsâ*n*ena, vâ*k*ibhi, *k*atubbhi, rattamahâbhi, ise (vocative), suvâmi = sâmi, maga = miga tumo = so, parovara = parâvara, bhûnahu = bhûtihanaka upaya, âmagandha, dhona, vyappatha, vyappathi, vevi*kkh*â

[1] Sir M. Coomâra Swâmy's translation of part of the book has been a great help to me. The Pâli text was published by the Pâli Text Society for 1884.

[2] C reads pagghasi.

visenibhûta, visenikatvâ, pa*t*iseniyanti. We also find tmesis as in the Vedas, for instance, v. 348, tamo v'assa nivuto sabbaloko; v. 1108, ki*m* su sa*m*yo*g*ano loko. Sometimes we meet with difficult and irregular constructions, and very condensed expressions. All this proves, I think, that these parts of the book are much older than the Suttas in which the language is not only fluent, but of which some verses are even singularly melodious.

2. In the contents of the Suttanipâta we have, I think, an important contribution to the right understanding of Primitive Buddhism, for we see here a picture not of life in monasteries, but of the life of hermits in its first stage. We have before us not the systematizing of the later Buddhist church, but the first germs of a system, the fundamental ideas of which come out with sufficient clearness. From the A*tth*akavagga especially it is evident where Buddha takes his stand in opposition to Philosophy (di*tth*i = dar*s*ana).

Indian society at the time of Buddha had two large and distinguished religious sects, Sama*n*as and Brâhma*n*as. This is apparent from several passages where they are mentioned together; for instance, Vinaya, ed. Oldenberg, II, p. 295; Grimblot, Sept Suttas Pâlis, p. ix, 8 &c., 118 &c., 158 &c., 306 &c., 309; Dhammapada, p. 392; Suttanipâta, vv. 99, 129, 189, 440, 529, 859, 1078; Sabhiyasutta, at the beginning; the Inscriptions of Asoka; Mahâbhâshya, II, 4, 9 (fol. 398 a); Lalita Vistara, pp. 309, l. 10, 318, l. 18, 320, l. 20; and lastly, Megasthenes (Schwanbeck, p. 45), δύο γένη φιλοσόφων, ὧν τοὺς μὲν Βραχμᾶνας καλεῖ, τοὺς δὲ Σαρμᾶνας.

Famous teachers arose and gathered around them flocks of disciples. As such are mentioned Pûra*n*a-Kassapa, Makkhali-Gosâla, A*g*ita-Kesakambali, Pakudha-Ka*kk*âyana, Sa*ñg*aya-Bela*tth*iputta, and Niga*nth*a-Nâtaputta[1]; see Suttanipâta, p. 85; Mahâparinibbânasutta, ed. Childers, p. 58; Vinaya II, p. 111; Grimblot, Sept Suttas Pâlis, p. 114, &c.; Milindapa*ñ*ha, ed. Trenckner, p. 4. Besides these there is Bâvari (Suttanipâta, p. 176), and his disciples A*g*ita, Tissametteyya, Pu*nn*aka, Mettagû, Dhotaka, Upasîva, Nanda,

[1] Cf. Indian Antiquary, 1880, p. 158.

Hemaka, Todeyya, Kappa, *G*atuka*nn*in, Bhadrâvudha, Udaya, Posâla, Mogharâ*g*an (Piṅgiya, vv. 1006–1008; Sela, p. 97), and *K*aṅkin, Târukkha, Pokkharasâti, *G*ânusso*n*i, Vâse*tth*a, and Bhâradvâ*g*a, p. 108.

We learn that there were four kinds of Sama*n*as, viz. Magga*g*inas, Maggadesakas (or Maggadesins, Magga*ggh*âyins), Magga*g*îvins, and Maggadûsins, vv. 83–88. Among these Sama*n*as disputes arose, vv. 828, 883–884; a number of philosophical systems were formed, and at the time of Buddha there were as many as sixty-three of them, v. 538. These systems are generally designated by di*tth*i, vv. 54, 151, 786, 837, 851, &c.; or by di*tth*igata, vv. 834, 836, 913; or by di*tth*asuta, v. 778; or by di*tth*a, suta, and muta, vv. 793, 813, 914; or by di*tth*a, suta, sîlavata[1], and muta, vv. 790, 797–798, 836, 887, 1080. The doctrines themselves are called di*tth*inivesa, v. 785; or nivesana, vv. 209, 470, 801, 846; or vini*kkh*aya, vv. 838, 866, 887, 894; and he who entertains any of them, is called nivissavâdin, vv. 910, 913.

What is said of the Sama*n*as seems mostly to hold good about the Brâhma*n*as also. They too are called disputatious, vâdasîla, v. 381, &c., p. 109; and three kinds of them are mentioned, viz. Titthiyas, Â*g*îvikas, and Niga*nth*as, vv. 380, 891–892. In contradistinction to the Sama*n*as the Brâhma*n*as are designated as Tevi*gg*as, vv. 594, 1019; they are Padakas, Veyyâkara*n*as, and perfect in *G*appa, Nigha*nd*u, Ketubha, Itihâsa, &c., v. 595, p. 97. They are called friends of the hymns, v. 139; well versed in the hymns, v. 976; and their principal hymn is Sâvitti[2], vv. 568, 456. They worship and make offerings to the fire, pp. 73, 20. In Brâhma*n*adhammikasutta the ancient and just Brâhma*n*as are described in opposition to the later

[1] I am not sure whether sîlavata is to be understood as one notion or two. It is generally written in one word, but at p. 108 Vâse*tth*a says, when one is virtuous and endowed with works, he is a Brâhma*n*a, yato kho bho sîlavâ *k*a hoti vatasampanno *k*a ettâvatâ kho brâhma*n*o hoti. Sîlavata, I presume, refers chiefly to the Brâhma*n*as.

[2] From v. 456 we see that Buddha has rightly read vare*n*iyam as the metre requires, but I must not omit to mention that the Commentator understands by Sâvitti the Buddhistic formula: Buddha*m* sara*n*a*m* ga*kkh*âmi, Dhamma*m* sara*n*a*m* ga*kkh*âmi, Sa*m*gha*m* sara*n*a*m* ga*kkh*âmi, which, like Sâvitti, contains twenty-four syllables.

Brâhma*n*as, who slay innocent cows and have acquired wealth through the favour of the kings, vv. 307, 308, 311, 302[1].

All these disputants hold fast to their own prejudiced views, v. 910. They say that purity comes from philosophical views, from tradition, and from virtuous works, and in many other ways, v. 1078, and that there is no bliss excepting by following their opinions, vv. 889, 891, 892.

Buddha himself has, it is true, sprung from the Sama*n*as: he is called Sama*n*a Gotama, p. 95; he shines like a sun in the midst of the Sama*n*as, v. 550; and intercourse with Sama*n*as is said to be the highest blessing, v. 265. But Buddha has overcome all their systems, v. 538; there is nothing which has not been seen, heard, or thought by him, and nothing which has not been understood by him, v. 1121. All the disputatious Brâhma*n*as do not overcome him in understanding, v. 380; and he asserts that no one is purified and saved by philosophy or by virtuous works, vv. 1079, 839. Sanctification, in fact, does not come from another, vv. 773, 790, 813; it can be attained only by going into the yoke with Buddha, v. 834; by believing in him and in the Dhamma of the Saints, vv. 183, 185, 370, 1142; on the whole, by being what Buddha is.

What then is Buddha?

First he is a Visionary, in the good sense of the word; his knowledge is intuitive, 'Seeing misery,' he says, 'in the philosophical views, without adopting any of them, searching for truth, I saw inward peace,' vv. 837, 207. And again, 'He, a conqueror unconquered, saw the Dhamma visibly, without any traditional instruction,' vv. 934, 1052, 1065. He teaches an instantaneous, an immediate religious life, vv. 567, 1136. He is called *k*akkhumat, endowed with an eye, clearly-seeing, vv. 160, 405, 540, 562, 596, 956, 992, 1028, 1095, 1115, 1127; samanta*k*akkhu, the all-seeing, vv. 1062, 1068; and as such he has become an eye to the world, v. 599. He sees the subtle meaning of things, vv. 376, 175; he is, in one word, Sambuddha, the perfectly-enlightened, vv. 177, 555, 596, 992; and by knowledge he

[1] Besides the religious Brâhma*n*as some secular Brâhma*n*as are mentioned, p. 11.

is delivered, vv. 1106, 727, 733. Existence is avi*gg*â, ignorance, v. 729; vi*gg*â, knowledge, is the extinction of the world, v. 730.

Secondly he is an Ascetic, a Muni[1], one that forsakes the world and wanders from the house to the houseless state, vv. 273, 375, 1003; because from house-life arises defilement, v. 206. An ascetic has no prejudiced ideas, v. 802; he has shaken off every philosophical view, v. 787; he does not enter into disputes, v. 887; he is not pleased nor displeased with anything, v. 813; he is indifferent to learning, v. 911; he does not cling to good and evil, vv. 520, 547, 790; he has cut off all passion and all desire, vv. 2, 795, 1130, 916; he is free from marks, v. 847; and possessionless, aki*ñk*ana, vv. 175, 454, 490, 620, 1058, 1062, 976, 1069, 1114. He is equable, v. 855; under all circumstances the same, v. 952; still as the deep water, v. 920; calm, vv. 459, 861. He has reached peace, vv. 837, 845, 919; he knows that bliss consists in peace, v. 933; he has gone to immortal peace, the unchangeable state of Nibbâna, v. 203. And how is this state brought about? By the destruction of consciousness, vv. 734-735. And how does consciousness cease? By the cessation of sensation, vv. 1109-1110.

1. What then is sin according to Buddha?

Subjectively sin is desire, in all its various forms, vv. 923, 1103; viz. desire for existence generally, vv. 776, 1059, 1067, and especially for name and form, i.e. individual existence, vv. 354, 1099. As long as man is led by desire he will be whirled about in existence, v. 740; for as long as there is birth, there will be death, v. 742. Existence is called the stream of death, v. 354; the realm of Mâra, vv. 164, 1145. Those who continually go to sa*m*sâra with birth and death, are the ignorant, v. 729.

[1] Buddha is sometimes styled the great Isi, vv. 1060, 1082; sometimes a Muni, vv. 164, 700; sometimes a Brâhma*n*a, v. 1064; sometimes a Bhikkhu, vv. 411, 415; and all these appellations are used synonymously, vv. 283, 284, 1064, 1066, 843, 844, 911, 912, 946, 220. Ascetic life is praised throughout the book, especially in the Uraga-, Muni-, Râhula-, Sammâparibbâ*g*aniya-, Dhammika-, Nâlaka-, Purâbheda-, Tuva*t*aka-, Attada*nd*a-, and Sâriputta-suttas.

But desire originates in the body, vv. 270, 1099; sin lies objectively in embodiment or matter, and consequently the human body is looked upon as a contemptible thing. See Vigayasutta, p. 32.

2. And what is bliss?

Subjectively, it is emancipation from desire by means of the peace that Buddha preaches, vv. 1065–1066, 1069, 1084, 1108, 838–839.

Objectively, it is emancipation from body and matter. One must destroy the elements of existence, upadhî, vv. 373, 546, 1050, 1056; and leave the body behind, that one may not come to exist again, vv. 1120, 1122, 761. The ignorant only create upadhî, v. 1050, and go again and again to samsâra, v. 729. The wise do not enter time, kappa, vv. 521, 535, 860; they look upon the world as void, v. 1118; hold that there is nothing really existing, v. 1069; and those whose minds are disgusted with a future existence, the wise who have destroyed their seeds (of existence), go out like a lamp, vv. 234, 353–354. As a flame, blown about by the violence of the wind, goes out, and cannot be reckoned (as existing), even so a Muni, delivered from name and body, disappears, and cannot be reckoned (as existing), v. 1073. For him who has disappeared, there is no form; that by which they say he is, exists for him no longer, v. 1075.

'Exert thyself, then,—O Dhotaka,' so said Bhagavat,—'being wise and thoughtful in this world, let one, having listened to my utterance, learn his own extinction,' v. 1061.

Tena h' âtappam karohi,—Dhotakâ 'ti Bhagavâ,—
idh' eva nipako sato
ito sutvâna nigghosam
sikkhe nibbânam attano.

With this short sketch of the contents of the Suttanipâta for a guide, I trust it will be easy to understand even the more obscure parts of the book.

V. FAUSBÖLL.

COPENHAGEN,
Sept. 13, 1880.

INTRODUCTION

TO THE SECOND EDITION OF

THE SUTTA-NIPÂTA.

I am glad to acknowledge that some of the corrections in this new translation I owe to the suggestions of Professor Rhys Davids and to the notes of the late Doctor Richard Morris in the Journal of the Pâli Text Society. In different difficult places I have added a few more extracts from the commentary 'Paramatthagotikâ,' for it is and has always been my principle to follow the commentaries, as far as I understand them, and I think that this is the only safe way to go at the beginning of a study like this; later, when we get a greater material to work from, we may perhaps in some places rid ourselves of the commentaries, still we must always be careful, and we must never think that we know better than a long tradition from guru to guru.

V. FAUSBÖLL.

COPENHAGEN.

I. URAGAVAGGA.

1. URAGASUTTA.

The Bhikkhu who discards all human passions is compared to a snake that casts his skin.—Text and translation in Fr. Spiegel's Anecdota Pâlica.

1. He who restrains his anger when it has arisen, as (they) by medicines (restrain) the poison of the snake spreading (in the body), that Bhikkhu leaves this and the further shore, as a snake (quits its) old worn out skin. (1)

2. He who has cut off passion entirely, as (they cut off) the lotus-flower growing in a lake, after diving (into the water), that Bhikkhu leaves this and the further shore, as a snake (quits its) old worn out skin. (2)

3. He who has cut off craving entirely, the flowing, the quickly running, after drying it up, that Bhikkhu leaves this and the further shore, as a snake (quits its) old worn out skin. (3)

4. He who has destroyed arrogance entirely, as the flood (destroys) a very frail bridge of reeds, that Bhikkhu leaves this and the further shore, as a snake (quits its) old worn out skin. (4)

5. He who has not found any essence in the existences, like one that looks for flowers on fig-trees, that Bhikkhu leaves this and the further shore, as a snake (quits its) old worn out skin. (5)

6. He in whose breast there are no feelings of anger, who has thus overcome reiterated existence, that Bhikkhu leaves this and the further shore, as a snake (quits its) old worn out skin. (6)

7. He whose doubts are scattered, cut off entirely inwardly, that Bhikkhu leaves this and the further shore, as a snake (quits its) old worn out skin. (7)

8. He who did not go too fast forward, nor was left behind, who overcame all this (world of) delusion, that Bhikkhu leaves this and the further shore, as a snake (quits its) old worn out skin. (8)

9. He who did not go too fast forward, nor was left behind, having seen that all this in the world is false, that Bhikkhu leaves this and the further shore, as a snake (quits its) old worn out skin. (9)

10. He who did not go too fast forward, nor was left behind, being free from covetousness, (seeing) that all this is false, that Bhikkhu leaves this and the further shore, as a snake (quits its) old worn out skin. (10)

11. He who did not go too fast forward, nor was left behind, being free from passion, (seeing) that all this is false, that Bhikkhu leaves this and the further shore, as a snake (quits its) old worn out skin. (11)

12. He who did not go too fast forward, nor was left behind, being free from hatred, (seeing) that all this is false, that Bhikkhu leaves this and the further shore, as a snake (quits its) old worn out skin. (12)

13. He who did not go too fast forward, nor was left behind, being free from folly, (seeing) that all this is false, that Bhikkhu leaves this and the further shore, as a snake (quits its) old worn out skin. (13)

14. He to whom there are no affections whatsoever, whose sins are extirpated from the root, that Bhikkhu leaves this and the further shore, as a snake (quits its) old worn out skin. (14)

15. He to whom there are no (sins) whatsoever originating in fear, which are the causes of coming back to this shore, that Bhikkhu leaves this and the further shore, as a snake (quits its) old worn out skin. (15)

16. He to whom there are no (sins) whatsoever originating in desire, which are the causes of binding (men) to existence, that Bhikkhu leaves this and the further shore, as a snake (quits its) old worn out skin. (16)

17. He who, having left the five obstacles, is free from suffering, has overcome doubt, and is without pain, that Bhikkhu leaves this and the further shore, as a snake (quits its) old worn out skin. (17)

Uragasutta is ended.

---

2. DHANIYASUTTA.

A dialogue between the rich herdsman Dhaniya and Buddha, the one rejoicing in his worldly security and the other in his religious belief.—This beautiful dialogue calls to mind the parable in the Gospel of St. Luke xii. 16. See a translation in Rhys Davids' Buddhism, 1896, p. 167.

1. 'I have boiled (my) rice, I have milked (my cows),'—so said the herdsman Dhaniya,—'I am living together with my fellows near the banks of the Mahî (river), (my) house is covered, the fire is kindled: therefore, if thou like, rain, O sky!' (18)

2. 'I am free from anger, free from stubbornness,'—so said Bhagavat,—'I am abiding for one night near the banks of the Mahî (river), my house

is uncovered, the fire (of passions) is extinguished: therefore, if thou like, rain, O sky!' (19)

3. 'Gad-flies are not to be found (with me),'—so said the herdsman Dhaniya,—'in meadows abounding with grass the cows are roaming, and they can endure rain when it comes: therefore, if thou like, rain, O sky!' (20)

4. '(By me) is made a well-constructed raft,'—so said Bhagavat,—'I have passed over (to Nibbâna), I have reached the further bank, having overcome the torrent (of passions); there is no (further) use for a raft: therefore, if thou like, rain, O sky!' (21)

5. 'My wife is obedient, not wanton,'—so said the herdsman Dhaniya,—'for a long time she has been living together (with me), she is winning, and I hear nothing wicked of her: therefore, if thou like, rain, O sky!' (22)

6. 'My mind is obedient, delivered (from all worldliness),'—so said Bhagavat,—'it has for a long time been highly cultivated and well-subdued, there is no longer anything wicked in me: therefore, if thou like, rain, O sky!' (23)

7. 'I support myself by my own earnings,'—so said the herdsman Dhaniya,—'and my children are (all) about me, healthy; I hear nothing wicked of them: therefore, if thou like, rain, O sky!' (24)

8. 'I am no one's servant,'—so said Bhagavat,—'with what I have gained I wander about in all the world, there is no need (for me) to serve: therefore, if thou like, rain, O sky!' (25)

9. 'I have cows, I have calves,'—so said the herdsman Dhaniya,—'I have cows in calf and heifers, and I have also a bull as lord over the cows: therefore, if thou like, rain, O sky!' (26)

10. 'I have no cows, I have no calves,'—so said Bhagavat,—'I have no cows in calf and no heifers, and I have no bull as a lord over the cows: therefore, if thou like, rain, O sky!' (27)

11. 'The stakes are driven in, and cannot be shaken,'—so said the herdsman Dhaniya,—'the ropes are made of mu*ñg*a grass, new and well-made, the cows will not be able to break them: therefore, if thou like, rain, O sky!' (28)

12. 'Having, like a bull, rent the bonds; having, like an elephant, broken through the galu*kkh*i creeper, I shall not again enter into a womb: therefore, if thou like, rain, O sky!' (29)

Then at once a shower poured down, filling both sea and land. Hearing the sky raining, Dhaniya spoke thus: (29 b)

13. 'No small gain indeed (has accrued) to us since we have seen Bhagavat; we take refuge in thee, O (thou who art) endowed with the eye (of wisdom); be thou our master, O great Muni!' (30)

14. 'Both my wife and myself are obedient; (if) we lead a holy life before Sugata, we shall conquer birth and death, and put an end to pain.' (31)

15. 'He who has sons has delight in sons,'—so said the wicked Mâra,—'he who has cows has delight likewise in cows; for upadhi (substance) is the delight of man, but he who has no upadhi has no delight.' (32)

16. 'He who has sons has care with (his) sons,'—so said Bhagavat,—'he who has cows has likewise care with (his) cows; for upadhi (is the cause of) people's cares, but he who has no upadhi has no care.' (33)

Dhaniyasutta is ended.

3. KHAGGAVISÂNASUTTA.

Family life and intercourse with others should be avoided, for society has all vices in its train; therefore one should leave the corrupted state of society and lead a solitary life.

1. Having laid aside the rod against all beings, and not hurting any of them, let no one wish for a son, much less for a companion, let him wander alone like a rhinoceros[1]. (34)

2. In him who has intercourse (with others) affections arise, (and then) the pain which follows affection; considering the misery that originates in affection let one wander alone like a rhinoceros. (35)

3. He who has compassion on his friends and confidential (companions) loses (his own) advantage, having a fettered mind; seeing this danger in friendship let one wander alone like a rhinoceros. (36)

4. Just as a large bamboo tree (with its branches) entangled (in each other, such is) the care one has with children and wife; (but) like the shoot of a bamboo not clinging (to anything) let one wander alone like a rhinoceros[2]. (37)

5. As a beast unbound in the forest goes feeding at pleasure, so let the wise man, considering (only his) own will, wander alone like a rhinoceros. (38)

6. There is (a constant) calling in the midst of company, both when sitting, standing, walking, and going away; (but) let one, looking (only) for freedom from desire and for following his own will, wander alone like a rhinoceros. (39)

7. There is sport and amusement in the midst of

[1] Comp. Dhp. v. 142. [2] Comp. Dhp. v. 345.

company, and for children there is great affection; (although) disliking separation from his dear friends, let one wander alone like a rhinoceros. (40)

8. He who is at home in (all) the four regions and is not hostile (to any one), being content with this or that, overcoming (all) dangers fearlessly, let him wander alone like a rhinoceros. (41)

9. Discontented are some pabba*g*itas (ascetics) also some gaha*tth*as (householders) dwelling in houses; let one, caring little about other people's children, wander alone like a rhinoceros. (42)

10. Removing the marks of a gihin (a householder) like a Kovilâra tree whose leaves are fallen, let one, after cutting off heroically the ties of a gihin, wander alone like a rhinoceros. (43)

11. If one acquires a clever companion, an associate righteous and wise, let him, overcoming all dangers, wander about with him glad and thoughtful[1]. (44)

12. If one does not acquire a clever companion, an associate righteous and wise, then as a king abandoning (his) conquered kingdom, let him wander alone like a rhinoceros[2]. (45)

13. Surely we ought to praise the good luck of having companions, the best (and such as are our) equals ought to be sought for; not having acquired such friends let one, enjoying (only) allowable things, wander alone like a rhinoceros[3]. (46)

14. Seeing bright golden (bracelets), well-wrought by the goldsmith, striking (against each other when there are) two on one arm, let one wander alone like a rhinoceros. (47)

[1] Comp. Dhp. v. 328. [2] Comp. Dhp. v. 329.
[3] Comp. Dhp. v. 61.

15. Thus (if I join myself) with another I shall swear or scold; considering this danger in future, let one wander alone like a rhinoceros. (48)

16. The sensual pleasures indeed, which are various, sweet, and charming, under their different shapes agitate the mind; seeing the misery (originating) in sensual pleasures, let one wander alone like a rhinoceros. (49)

17. These (pleasures are) to me calamities, boils, misfortunes, diseases, sharp pains, and dangers; seeing this danger (originating) in sensual pleasures, let one wander alone like a rhinoceros. (50)

18. Both cold and heat, hunger and thirst, wind and a burning sun, and gad-flies and snakes—having overcome all these things, let one wander alone like a rhinoceros[1]. (51)

19. As the elephant, the strong, the spotted, the large, after leaving the herd walks at pleasure in the forest, even so let one wander alone like a rhinoceros. (52)

20. For him who delights in intercourse (with others, even) that is inconvenient which tends to temporary deliverance; reflecting on the words of (Buddha) the kinsman of the Âdi*kk*a family, let one wander alone like a rhinoceros. (53)

21. The harshness of the (philosophical) views I have overcome, I have acquired self-command, I have attained to the way (leading to perfection), I am in possession of knowledge, and not to be led by others; so speaking, let one wander alone like a rhinoceros. (54)

22. Without covetousness, without deceit, without

[1] Comp. *G*âtaka I, p. 93.

craving, without detraction, having got rid of passions and folly, being free from desire in all the world, let one wander alone like a rhinoceros. (55)

23. Let one avoid a wicked companion who teaches what is useless and has gone into what is wrong, let him not cultivate (the society of) one who is devoted (to and) lost in sensual pleasures, let one wander alone like a rhinoceros. (56)

24. Let one cultivate (the society of) a friend who is learned and keeps the Dhamma, who is magnanimous and wise; knowing the meaning (of things and) subduing his doubts, let one wander alone like a rhinoceros. (57)

25. Not adorning himself, not looking out for sport, amusement, and the delight of pleasure in the world, (on the contrary) being loath of a life of dressing, speaking the truth, let one wander alone like a rhinoceros. (58)

26. Having left son and wife, father and mother, wealth, and corn, and relatives, the different objects of desire, let one wander alone like a rhinoceros. (59)

27. 'This is a tie, in this there is little happiness, little enjoyment, but more of pain, this is a fish-hook,' so having understood, let a thoughtful man wander alone like a rhinoceros. (60)

28. Having torn the ties, having broken the net as a fish in the water, being like a fire not returning to the burnt place, let one wander alone like a rhinoceros. (61)

29. With downcast eyes, and not prying[1], with his senses guarded, with his mind protected free from

---

[1] Na *k*a pâdalolo ti ekassa duliyo dvinna*m* tatiyo ti eva*m* ga*n*amag*gh*am pavisitukâmatâya ka*nd*ûyamânapâdo viya abhavanto dîgha*k*ârika-anavattha*k*ârikavirato vâ. Commentator.

passion, not burning (with lust), let one wander alone like a rhinoceros. (62)

30. Removing the characteristics of a gihin (householder), like a Pâri*kh*atta tree whose leaves are cut off, clothed in a yellow robe after wandering away (from his house), let one wander alone like a rhinoceros. (63)

31. Not being greedy of sweet things, not being unsteady, not supporting others, going begging from house to house, having a mind which is not fettered to any household, let one wander alone like a rhinoceros. (64)

32. Having left the five obstacles of the mind, having dispelled all sin, being independent, having cut off the sin of desire, let one wander alone like a rhinoceros. (65)

33. Having thrown behind (himself bodily) pleasure and pain, and previously (mental) joy and distress, having acquired equanimity, tranquillity, purity, let one wander alone like a rhinoceros. (66)

34. Strenuous for obtaining the supreme good (i.e. Nibbâna), with a mind free from attachment, not living in idleness, being firm, endowed with bodily and mental strength, let one wander alone like a rhinoceros. (67)

35. Not abandoning seclusion and meditation, always wandering in (accordance with) the Dhammas[1], seeing misery in the existences, let one wander alone like a rhinoceros[2]. (68)

36. Wishing for the destruction of desire (i.e. Nibbâna), being careful, no fool, learned, strenuous, considerate, restrained, energetic, let one wander alone like a rhinoceros. (69)

[1] Dhammesu ni*kk*a*m* anudhamma*k*ârî. [2] Comp. Dhp. v. 20.

37. Like a lion not trembling at noises, like the wind not caught in a net, like a lotus not stained by water, let one wander alone like a rhinoceros. (70)

38. As a lion strong by his teeth, after overcoming (all animals), wanders victorious as the king of the animals, and haunts distant dwelling-places[1], (even so) let one wander alone like a rhinoceros. (71)

39. Cultivating in (due) time kindness, equanimity, compassion, deliverance, and rejoicing (with others), unobstructed by the whole world, let one wander alone like a rhinoceros. (72)

40. Having abandoned both passion and hatred and folly, having rent the ties, not trembling in the loss of life, let one wander alone like a rhinoceros[2]. (73)

41. They cultivate (the society of others) and serve them for the sake of advantage; friends without a motive are now difficult to get, men know their own profit and are impure; (therefore) let one wander alone like a rhinoceros. (74)

Khaggavisâ*n*asutta is ended.

---

4. KASIBHÂRADVÂ*G*ASUTTA.

The Brâhma*n*a Kasibhâradvâ*g*a reproaches Gotama with idleness, but the latter convinces him that he (Buddha) also works, and so the Brâhma*n*a is converted, and finally becomes a saint. Compare Sp. Hardy, A Manual of Buddhism, p. 214; Gospel of St. John v. 17.

So it was heard by me:

At one time Bhagavat dwelt in Magadha at Dakkhi*n*âgiri in the Brâhma*n*a village Ekana*l*â. And at

---

[1] Pantânîti dûrâni senâsanânîti vasati*tth*ânânî. Commentator.

[2] Comp. Dhp. v. 20.

that time the Brâhma*n*a Kasibhâradvâ*g*a's five hundred ploughs were tied (to the yokes) in the sowing season. Then Bhagavat, in the morning, having put on his raiment and taken his bowl and robes, went to the place where the Brâhma*n*a Kasibhâradvâ*g*a's work (was going on). At that time the Brâhma*n*a Kasibhâradvâ*g*a's distribution of food took place. Then Bhagavat went to the place where the distribution of food took place, and having gone there, he stood apart. The Brâhma*n*a Kasibhâradvâ*g*a saw Bhagavat standing there to get alms, and having seen him, he said this to Bhagavat:

'I, O Sama*n*a, both plough and sow, and having ploughed and sown, I eat; thou also, O Sama*n*a, shouldst plough and sow, and having ploughed and sown, thou shouldst eat.'

'I also, O Brâhma*n*a, both plough and sow, and having ploughed and sown, I eat,' so said Bhagavat.

'Yet we do not see the yoke, or the plough, or the ploughshare, or the goad, or the oxen of the venerable Gotama.'

And then the venerable Gotama spoke in this way:

'I also, O Brâhma*n*a, both plough and sow, and having ploughed and sown, I eat,' so said Bhagavat.

Then the Brâhma*n*a Kasibhâradvâ*g*a addressed Bhagavat in a stanza:

1. 'Thou professest to be a ploughman, and yet we do not see thy ploughing; asked about (thy) ploughing, tell us (of it), that we may know thy ploughing.' (75)

2. Bhagavat answered: 'Faith is the seed, penance the rain, understanding my yoke and plough, modesty the pole of the plough, mind the tie, thoughtfulness my ploughshare and goad. (76)

3. 'I am guarded in respect of the body, I am guarded in respect of speech, temperate in food; I make truth to cut away (weeds), tenderness is my deliverance. (77)

4. 'Exertion is my beast of burden; carrying (me) to Nibbâna he goes without turning back to the place where having gone one does not grieve. (78)

5. 'So this ploughing is ploughed, it bears the fruit of immortality; having ploughed this ploughing one is freed from all pain.' (79)

Then the Brâhma*n*a Kasibhâradvâ*g*a, having poured rice-milk into a golden bowl, offered it to Bhagavat, saying, 'Let the venerable Bhagavat eat of the rice-milk; the venerable is a ploughman, for the venerable Gotama ploughs a ploughing that bears the fruit of immortality.'

6. Bhagavat said: 'What is acquired by reciting stanzas is not to be eaten by me; this is, O Brâhma*n*a, not the Dhamma of those that see rightly; Buddha rejects what is acquired by reciting stanzas, this is the conduct (of Buddhas) as long as the Dhamma exists. (80)

7. 'One who is an accomplished great Isi, whose passions are destroyed and whose misbehaviour has ceased, thou shouldst serve with other food and drink, for this is the field for one who looks for good works[1].' (81)

'To whom then, O Gotama, shall I give this rice-milk?' so said Kasibhâradvâ*g*a.

'I do not see, O Brâhma*n*a, in the world (of men) and gods and Mâras and Brahmans, amongst beings comprising gods and men, and Sama*n*as and Brâh-

[1] Cf. Sundarikabhâradvâ*g*a, v. 28.

ma*n*as, any by whom this rice-milk when eaten can be properly digested with the exception of Tathâgata, or a disciple of Tathâgata. Therefore, O Brâhma*n*a, thou shalt throw this rice-milk in (a place where there is) little grass, or cast it into water with no worms,' so said Bhagavat.

Then the Brâhma*n*a Kasibhâradvâ*g*a threw the rice-milk into some water with no worms. Then the rice-milk thrown into the water splashed, hissed, smoked in volumes; for as a ploughshare that has got hot during the day when thrown into the water splashes, hisses, and smokes in volumes, even so the rice-milk (when) thrown into the water splashed, hissed, and smoked in volumes.

Then the Brâhma*n*a Kasibhâradvâ*g*a alarmed and terrified went up to Bhagavat, and after having approached and fallen with his head at Bhagavat's feet, he said this to Bhagavat:

'It is excellent, O venerable Gotama! It is excellent, O venerable Gotama! As one raises what has been overthrown, or reveals what has been hidden, or tells the way to him who has gone astray, or holds out an oil lamp in the dark that those who have eyes may see the objects, even so by the venerable Gotama in manifold ways the Dhamma (has been) illustrated. I take refuge in the venerable Gotama and in the Dhamma and in the Assembly of Bhikkhus; I wish to receive the pabba*gg*â, I wish to receive the upasampadâ (the robe and the orders) from the venerable Gotama,' so said Kasibhâradvâ*g*a.

Then the Brâhma*n*a Kasibhâradvâ*g*a received the pabba*gg*â from Bhagavat, and he received also the upasampadâ; and the venerable Bhâradvâ*g*a having lately received the upasampadâ, leading a solitary retired, strenuous, ardent, energetic life, lived after having in a short time in this existence by his own understanding ascertained and possessed himself of that highest perfection of a religious life for the sake of which men of good family rightly wander away from their houses to a houseless state. 'Birth had been destroyed, a religious life had been led, what was to be done had been done, there was nothing else (to be done) for this existence,' so he perceived, and the venerable Bhâradvâ*g*a became one of the arahats (saints).

Kasibhâradvâ*g*asutta is ended.

---

5. *K*UNDASUTTA.

Buddha describes the four different kinds of Sama*n*as to *K*unda, the smith.

1. 'I ask the Muni of great understanding,'—so said *K*unda, the smith,—'Buddha, the lord of the Dhamma, who is free from craving, the best of bipeds, the most excellent of charioteers, how many (kinds of) Sama*n*as are there in the world; pray tell me that?' (82)

2. 'There are four (kinds of) Sama*n*as, (there is) not a fifth, O *K*unda,'—so said Bhagavat,—'these I will reveal to thee, being asked in person; (they are) Magga*g*inas and Maggadesakas, Magga*g*îvins and Maggadûsins.' (83)

3. 'Whom do the Buddhas call a Magga*g*ina?'—so said *K*unda, the smith,—'How is a Magga*ggh*âyin

unequalled? Being asked, describe to me a Maggagîvin, and reveal to me a Maggadûsin.' (84)

4. Bhagavat said: 'He who has overcome doubt, is without pain, delights in Nibbâna, is free from greed, a leader of the world of men and gods, such a one the Buddhas call a maggagina (that is, victorious by the way). (85)

5. 'He who in this world having known the best (i.e. Nibbâna) as the best, expounds and explains here the Dhamma, him, the doubt-cutting Muni, without desire, the second Bhikkhu they call a maggadesin (that is, teaching the way). (86)

6. 'He who lives in the way that has so well been taught in the Dhammapada, and is restrained, attentive, cultivating blameless words, him the third Bhikkhu they call a maggagîvin (that is, living in the way). (87)

7. 'He who although counterfeiting the virtuous is forward, disgraces families, is impudent, deceitful, unrestrained, a babbler, walking in disguise, such a one is a maggadûsin (that is, defiling the way)[1]. (88)

8. 'He who has penetrated these (four Samanas), who is a householder, possessed of knowledge, a pupil of the venerable ones, wise, having known that they all are such,—having seen so, his faith is not lost; for how could he make the undepraved equal to the depraved and the pure equal to the impure?' (89)

*K*undasutta is ended.

[1] Comp. *G*âtaka II, p. 281.

6. PARÂBHAVASUTTA.

A dialogue between a deity and Buddha on the things by which a man loses and those by which he gains in this world.—Text by Grimblot, in Journal Asiatique, t. xviii (1871), p. 237; translation by L. Feer, in Journal Asiatique, t. xviii (1871), p. 309, and by Gogerly, reprinted in Journal Asiatique, t. xx (1872), p. 226.

So it was heard by me:

At one time Bhagavat dwelt at Sâvatthî, in *G*etavana, in the park of Anâthapi*nd*ika. Then when the night had come, a certain deity of a beautiful appearance, having illuminated the whole *G*etavana, went up to Bhagavat, and having approached and saluted him, he stood apart, and standing apart that deity addressed Bhagavat in stanzas:

1. 'We ask (thee), Gotama, about a man that suffers loss; having come to ask, Bhagavat, (tell us) what is the cause (of loss) to the losing (man).' (90)

2. Bhagavat: 'The winner is easily known, easily known (is also) the loser: he who loves Dhamma is the winner, he who hates Dhamma is the loser.' (91)

3. Deity: 'We know this to be so, this is the first loser; tell (us) the second, O Bhagavat, what is the cause (of loss) to the losing (man).' (92)

4. Bhagavat: 'Wicked men are dear to him, he does not do anything that is dear to the good, he approves of the Dhamma of the wicked,—that is the cause (of loss) to the losing (man).' (93)

5. Deity: 'We know this to be so, this is the second loser; tell us the third, O Bhagavat, what is the cause (of loss) to the losing (man).' (94)

6. Bhagavat: 'The man who is drowsy, fond of society and without energy, lazy, given to anger,—that is the cause (of loss) to the losing (man).' (95)

7. Deity: '"We know this to be so, this is the third loser; tell us the fourth, O Bhagavat, what is the cause (of loss) to the losing (man).' (96)

8. Bhagavat: 'He who being rich does not support mother or father who are old or past their youth,—that is the cause (of loss) to the losing (man).' (97)

9. Deity: 'We know this to be so, this is the fourth loser; tell us the fifth, O Bhagavat, what is the cause (of loss) to the losing (man).' (98)

10. Bhagavat: 'He who by falsehood deceives either a Brâhma*n*a or a Sama*n*a or any other mendicant,—that is the cause (of loss) to the losing (man).' (99)

11. Deity: 'We know this to be so, this is the fifth loser; tell us the sixth, O Bhagavat, what is the cause (of loss) to the losing (man).' (100)

12. Bhagavat: 'The man who is possessed of much property, who has gold and food, (and still) enjoys alone his sweet things,—that is the cause (of loss) to the losing (man).' (101)

13. Deity: 'We know this to be so, this is the sixth loser; tell us the seventh, O Bhagavat, what is the cause (of loss) to the losing (man).' (102)

14. Bhagavat: 'The man who proud of his birth, of his wealth, and of his family, despises his relatives,—that is the cause (of loss) to the losing (man).' (103)

15. Deity: 'We know this to be so, this is the seventh loser; tell us the eighth, O Bhagavat, what is the cause (of loss) to the losing (man).' (104)

16. Bhagavat: 'The man who given to women, to strong drink, and to dice, wastes whatever he has gained,—that is the cause (of loss) to the losing (man).' (105)

17. Deity: 'We know this to be so, this is the eighth loser; tell us the ninth, O Bhagavat, what is the cause (of loss) to the losing (man).' (106)

18. Bhagavat: 'He who, not satisfied with his own wife, is seen with harlots and the wives of others,—that is the cause (of loss) to the losing (man).' (107)

19. Deity: 'We know this to be so, this is the ninth loser; tell us the tenth, O Bhagavat, what (is) the cause (of loss) to the losing (man).' (108)

20. Bhagavat: 'The man who past his youth, brings home a woman with breasts like the timbaru fruit, and for jealousy of her cannot sleep,—that is the cause (of loss) to the losing (man).' (109)

21. Deity: 'We know this to be so, this is the tenth loser; tell us the eleventh, O Bhagavat, what is the cause (of loss) to the losing (man).' (110)

22. Bhagavat: 'He who places in supremacy a woman given to drink and squandering, or a man of the same kind,—that is the cause (of loss) to the losing (man).' (111)

23. Deity: 'We know this to be so, this is the eleventh loser; tell us the twelfth, O Bhagavat, what is the cause (of loss) to the losing (man).' (112)

24. Bhagavat: 'He who has little property, (but) great craving, is born in a Khattiya family and wishes for the kingdom in this world,—that is the cause (of loss) to the losing (man).' (113)

25. Having taken into consideration these losses in the world, the wise, venerable man, who is endowed with insight, cultivates the happy world (of the gods). (114)

Parâbhavasutta is ended.

7. VASALASUTTA.

The Brâhma*n*a Aggikabhâradvâ*g*a is converted by Buddha, after hearing his definition of an outcast, illustrated by the story of Mâtaṅga, told in the Mâtaṅga*g*âtaka. Comp. Sp. Hardy, The Legends and Theories of the Buddhists, p. 49.—Text and translation in Alwis's Buddhist Nirvâ*n*a, p. 119.

So it was heard by me:

At one time Bhagavat dwelt at Sâvatthî, in *G*etavana, in the park of Anâthapi*nd*ika. Then Bhagavat having put on his raiment in the morning, and having taken his bowl and his robes, entered Sâvatthî for alms.

Now at that time in the house of the Brâhma*n*a Aggikabhâradvâ*g*a the fire was blazing, the offering brought forth. Then Bhagavat going for alms from house to house in Sâvatthî went to the house of the Brâhma*n*a Aggikabhâradvâ*g*a. The Brâhma*n*a Aggikabhâradvâ*g*a saw Bhagavat coming at a distance, and seeing him he said this: 'Stay there, O Shaveling; (stay) there, O Sama*n*aka (i. e. wretched Sama*n*a); (stay) there, O Vasalaka (i. e. outcast)!'

This having been said, Bhagavat replied to the Brâhma*n*a Aggikabhâradvâ*g*a: 'Dost thou know, O Brâhma*n*a, an outcast, or the things that make an outcast?'

'No, O venerable Gotama, I do not know an outcast, or the things that make an outcast; let the venerable Gotama teach me this so well that I may know an outcast, or the things that make an outcast.'

'Listen then, O Brâhma*n*a, attend carefully, I will tell (thee).'

'Even so, O venerable one,' so the Brâhma*n*a Aggikabhâradvâ*g*a replied to Bhagavat.

Then Bhagavat said this:

1. 'The man who is angry and bears hatred, who is wicked and hypocritical, who has embraced wrong views, who is deceitful, let one know him as an outcast. (115)

2. 'Whosoever in this world harms living beings, whether once or twice born, and in whom there is no compassion for living beings, let one know him as an outcast. (116)

3. 'Whosoever destroys or lays siege to villages and towns, and is known as an enemy, let one know him as an outcast. (117)

4. 'Be it in the village or in the wood, whosoever appropriates by theft what is the property of others and what has not been given, let one know him as an outcast. (118)

5. 'Whosoever, having really contracted a debt, runs away when called upon (to pay), saying, "There is no debt (that I owe) thee," let one know him as an outcast. (119)

6. 'Whosoever for love of a trifle having killed a man going along the road, takes the trifle, let one know him as an outcast. (120)

7. 'The man who for his own sake or for that of others or for the sake of wealth speaks falsely when asked as a witness, let one know him as an outcast. (121)

8. 'Whosoever is seen with the wives of relatives or of friends either by force or with their consent, let one know him as an outcast. (122)

9. 'Whosoever being rich does not support mother or father when old and past their youth, let one know him as an outcast. (123)

10. 'Whosoever strikes or by words annoys mother

or father, brother, sister, or mother-in-law, let one know him as an outcast. (124)

11. 'Whosoever, being asked about what is good, teaches what is bad and advises (another, while) concealing (something from him), let one know him as an outcast. (125)

12. 'Whosoever, having committed a bad deed, hopes (saying), "Let no one know me" (as having done it, who is) a dissembler, let one know him as an outcast. (126)

13. 'Whosoever, having gone to another's house and partaken of his good food, does not in return honour him when he comes, let one know him as an outcast. (127)

14. 'Whosoever by falsehood deceives either a Brâhma*n*a or a Sama*n*a or any other mendicant, let one know him as an outcast. (128)

15. 'Whosoever by words annoys either a Brâhma*n*a or a Sama*n*a when meal-time has come and does not give (him anything), let one know him as an outcast. (129)

16. 'Whosoever enveloped in ignorance in this world predicts what is not (to take place), coveting a trifle, let one know him as an outcast. (130)

17. 'Whosoever exalts himself and despises others, being mean by his pride, let one know him as an outcast. (131)

18. 'Whosoever is a provoker and is avaricious, has sinful desires, is envious, wicked, shameless, and fearless of sinning, let one know him as an outcast. (132)

19. 'Whosoever reviles Buddha or his disciple, be he a wandering mendicant (paribbâ*g*a) or a householder (gaha*tth*a), let one know him as an outcast. (133)

20. 'Whosoever without being a saint (arahat) pretends to be a saint, (and is) a thief in all the worlds including that of Brahman, he is indeed the lowest outcast; (all) these who have been described by me to you are indeed called outcasts. (134)

21. 'Not by birth does one become an outcast, not by birth does one become a Brâhma*n*a; by deeds one becomes an outcast, by deeds one becomes a Brâhma*n*a. (135)

22. 'Know ye this in the way that this example of mine (shows): There was a *K*a*nd*âla of the Sopâka caste, well known as Mâtaṅga. (136)

23. 'This Mâtaṅga reached the highest fame, such as was very difficult to obtain, and many Khattiyas and Brâhma*n*as went to serve him. (137)

24. 'He having mounted the vehicle of the gods, (and entered) the high road (that is) free from dust, having abandoned sensual desires, went to the Brahma world. (138)

25. 'His birth did not prevent him from being re-born in the Brahma world; (on the other hand) there are Brâhma*n*as, born in the family of preceptors, friends of the hymns (of the Vedas). (139)

26. 'But they are continually caught in sinful deeds, and are to be blamed in this world, while in the coming (world) hell (awaits them); birth does not save them from hell nor from blame. (140)

27. '(Therefore) not by birth does one become an outcast, not by birth does one become a Brâhma*n*a, by deeds one becomes an outcast, by deeds one becomes a Brâhma*n*a.' (141)

This having been said, the Brâhma*n*a Aggikabhâradvâ*g*a answered Bhagavat as follows:

'Excellent, O venerable Gotama! Excellent, O

venerable Gotama! As one, O venerable Gotama, raises what has been overthrown, or reveals what has been hidden, or tells the way to him who has gone astray, or holds out an oil lamp in the dark that those who have eyes may see the objects, even so by the venerable Gotama in manifold ways the Dhamma has been illustrated; I take refuge in the venerable Gotama and in the Dhamma and in the Assembly of Bhikkhus. Let the venerable Gotama accept me as an upâsaka (a follower, me) who henceforth for all my life have taken refuge (in him).'

Vasalasutta is ended.

---

8. METTASUTTA.

A peaceful mind and goodwill towards all beings are praised.—Text by Grimblot in Journal Asiatique, t. xviii (1871), p. 250, and by Childers in Khuddaka Pâ*th*a, p. 15; translation (?) by Gogerly in the Ceylon Friend, 1839, p. 211, by Childers in Kh. Pâ*th*a and by L. Feer in Journal Asiatique, t. xviii (1871), p. 328.

1. Whatever is to be done by one who is skilful in seeking (what is) good, having attained that tranquil state (of Nibbâna):—Let him be able and upright and conscientious and of soft speech, gentle, not proud, (142)

2. And contented and easily supported and having few cares, unburdened and with his senses calmed and wise, not arrogant, without (showing) greediness (when going his round) in families. (143)

3. And let him not do anything mean for which others who are wise might reprove (him); may all beings be happy and secure, may they be happy-minded. (144)

4. Whatever living beings there are, either feeble or strong, all either long or great, middle-sized, short, small or large, (145)

5. Either seen or which are not seen, and which live far (or) near, either born or seeking birth, may all creatures be happy-minded. (146)

6. Let no one deceive another, let him not despise (another) in any place, let him not out of anger or resentment wish harm to another. (147)

7. As a mother at the risk of her life watches over her own child, her only child, so also let every one cultivate a boundless (friendly) mind towards all beings. (148)

8. And let him cultivate goodwill towards all the world, a boundless (friendly) mind, above and below and across, unobstructed, without hatred, without enmity. (149)

9. Standing, walking or sitting or lying, as long as he be awake, let him devote himself to this mind; this (way of) living they say is the best in this world. (150)

10. He who, not having embraced (philosophical) views, is virtuous, endowed with (perfect) vision, after subduing greediness for sensual pleasures, will never again go to a mother's womb. (151)

Mettasutta is ended.

9. HEMAVATASUTTA.

A dialogue between two Yakkhas on the qualities of Buddha. They go to Buddha, and after having their questions answered they, together with ten hundred Yakkhas, become the followers of Buddha.

1. 'To-day is the fifteenth, a fast day; a lovely

night has come,'—so said the Yakkha Sâtâgira,—'let us (go and) see the renowned Master Gotama.' (152)

2. 'Is the mind of such a one well disposed towards all beings?'—so said the Yakkha Hemavata,—'are his thoughts restrained as to things wished for or not wished for?' (153)

3. 'His mind is well disposed towards all beings, (the mind) of such a one,'—so said the Yakkha Sâtâgira,—'and his thoughts are restrained as to things wished for or not wished for.' (154)

4. 'Does he not take what has not been given (to him)?'—so said the Yakkha Hemavata,—'is he self-controlled (in his behaviour) to living beings? is he far from (a state of) carelessness? does he not abandon meditation?' (155)

5. 'He does not take what has not been given (to him),'—so said the Yakkha Sâtâgira,—'and he is self-controlled (in his behaviour) to living beings, and he is far from (a state of) carelessness; Buddha does not abandon meditation.' (156)

6. 'Does he not speak falsely?'—so said the Yakkha Hemavata,—'is he not harsh-spoken? does he not utter slander? does he not talk nonsense?' (157)

7. 'He does not speak falsely,'—so said the Yakkha Sâtâgira,—'he is not harsh-spoken, he does not utter slander, with judgment he utters what is good sense.' (158)

8. 'Is he not given to sensual pleasures?'—so said the Yakkha Hemavata,—'is his mind undisturbed? has he overcome folly? does he see clearly in (all) things (dhammas)?' (159)

9. 'He is not given to sensual pleasures,'—so said the Yakkha Sâtâgira,—'and his mind is undis-

turbed; he has overcome all folly; Buddha sees clearly in (all) things.' (160)

10. 'Is he endowed with knowledge?'—so said the Yakkha Hemavata,—'is his conduct pure? have his passions been destroyed? is there no new birth (for him)?' (161)

11. 'He is endowed with knowledge,'—so said the Yakkha Sâtâgira,—'and his conduct is pure; all his passions have been destroyed; there is no new birth for him. (162)

12. 'The mind of the Muni is accomplished in deed and word; Gotama, who is accomplished by his knowledge and conduct, let us (go and) see. (163)

13. 'Come, let us (go and) see Gotama, who has legs like an antelope, who is thin, who is wise, living on little food, not covetous, the Muni who is meditating in the forest. (164)

14. 'Having gone to him who is like a lion, a lonely wandering elephant, and who does not look for sensual pleasures, let us ask about the (means of) deliverance from the snares of death. (165)

15. 'Let us ask Gotama, the preacher, the expounder, who has penetrated all things, Buddha who has overcome hatred and fear.' (166)

16. 'In what has the world originated?'—so said the Yakkha Hemavata,—'with what is the world intimate? by what is the world afflicted, after having grasped at what?' (167)

17. 'In six the world has originated, O Hemavata,'—so said Bhagavat,—'with six it is intimate, by six the world is afflicted, after having grasped at six.' (168)

18. Hemavata said: 'What is the grasping by

which the world is afflicted? Asked about salvation, tell (me) how one is released from pain?' (169)

19. Bhagavat said: 'Five pleasures of sense are said to be in the world, with (the pleasure of) the mind as the sixth; having divested oneself of desire for these, one is thus released from pain. (170)

20. 'This salvation of the world has been told to you truly, this I tell you: thus one is released from pain.' (171)

21. Hemavata said: 'Who in this world crosses the stream (of existence)? who in this world crosses the sea? who does not sink into the deep, where there is no footing and no support?' (172)

22. Bhagavat said: 'He who is always endowed with virtue, possessed of understanding, well composed, reflecting within himself, and thoughtful, crosses the stream that is difficult to cross. (173)

23. 'He who is disgusted with sensual pleasures, who has overcome all bonds and destroyed joy, such a one does not sink into the deep.' (174)

24. Hemavata said: 'He who is endowed with a profound understanding, seeing what is subtile, possessing nothing, not clinging to sensual pleasures, behold him who is in every respect liberated, the great Isi, walking in the divine path. (175)

25. 'He who has got a great name, sees what is subtile, imparts understanding, and does not cling to the abode of sensual pleasures, behold him, the all-knowing, the wise, the great Isi, walking in the noble path. (176)

26. 'A good sight indeed (has met) us to-day, a good daybreak, a beautiful rising, (for) we have seen the perfectly enlightened (sambuddham), who has crossed the stream, and is free from passion. (177)

27. 'These ten hundred Yakkhas, possessed of supernatural power and of fame, they all take refuge in thee, thou art our incomparable Master. (178)

28. 'We will wander about from village to village, from mountain to mountain, worshipping the perfectly enlightened and the perfection of the Dhamma[1].' (179)

Hemavatasutta is ended.

---

10. ÂLAVAKASUTTA.

The Yakkha Â*l*avaka first threatens Buddha, then puts some questions to him which Buddha answers, whereupon Â*l*avaka is converted.

So it was heard by me:

At one time Bhagavat dwelt at Â*l*avî, in the realm of the Yakkha Â*l*avaka. Then the Yakkha Â*l*avaka went to the place where Bhagavat dwelt, and having gone there he said this to Bhagavat:

'Come out, O Sama*n*a!'

'Yes, O friend!' so saying Bhagavat came out.

'Enter, O Sama*n*a!'

'Yes, O friend!' so saying Bhagavat entered.

A second time the Yakkha Â*l*avaka said this to Bhagavat: 'Come out, O Sama*n*a!'

'Yes, O friend!' so saying Bhagavat came out.

'Enter, O Sama*n*a!'

'Yes, O friend!' so saying Bhagavat entered.

A third time the Yakkha Â*l*avaka said this to Bhagavat: 'Come out, O Sama*n*a!'

'Yes, O friend!' so saying Bhagavat came out.

'Enter, O Sama*n*a!'

---

[1] Dhammassa *k*a sudhammatam.

'Yes, O friend!' so saying Bhagavat entered.

A fourth time the Yakkha Â*l*avaka said this to Bhagavat: 'Come out, O Sama*n*a!'

'I shall not come out to thee, O friend, do what thou pleasest.'

'I shall ask thee a question, O Sama*n*a, if thou canst not answer it, I will either scatter thy thoughts or cleave thy heart, or take thee by thy feet and throw thee over to the other shore of the Gaṅgâ.'

'I do not see, O friend, any one in this world nor in the world of gods, Mâras, Brahmans, amongst the beings comprising gods, men, Sama*n*as, and Brâhma*n*as, who can either scatter my thoughts or cleave my heart, or take me by the feet and throw me over to the other shore of the Gaṅgâ; however, O friend, ask what thou pleasest.'

Then the Yakkha Â*l*avaka addressed Bhagavat in stanzas:

1. 'What in this world is the best property for a man? what, being well done, conveys happiness? what is indeed the sweetest of sweet things? how lived do they call life the best?' (180)

2. Bhagavat said: 'Faith is in this world the best property for a man; Dhamma, well observed, conveys happiness; truth indeed is the sweetest of things; and that life they call the best which is lived with understanding.' (181)

3. Â*l*avaka said: 'How does one cross the stream (of existence)? how does one cross the sea? how does one conquer pain? how is one purified?' (182)

4. Bhagavat said: 'By faith one crosses the stream, by zeal the sea, by exertion one conquers pain, by understanding one is purified.' (183)

5. Â*l*avaka said: 'How does one obtain understanding? how does one acquire wealth? how does one obtain fame? how does one bind friends (to himself)? how does one not grieve passing away from this world to the other?' (184)

6. Bhagavat said: 'He who believes in the Dhamma of the venerable ones as to the acquisition of Nibbâna, will obtain understanding from his desire to hear, being zealous and discerning. (185)

7. 'He who does what is proper, who takes the yoke (upon him and) exerts himself, will acquire wealth, by truth he will obtain fame, and being charitable he will bind friends (to himself). (186)

8. 'He who is faithful and leads the life of a householder, and possesses the following four Dhammas (virtues), truth, justice (dhamma), firmness, and liberality,—such a one indeed does not grieve when passing away. (187)

9. 'Pray, ask also other Sama*n*as and Brâhma*n*as far and wide, whether there is found in this world anything greater than truth, self-restraint, liberality, and forbearance.' (188)

10. Â*l*avaka said: 'Why should I now ask Sama*n*as and Brâhma*n*as far and wide? I now know what is my future good. (189)

11. 'For my good Buddha came to live at Â*l*avî; now I know where (i. e. on whom bestowed) a gift will bear great fruit. (190)

12. 'I will wander about from village to village, from town to town, worshipping the perfectly enlightened (sambuddha) and the perfection of the Dhamma.' (191)

Â*l*avakasutta is ended.

11. VI*G*AYASUTTA.

A reflection on the worthlessness of the human body; a follower of Buddha only sees the body as it really is, and consequently goes to Nibbâna. Comp. *G*âtaka I, p. 146.

1. If either walking or standing, sitting or lying, any one contracts (or) stretches (his body, then) this is the motion of the body. (192)

2. The body which is put together with bones and sinews, plastered with membrane and flesh, and covered with skin, is not seen as it really is. (193)

3. It is filled with the intestines, the stomach, the lump of the liver, the abdomen, the heart, the lungs, the kidneys, the spleen. (194)

4. With mucus, saliva, perspiration, lymph, blood, the fluid that lubricates the joints, bile, and fat. (195)

5. Then in nine streams impurity flows always from it; from the eye the eye-excrement, from the ear the ear-excrement, (196)

6. Mucus from the nose, through the mouth it ejects at one time bile and (at other times) it ejects phlegm, and from (all) the body come sweat and dirt. (197)

7. Then its hollow head is filled with the brain. A fool led by ignorance thinks it a fine thing. (198)

8. And when it lies dead, swollen and livid, discarded in the cemetery, relatives do not care (for it). (199)

9. Dogs eat it and jackals, wolves and worms; crows and vultures eat it, and what other living creatures there are. (200)

10. The Bhikkhu possessed of understanding in this world, having listened to Buddha's words, he

certainly knows it (i. e. the body) thoroughly, for he sees it as it really is. (201)

11. As this (living body is) so is that (dead one), as this is so that (will be); let one put away desire for the body, both as to its interior and as to its exterior. (202)

12. Such a Bhikkhu who has turned away from desire and attachment, and is possessed of understanding in this world, has (already) gone to the immortal peace, the unchangeable state of Nibbâna. (203)

13. This (body) with two feet is cherished (although) impure, ill-smelling, filled with various kinds of stench, and trickling here and there. (204)

14. He who with such a body thinks to exalt himself or despises others—what else (is this) but blindness? (205)

Vigayasutta is ended.

12. MUNISUTTA.

Definition of a Muni.

1. From acquaintanceship arises fear, from house-life arises defilement; the houseless state, freedom from acquaintanceship—this is indeed the view of a Muni. (206)

2. Whosoever, after having uprooted his (sin that has) arisen, would not replant it and would not allow it to grow up (again), him the solitarily wandering they call a Muni; such a great Isi has seen the state of peace. (207)

3. Having considered the causes (of sin, and) having discerned the seed, let him not allow any desire (sin, &c.) for it (to arise again); such a Muni

who sees the end of birth and destruction (i.e. Nibbâna), after leaving reasoning behind, does not enter the number (of living beings). (208)

4. He who has penetrated all the resting-places[1] (of the mind, and) does not wish for any of them,—such a Muni indeed, free from covetousness and free from greediness, strives no longer, for he has reached the other shore. (209)

5. The man who has overcome everything, who knows everything, who is possessed of a good understanding, undefiled in all things (dhamma), abandoning everything, liberated in the destruction of desire (i.e. Nibbâna), him the wise style a Muni[2]. (210)

6. The man who has the strength of understanding, is endowed with virtue and (holy) works, is composed, delights in meditation, is thoughtful, free from ties, free from harshness (akhila), and free from passion, him the wise style a Muni. (211)

7. The Muni that wanders solitarily, the zealous, that is not shaken by blame and praise, like a lion not trembling at noises, like the wind not caught in a net, like a lotus not soiled by water, leading others, not led by others, him the wise style a Muni. (212)

8. Whosoever becomes firm as the post in a bathing-place, in whom others acknowledge propriety of speech, who is free from passion, and (endowed) with well-composed senses, such a one the wise style a Muni. (213)

9. Whosoever is firm, like a straight shuttle, and is disgusted with evil actions, reflecting on what is just and unjust, him the wise style a Muni. (214)

---

[1] Nivesanâni.. Comp. Du*tth*aka, v. 6.

[2] Comp. Dhp. v. 353.

10. Whosoever is self-restrained and does not do evil, is a young or middle-aged Muni, self-subdued, one that should not be provoked (as) he does not provoke any, him the wise style a Muni. (215)

11. Whosoever, living upon what is given by others, receives a lump of rice from the top, from the middle or from the rest (of the vessel, and) does not praise (the giver) nor speak harsh words, him the wise style a Muni. (216)

12. The Muni that wanders about abstaining from sexual intercourse, who in his youth is not fettered in any case, is abstaining from the insanity of pride, liberated, him the wise style a Muni. (217)

13. The man who having penetrated the world, sees the highest truth, such a one, after crossing the stream and sea (of existence), who has cut off all ties, is independent, free from passion, him indeed the wise style a Muni. (218)

14. Two whose mode of life and occupation are quite different, are not equal: a householder maintaining a wife, and an unselfish virtuous man. A householder (is intent) upon the destruction of other living creatures, being unrestrained; but a Muni always protects living creatures, being restrained. (219)

15. As the crested bird with the blue neck (the peacock) never attains the swiftness of the swan, even so a householder does not equal a Bhikkhu, a secluded Muni meditating in the wood. (220)

Munisutta is ended.

Uragavagga is ended.

II. *K*ÛLAVAGGA.

1. RATANASUTTA.

For all beings salvation is only to be found in Buddha, Dhamma, and Saṅgha. — Text and translation in Childers' Khuddaka Pâ*th*a, p. 6.

1. Whatever spirits have come together here, either belonging to the earth or living in the air, let all spirits be happy, and then listen attentively to what is said. (221)

2. Therefore, O spirits, do ye all pay attention, show kindness to the human race who both day and night bring their offerings; therefore protect them strenuously. (222)

3. Whatever wealth there be here or in the other world, or whatever excellent jewel in the heavens, it is certainly not equal to Tathâgata. This excellent jewel (is found) in Buddha, by this truth may there be salvation. (223)

4. The destruction (of passion), the freedom from passion, the excellent immortality which Sakyamuni attained (being) composed,—there is nothing equal to that Dhamma. This excellent jewel (is found) in the Dhamma, by this truth may there be salvation. (224)

5. The purity which the best of Buddhas praised, the meditation which they call uninterrupted, there is no meditation like this. This excellent jewel (is

found) in the Dhamma, by this truth may there be salvation. (225)

6. The eight persons that are praised by the righteous[1], and make these four pairs, they are worthy of offerings, (being) Sugata's disciples; what is given to these will bear great fruit. This excellent jewel (is found) in the Assembly (saṅgha), by this truth may there be salvation. (226)

7. Those who have applied themselves studiously with a firm mind and free from desire to the commandments of Gotama, have obtained the highest gain, having merged into immortality, and enjoying happiness after getting it for nothing. This excellent jewel (is found) in the Assembly, by this truth may there be salvation. (227)

8. As a post in the front of a city gate is firm in the earth and cannot be shaken by the four winds, like that I declare the righteous man to be who, having penetrated the noble truths, sees (them clearly). This excellent jewel (is found) in the Assembly, by this truth may there be salvation. (228)

9. Those who understand the noble truths well taught by the profoundly wise (i. e. Buddha), though they be greatly distracted, will not (have to) take the eighth birth. This excellent jewel (is found) in the Assembly, by this truth may there be salvation. (229)

10. On his (attaining the) bliss of (the right) view three things (dhammas) are left behind (by him): conceit and doubt and whatever he has got of virtue and (holy) works. He is released also from the four hells, and he is incapable of committing the six

[1] The Commentator: satam pasatthâ ti sappurisehi buddhapa*kk*ekabuddhasâvakehi a*ññ*ehi *k*a devamanussehi pasatthâ.

deadly sins. This excellent jewel (is found) in the Assembly, by this truth may there be salvation. (230)

11. Even if he commit a sinful deed by his body, or in word or in thought, he is incapable of concealing it, (for) to conceal is said to be impossible for one that has seen the state (of Nibbâna). This excellent jewel (is found) in the Assembly, by this truth may there be salvation. (231)

12. As in a clump of trees with their tops in bloom in the first heat of the hot month, so (Buddha) taught the excellent Dhamma leading to Nibbâna to the greatest benefit (for all). This excellent jewel (is found) in Buddha, by this truth may there be salvation. (232)

13. The excellent one who knows what is excellent, who gives what is excellent, and who brings what is excellent, the incomparable one taught the excellent Dhamma. This excellent jewel (is found) in Buddha, by this truth may there be salvation. (233)

14. The old is destroyed, the new has not arisen, those whose minds are disgusted with a future existence, the wise who have destroyed their seeds (of existence, and) whose desires do not increase, go out like this lamp. This excellent jewel (is found) in the Assembly, by this truth may there be salvation. (234)

15. Whatever spirits have come together here, either belonging to the earth or living in the air, let us worship the perfect (tathâgata) Buddha, revered by gods and men; may there be salvation. (235)

16. Whatever spirits have come together here, either belonging to the earth or living in the air, let us worship the perfect (tathâgata) Dhamma, revered by gods and men; may there be salvation. (236)

17. Whatever spirits have come together here,

either belonging to the earth or living in the air, let us worship the perfect (tathâgata) Saṅgha, revered by gods and men; may there be salvation. (237)

Ratanasutta is ended.

---

2. ÂMAGANDHASUTTA.

A bad mind and wicked deeds are what defiles a man; no outward observances can purify him. Comp. Gospel of St. Matthew xv. 10.

1. Âmagandhabrâhma*n*a: 'Those who eat sâmâka, *k*iṅgûlaka, and *k*înaka, pattaphala, mûlaphala, and gaviphala (different sorts of grass, leaves, roots, &c.), justly obtained of the just, do not speak falsehood, (nor are they) desirous of sensual pleasures. (238)

2. 'He who eats what has been well prepared, well dressed, what is pure and excellent, given by others, he who enjoys food made of rice, eats, O Kassapa, Âmagandha (what defiles one). (239)

3. '(The charge of) Âmagandha does not apply to me,' so thou sayest, 'O Brahman (brahmabandhu, although) enjoying food (made) of rice together with the well-prepared flesh of birds. I ask thee, O Kassapa, the meaning of this, of what description (is then) thy Âmagandha?' (240)

4. Kassapabuddha: 'Destroying living beings, killing, cutting, binding, stealing, speaking falsehood, fraud and deception, worthless reading[1], intercourse with another's wife;—this is Âmagandha, but not the eating of flesh. (241)

---

[1] Agg*h*enakugg*a*n ti niratthakânattha*g*anakaganthapariyâpu*n*ana*m*. Commentator.

5. 'Those persons who in this world are unrestrained in (enjoying) sensual pleasures, greedy of sweet things, associated with what is impure, sceptics (natthikadi*tth*i), unjust, difficult to follow;—this is Âmagandha, but not the eating of flesh. (242)

6. 'Those who are rough, harsh, backbiting, treacherous, merciless, arrogant, and (who being) illiberal do not give anything to any one;—this is Âmagandha, but not the eating of flesh. (243)

7. 'Anger, intoxication, obstinacy, bigotry, deceit, envy, grandiloquence, pride and conceit, intimacy with the unjust;—this is Âmagandha, but not the eating of flesh. (244)

8. 'Those who in this world are wicked, and such as do not pay their debts, are slanderers, false in their dealings, counterfeiters, those who in this world being the lowest of men commit sin;—this is Âmagandha, but not the eating of flesh. (245)

9. 'Those persons who in this world are unrestrained (in their behaviour) towards living creatures, who are bent upon injuring after taking others' (goods), wicked, cruel, harsh, disrespectful;—this is Âmagandha, but not the eating of flesh. (246)

10. 'Those creatures who are greedy of these (living beings, who are) hostile, offending; always bent upon (evil) and therefore, when dead, go to darkness and fall with their heads downwards into hell;—this is Âmagandha, but not the eating of flesh. (247)

11. 'Neither the flesh of fish, nor fasting, nor nakedness, nor tonsure, nor matted hair, nor dirt, nor rough skins, nor the worshipping of the fire, nor the many immortal penances in the world, nor hymns, nor oblations, nor sacrifice, nor observance of the

seasons, purify a mortal who has not conquered his doubt[1]. (248)

12. 'The wise man wanders about with his organs of sense guarded, and his senses conquered, standing firm in the Dhamma, delighting in what is right and mild; having overcome all ties and left behind all pain, he does not cling to what is seen and heard.' (249)

13. Thus the Bhagavat (Kassapa) preached this subject again and again, (and the Brâhma*n*a) who was accomplished in the hymns (of the Vedas) understood it; the Muni who is free from defilement, independent, and difficult to follow, made it clear in various stanzas. (250)

14. Having heard the Buddha's well-spoken words, which are free from defilement and send away all pain, he worshipped the Tathâgata's (feet) in humility, and took orders at once. (251)

Âmagandhasutta is ended.

---

3. HIRISUTTA.

On true friendship.

1. He who transgresses and despises modesty, who says, 'I am a friend,' but does not undertake any work that can be done, know (about) him: 'he is not my (friend).' (252)

2. Whosoever uses pleasing words to friends without effect[2], him the wise know as one that (only) talks, but does not do anything. (253)

3. He is not a friend who always eagerly suspects

---

[1] Comp. Dhp. v. 141.

[2] Ananvayan ti ya*m* attha*m* dassâmi karissâmîti bhâsati tena ananugata*m*. Commentator.

a breach and looks out for faults; but he with whom he dwells as a son at the breast (of his mother), he is indeed a friend that cannot be severed (from him) by others. (254)

4. He who hopes for fruit, cultivates the energy that produces joy and the pleasure that brings praise, (while) carrying the human yoke. (255)

5. Having tasted the sweetness of seclusion and tranquillity one becomes free from fear and free from sin, drinking in the sweetness of the Dhamma[1]. (256)

Hirisutta is ended.

4. MAHÂMAṄGALASUTTA.

Buddha defines the highest blessing to a deity.—Text by Grimblot in Journal Asiatique, t. xviii (1871), p. 229, and by Childers in Kh. Pâ*th*a, p. 4; translation by Gogerly in the Ceylon Friend, 1839, p. 208; by Childers in Kh. Pâ*th*a, p. 4; and by L. Feer in Journal Asiatique, t. xviii (1871), p. 296.

So it was heard by me:

At one time Bhagavat dwelt at Sâvatthî, in *G*etavana, in the park of Anâthapi*nd*ika. Then, when the night had come near, a deity of beautiful appearance, having illuminated the whole *G*etavana, approached Bhagavat, and having approached and saluted him, he stood apart, and standing apart that deity addressed Bhagavat in a stanza:

1. 'Many gods and men have devised blessings, longing for happiness, tell thou (me) the highest blessing.' (257)

2. Buddha said: 'Not cultivating (the society of) fools, but cultivating (the society of) wise men, wor-

[1] Comp. Dhp. v. 205.

shipping those that are to be worshipped, this is the highest blessing. (258)

3. 'To live in a suitable country, to have done good deeds in a former (existence), and a thorough study of one's self, this is the highest blessing. (259)

4. 'Great learning and skill, well-learnt discipline, and well-spoken words, this is the highest blessing. (260)

5. 'Waiting on mother and father, protecting child and wife, and a quiet calling, this is the highest blessing. (261)

6. 'Giving alms, living religiously, protecting relatives, blameless deeds, this is the highest blessing. (262)

7. 'Ceasing and abstaining from sin, refraining from intoxicating drink, perseverance in the Dhammas, this is the highest blessing. (263)

8. 'Reverence and humility, contentment and gratitude, the hearing of the Dhamma at due seasons, this is the highest blessing. (264)

9. 'Patience and pleasant speech, intercourse with Sama*n*as, religious conversation at due seasons, this is the highest blessing. (265)

10. 'Penance and chastity, discernment of the noble truths, and the realisation of Nibbâna, this is the highest blessing. (266)

11. 'He whose mind is not shaken (when he is) touched by the things of the world (lokadhamma), (but remains) free from sorrow, free from defilement, and secure, this is the highest blessing. (267)

12. 'Those who, having done such (things), are undefeated in every respect, walk in safety everywhere, theirs is the highest blessing.' (268)

Mahâmangala is ended.

5. SÛ*K*ILOMASUTTA.

The Yakkha Sû*k*iloma threatens to harm Buddha, if he cannot answer his questions. Buddha answers that all passions proceed from the body.

So it was heard by me:

At one time Bhagavat dwelt at Gayâ (seated) on a stone seat in the realm of the Yakkha Sû*k*iloma. And at that time the Yakkha Khara and the Yakkha Sû*k*iloma passed by, not far from Bhagavat. And then the Yakkha Khara said this to the Yakkha Sû*k*iloma: 'Is this man a Sama*n*a?'

Sû*k*iloma answered: 'He is no Sama*n*a, he is a Sama*n*aka (a wretched Sama*n*a); however I will ascertain whether he is a Sama*n*a or a Sama*n*aka.'

Then the Yakkha Sû*k*iloma went up to Bhagavat, and having gone up to him, he brushed against Bhagavat's body. Then Bhagavat took away his body. Then the Yakkha Sû*k*iloma said this to Bhagavat: 'O Sama*n*a, art thou afraid of me?'

Bhagavat answered: 'No, friend, I am not afraid of thee, but thy touching me is sinful.'

Sû*k*iloma said: 'I will ask thee a question, O Sama*n*a; if thou canst not answer it I will either scatter thy thoughts or cleave thy heart, or take thee by the feet and throw thee over to the other shore of the Gaṅgâ.'

Bhagavat answered: 'I do not see, O friend, neither in this world together with the world of the Devas, Mâras, Brahmans, nor amongst the generation of Sama*n*a and Brâhma*n*as, gods and men, the one who can either scatter my thoughts or cleave my heart, or take me by the feet and throw me over to the other shore of the Gaṅgâ. However ask, O friend, what thou pleasest.' Then the Yakkha Sûkiloma addressed Bhagavat in a stanza:

1. 'What origin have passion and hatred, disgust, delight, and horror? wherefrom do they arise? whence arising do doubts vex the mind, as boys vex a crow?' (269)

2. Buddha said: 'Passion and hatred have their origin from this (body), disgust, delight, and horror arise from this body; arising from this (body) doubts vex the mind, as boys vex a crow. (270)

3. 'They originate in desire, they arise in self, like the shoots of the banyan tree; far and wide they are connected with sensual pleasures, like the mâluvâ creeper spread in the wood. (271)

4. 'Those who know whence it (sin) arises, drive it away. Listen, O Yakkha! They cross over this stream that is difficult to cross, and has not been crossed before, with a view to not being born again.' (272)

Sûkilomasutta is ended.

---

6. DHAMMAKARIYASUTTA OR KAPILASUTTA.

The Bhikkhus are admonished to rid themselves of sinful persons, and advised to lead a pure life.

1. A just life, a religious life, this they call the best gem, if any one has gone forth from house-life to a houseless life. (273)

2. But if he be harsh-spoken, and like a beast delighting in injuring (others), then the life of such a one is very wicked, and he increases his own pollution. (274)

3. A Bhikkhu who delights in quarrelling and is shrouded in folly, does not understand the Dhamma that is preached and taught by Buddha. (275)

4. Injuring his own cultivated mind, and led by ignorance, he does not understand that sin is the way leading to hell. (276)

5. Having gone to calamity, from womb to womb, from darkness to darkness, such a Bhikkhu verily, after passing away, goes to pain (277)

6. As when there is a pit of excrement (that has become) full during a number of years,—he who should be such a one full of sin is difficult to purify. (278)

7. Whom you know to be such a one, O Bhikkhus, (a man) dependent on a house, having sinful desires, sinful thoughts, and being with sinful deeds and objects, (279)

8. Him do avoid, being all in concord; blow him away as sweepings, put him away as rubbish. (280)

9. Then remove as chaff those that are no Samanas, (but only) think themselves, blowing away those that have sinful desires and those with sinful deeds and objects. (281)

10. Be pure and live together with the pure, being thoughtful; then agreeing (and) wise you will put an end to pain. (282)

Dhammakariyasutta is ended.

---

7. BRÂHMANADHAMMIKASUTTA.

Wealthy Brâhmanas come to Buddha, asking about the customs of the ancient Brâhmanas. Buddha describes their mode of life and the change wrought in them by seeing the king's riches, and furthermore, how they induced the king to commit the sin of having living creatures slain at sacrifices. On hearing Buddha's enlightened discourse the wealthy Brâhma*n*as are converted. Compare, Sp. Hardy's Legends, p. 46.

So it was heard by me:

At one time Bhagavat dwelt at Sâvatthî, in *G*eta-vana, in the park of Anâthapi*nd*ika. Then many wealthy Brâhma*n*as of Kosala, decrepit, elderly, old, advanced in age, or arrived at extreme old age, went to Bhagavat, and having gone to him they talked pleasantly with him, and after having had some pleasant and remarkable talk with him, they sat down apart. Sitting down apart these wealthy Brâhma*n*as said this to Bhagavat: 'O venerable Gotama, are the Brâhma*n*as now-a-days seen (engaged) in the Brâhmanical customs (dhamma) of the ancient Brâhma*n*as?'

Bhagavat answered: 'The Brâhma*n*as now-a-days, O Brâhma*n*as, are not seen (engaged) in the Brâhmanical customs of the ancient Brâhma*n*as.'

The Brâhma*n*as said: 'Let the venerable Gotama tell us the Brâhmanical customs of the ancient Brâhma*n*as, if it is not inconvenient to the venerable Gotama.'

Bhagavat answered: 'Then listen, O Brâhma*n*as, pay great attention, I will speak.'

'Yes,' so saying the wealthy Brâhma*n*as listened to Bhagavat. Bhagavat said this:

1. The old sages (isayo) were self-restrained, penitent; having abandoned the objects of the five senses, they studied their own welfare. (283)

2. There were no cattle for the Brâhma*n*as, nor gold, nor corn, (but) the riches and corn of meditation were for them, and they kept watch over the best treasure. (284)

3. What was prepared for them and placed as food at the door, they thought was to be given to those that seek for what has been prepared by faith. (285)

4. With garments variously coloured, with beds and abodes, prosperous people from the provinces and the whole country worshipped those Brâhma*n*as. (286)

5. Inviolable were the Brâhma*n*as, invincible, protected by the Dhamma, no one opposed them (while standing) at the doors of the houses anywhere. (287)

6. For forty-eight years they practised juvenile chastity, the Brâhma*n*as formerly went in search of science and exemplary conduct. (288)

7. The Brâhma*n*as did not marry (a woman belonging to) another (caste), nor did they buy a wife; they chose living together in mutual love after having come together. (289)

8. Excepting from the time about the cessation of the menstruation else the Brâhma*n*as did not indulge in sexual intercourse. (290)

9. They praised chastity and virtue, rectitude, mildness, penance, tenderness, compassion, and patience. (291)

10. He who was the best of them, a strong Brâhma*n*a, did not (even) in sleep indulge in sexual intercourse. (292)

11. Imitating his practices some wise men in this world praised chastity, virtue, and patience. (293)

12. Having asked for rice, beds, garments, butter, and oil, and gathered them justly, they made sacrifices out of them, and when the sacrifice came on, they did not kill cows. (294)

13. Like unto a mother, a father, a brother, and

other relatives the cows are our best friends, in which medicines are produced. (295)

14. They give food, and they give strength, they likewise give (a good) complexion and happiness; knowing the real state of this, they did not kill cows. (296)

15. They were graceful, large, handsome, renowned, Brâhma*n*as by nature, zealous for their several works; as long as they lived in the world, this race prospered. (297)

16. But there was a change in them: after gradually seeing the king's prosperity and adorned women, (298)

17. Well-made chariots drawn by noble horses, carpets in variegated colours, palaces and houses, divided into compartments and measured out, (299)

18. The great human wealth, attended with a number of cows, and combined with a flock of beautiful women, the Brâhma*n*as became covetous. (300)

19. They then, in this matter, having composed hymns, went to Okkâka, and said: 'Thou hast much wealth and corn, sacrifice, (for) great is thy property, sacrifice, (for) great is thy wealth.' (301)

20. And then the king, the lord of chariots, instructed by the Brâhma*n*as, brought about assamedha, purisamedha, sammâpâsa, and vâ*k*âpeyya without any hinderance, and having offered these sacrifices he gave the Brâhma*n*as wealth: (302)

21. Cows, beds, garments, and adorned women, and well-made chariots, drawn by noble horses, carpets in variegated colours, (303)

22. Beautiful palaces, well divided into compartments; and having filled these with different (sorts of) corn, he gave this wealth to the Brâhma*n*as. (304)

23. And they having thus received wealth wished

for a store, and the craving of those who had given way to (their) wishes increased still more; they then, in this matter, having composed hymns, went again to Okkâka, and said: (305)

24. 'As water, earth, gold, wealth, and corn, even so are there cows for men, for this is a requisite for living beings; sacrifice, (for) great is thy property, sacrifice, (for) great is thy wealth.' (306)

25. And then the king, the lord of chariots, instructed by the Brâhma*n*as, caused many hundred thousand cows to be slain in offerings. (307)

26. Not with their feet, nor with their horns do the cows hurt (any one in any way, being like goats tender (and) yielding vessels (of milk)—(still) seizing them by the horns the king caused them to be slain with a weapon. (308)

27. Then the gods, the forefathers, Inda, the Asuras, and the Rakkhasas cried out: 'This is injustice,' because of the weapon falling on the cows. (309)

28. There were formerly three diseases: desire, hunger, and decay, but from the slaying of cattle there came ninety-eight. (310)

29. This injustice of (using) violence that has come down (to us), was old; innocent (cows) are slain, the sacrificing (priests) have fallen off from the Dhamma. (311)

30. So this old and mean Dhamma is blamed by the wise; where people see such a one, they blame the sacrificing priest. (312)

31. So Dhamma being lost, the Suddas and the Vessikas disagreed, the Khattiyas disagreed in manifold ways, the wife despised her husband. (313)

32. The Khattiyas and the Brâhma*n*as and those others who had been protected by their castes, after

doing away with their disputes on descent, fell into the power of sensual pleasures. (314)

This having been said, those wealthy Brâhma*n*as said to Bhagavat as follows:

'It is excellent, O venerable Gotama! It is excellent, O venerable Gotama! As one raises what has been overthrown, or reveals what has been hidden, or tells the way to him who has gone astray, or holds out an oil lamp in the dark that those who have eyes may see the objects, even so by the venerable Gotama in manifold ways the Dhamma has been illustrated; we take refuge in the venerable Gotama, in the Dhamma, and in the Assembly of Bhikkhus; may the venerable Gotama receive us as followers (upâsaka), who from this day for life have taken refuge (in him).'

Brâhma*n*adhammikasutta is ended.

---

8. NÂVÂSUTTA.

On choosing a good and learned teacher.

1. A man should worship him from whom he learns the Dhamma, as the gods (worship) Inda; the learned man being worshipped and pleased with him, makes the (highest) Dhamma manifest. (315)

2. Having heard and considered that (Dhamma), the wise man practising the Dhamma that is in accordance with the (highest) Dhamma, becomes learned, expert, and skilful, strenuously associating with such a (learned teacher). (316)

3. He who serves a low (teacher), a fool who has not understood the meaning, and who is envious, goes to death, not having overcome doubt, and not having understood the Dhamma. (317)

4. As a man, after descending into a river, a turgid water with a rapid current, is borne along following the current,—how will he be able to put others across? (318)

5. Even so how will a man, not having understood the Dhamma, and not attending to the explanation of the learned and not knowing it himself, not having overcome doubt, be able to make others understand it? (319)

6. As one, having gone on board a strong ship, provided with oars and rudder, carries across in it many others, knowing the way to do it, and being expert and thoughtful, (320)

7. So also he who is accomplished, of a cultivated mind, learned, intrepid, makes others endowed with attention and assiduity understand it, knowing (it himself). (321)

8. Therefore indeed one should cultivate (the society of) a good man, who is intelligent and learned; he who leads a regular life, having understood what is good and penetrated the Dhamma, will obtain happiness. (322)

Nâvâsutta is ended.

---

9. KIMSÎLASUTTA.

How to obtain the highest good.

1. By what virtue, by what conduct, and performing what works, will a man be perfectly established (in the commandments) and obtain the highest good? (323)

2. Let him honour old people, not be envious,

let him know the (right) time for seeing his teacher, and knowing the (right) moment let him assiduously listen to his religious discourses pronounced (and) to his well-spoken (words). (324)

3. Let him in due time go to the presence of his teacher, let him be humble after casting away obstinacy, let him remember and practise what is good, the Dhamma, self-restraint, and chastity. (325)

4. Let his pleasure-garden be the Dhamma, let him delight in the Dhamma, let him stand fast in the Dhamma, let him know how to enquire into the Dhamma, let him not raise any dispute that pollutes the Dhamma, and let him spend his time in (speaking) well-spoken truths[1]. (326)

5. Having abandoned ridiculous talk, lamentation, corruption, deceit, hypocrisy, greediness and haughtiness, clamour and harshness, depravity and foolishness, let him live free from infatuation, with a steady mind. (327)

6. The words, the essence of which is understood, are well spoken, and what is heard, if understood, contains the essence of meditation; but the understanding and learning of the man who is hasty and careless, does not increase. (328)

7. Those who delight in the Dhamma, proclaimed by the venerable ones, are unsurpassed in speech, mind and work, they are established in peace, tenderness and meditation, and have gone to the essence of learning and understanding. (329)

Ki*m*sîlasutta is ended.

[1] Comp. Dhp. v. 364.

10. U*TTH*ÂNASUTTA.

Advice not to be lukewarm and slothful. (See a free translation in Rhys Davids' Buddhism, 1896, p. 170.)

1. Rise, sit up, what is the use of your sleeping; to those who are sick, pierced by the arrow (of pain), and suffering, what sleep is there? (330)

2. Rise, sit up, learn steadfastly for the sake of peace, let not the king of death, knowing you to be indolent (pamatta), befool you and lead you into his power. (331)

3. Conquer this desire which gods and men stand wishing for and are dependent upon, let not the (right) moment pass by you; for those who have let the (right) moment pass, will grieve when they have been consigned to hell. (332)

4. Indolence (pamâda) is defilement, continued indolence is defilement; by earnestness (appamâda) and knowledge let one pull out his arrow (of passion). (333)

U*tth*ânasutta is ended.

11. RÂHULASUTTA.

Buddha recommends the life of a recluse to Râhula, and admonishes him to turn his mind away from the world and to be moderate.

1. Bhagavat said: 'Dost thou not despise the wise man, from living with him constantly? Is he who holds up a torch to mankind honoured by thee?' (334)

2. Râhula: 'I do not despise the wise man, from living with him constantly; he who holds up a torch to mankind is always honoured by me.' (335)

Vatthugâthâ.

3. Bhagavat: 'Having abandoned the objects of the five senses, the beautiful, the charming, and gone out from thy house with faith, do thou put an end to pain. (336)

4. 'Cultivate (the society of) virtuous friends and a distant dwelling-place, secluded and quiet; be moderate in food[1]. (337)

5. 'Robes, alms (in bowl), requisites (for the sick), a dwelling-place,—do not thirst after these (things), that thou mayest not go back to the world again. (338)

6. 'Be subdued according to the precepts, and as to the five senses, be attentive as regards thy body, and be full of disgust (with the world). (339)

7. 'Avoid signs, what is pleasant and is accompanied with passion, turn thy mind undisturbed and well composed to what is not pleasant. (340)

8. 'Cherish what is signless, leave the inclinations for pride; then by sacrificing thy pride thou shalt wander calm.' (341)

So Bhagavat repeatedly admonished the venerable Râhula with these stanzas.

Râhulasutta is ended.

---

12. VAṄGÎSASUTTA.

Vaṅgîsa desires to know the fate of Nigrodhakappa, whether he has been completely extinguished, or whether he is still with some elements of existence left behind. He is answered by Buddha.

So it was heard by me:

At one time Bhagavat dwelt at Â*l*avî, in the

---

[1] Comp. Dhp. v. 185 and v. 375.

temple of Aggâ*l*ava. At that time the teacher of the venerable Vaṅgîsa, the Thera, by name Nigrodhakappa, had attained bliss not long before (a*k*iraparinibbuta). Then this reflection occurred to the venerable Vaṅgîsa, while retired and meditating:

Whether my teacher be blessed (parinibbuta) or whether he be not blessed. Then the venerable Vaṅgîsa, at the evening time, coming forth from his retirement went to Bhagavat, and having gone to him he sat down apart after saluting him, and sitting down apart the venerable Vaṅgîsa said this to Bhagavat:

'Lord, while retired and meditating, this reflection occurred to me here: Whether my teacher be blessed or whether he be not blessed.'

Then the venerable Vaṅgîsa, rising from his seat, throwing his robe over one shoulder and bending his joined hands towards Bhagavat, addressed him in stanzas:

1 'We ask the Master of excellent understanding: he who in this world had cut off doubt, died at Aggâ*l*ava, a Bhikkhu, well known, famous, and of a calm mind. (342)

2. 'The name "Nigrodhakappa" was given to that Brâhma*n*a by thee, O Bhagavat; he wandered about worshipping thee, having liberation in view, strong, O thou who seest Nibbâna. (343)

3. 'O Sakka, thou all-seeing, we all wish to learn (something about) this disciple; our ears are ready to hear, thou art our Master, thou art incomparable. (344)

4. 'Cut off our doubt, tell me of him, inform us of the blessed, O thou of great understanding; speak

in the midst of us, O thou all-seeing, as the thousand-eyed Sakka (speaks in the midst) of the gods. (345)

5. 'Whatever ties there are in this world (constituting) the way to folly, combined with ignorance, forming the seat of doubt, they do not exist before Tathâgata, for he is the best eye of men. (346)

6. 'If a man does not for ever dispel the sin as the wind (dispels) a mass of clouds, all the world will be enveloped in darkness, not even illustrious men will shine. (347)

7. 'Wise men are light-bringers, therefore, O wise man, I consider thee as such a one; we have come to him who beholds meditation, reveal Kappa to us in the assembly. (348)

8. 'Uplift quickly, O thou beautiful one, thy beautiful voice, like the swans drawing up (their necks), sing softly with a rich and well-modulated voice; we will all listen to thee attentively. (349)

9. 'Having earnestly called upon him who has completely left birth and death behind and shaken off (sin), I will make him proclaim the Dhamma, for ordinary people cannot do what they want, but the Tathâgatas act with a purpose. (350)

10. 'This full explanation by thee, the perfectly wise, is accepted, this last clasping of the hands is well bent, O thou of high wisdom, knowing (Kappa's transmigration), do not delude us. (351)

11. 'Having perfectly[1] comprehended the Dhamma of the venerable ones, do not delude (us), O thou of unsurpassed strength, knowing (everything); as one in the hot season pained by the heat (longs for)

[1] Parovaran ti lokuttaralokiyavasena sundarâsundara*m* dûre santika*m* vâ. Commentator.

water, so I long for thy words; send a shower of learning. (352)

12. 'The rich religious life which Kappâyana led, has not that been in vain (to him), has he been (completely) extinguished, or is he still with some elements of existence (left behind)? How he was liberated, that we want to hear.' (353)

13. Bhagavat: 'He cut off the craving for name and form in this world,'—so said Bhagavat,—'Ka*n*ha's (i.e. Mâra's) stream, adhered to for a long time, he crossed completely birth and death,' so said Bhagavat, the best of the five (Brâhma*n*as, pa*ñk*avaggiyâ). (354)

14. Vaṅgîsa: 'Having heard thy word, O thou the best of the Isis, I am pleased; not in vain have I asked, the Brâhma*n*a did not deceive me. (355)

15. 'As he talked so he acted, he was a (true) disciple of Buddha, he cut asunder the outspread strong net of deceitful death. (356)

16. 'Kappiya (Kappâyana) saw, O Bhagavat, the beginning of attachment, Kappâyana verily crossed the realm of death, which is very difficult to cross.' (357)

Vaṅgîsasutta is ended.

---

13. SAMMÂPARIBBÂ*G*ANIYASUTTA.

The right path for a Bhikkhu.

1. 'We will ask the Muni of great understanding, who has crossed, gone to the other shore, is blessed (parinibbuta), and of a firm mind: How does a Bhikkhu wander rightly in the world, after having

gone out from his house and driven away desire?' (358)

2. 'He whose (ideas of) omens, meteors, dreams and signs are destroyed,'—so said Bhagavat,—'such a Bhikkhu who has abandoned the sinful omens, wanders rightly in the world. (359)

3. 'Let the Bhikkhu subdue his passion for human and divine pleasures, then after conquering existence and understanding the Dhamma, such a one will wander rightly in the world. (360)

4. 'Let the Bhikkhu, after casting behind him slander and anger, abandon avarice and be free from compliance and opposition, then such a one will wander rightly in the world. (361)

5. 'He who having left behind both what is agreeable and what is disagreeable, not seizing upon anything, is independent in every respect and liberated from bonds, such a one will wander rightly in the world. (362)

6. 'He does not see any essence in the Upadhis, having subdued his wish and passion for attachments, he is independent and not to be led by others, such a one will wander rightly in the world. (363)

7. 'He who is not opposed (to any one) in word, thought or deed, who, after having understood the Dhamma perfectly, longs for the state of Nibbâna, such a one will wander rightly in the world. (364)

8. 'He who thinking "he salutes me" is not elated, the Bhikkhu who, although abused, does not reflect (upon it, and) having received food from others does not get intoxicated (with pride), such a one will wander rightly in the world. (365)

9. 'The Bhikkhu who, after leaving behind covetousness and existence, is disgusted with cutting and

binding (others), he who has overcome doubt, and is without pain, such a one will wander rightly in the world. (366)

10. 'And knowing what becomes him, the Bhikkhu will not harm any one in the world, understanding the Dhamma thoroughly, such a one will wander rightly in the world. (367)

11. 'He to whom there are no affections whatsoever, whose sins are extirpated from the root, he free from desire and not longing (for anything), such a one will wander rightly in the world. (368)

12. 'He whose passions have been destroyed, who is free from pride, who has overcome all the path of passion, is subdued, perfectly happy (parinibbuta), and of a firm mind, such a one will wander rightly in the world. (369)

13. 'The believer, possessed of knowledge, seeing the way (leading to Nibbâna), who is no partisan amongst the partisans (of the sixty-two philosophical views), wise after subduing covetousness, hatred, such a one will wander rightly in the world. (370)

14. 'He who is pure and victorious, who has removed the veil (of the world), who is subdued in the Dhammas, has gone to the other shore, is without desire, and skilled in the knowledge of the cessation of the Sa*m*khâras, such a one will wander rightly in the world. (371)

15. 'He who has overcome time (kappâtîta) in the past and in the future, is of an exceedingly pure understanding, liberated from all the dwelling-places (of the mind), such a one will wander rightly in the world. (372)

16. 'Knowing the step (of the four truths), understanding the Dhamma, seeing clearly the abandon-

ment of the passions from the destruction of all the elements of existence (upadhî), such a one will wander rightly in the world.' (373)

17. 'Certainly, O Bhagavat, it is so: whichever Bhikkhu lives in this way, subdued and having overcome all bonds, such a one will wander rightly in the world.' (374)

Sammâparibbâ*g*aniyasutta is ended.

---

14. DHAMMIKASUTTA.

Buddha shows Dhammika what the life of a Bhikkhu and what the life of a householder ought to be.

So it was heard by me:

At one time Bhagavat dwelt at Sâvatthî, in *G*etavana, in the park of Anâthapi*nd*ika. Then the follower (upâsaka) Dhammika, together with five hundred followers, went to Bhagavat, and having gone to Bhagavat and saluted him, he sat down apart; sitting down apart the follower Dhammika addressed Bhagavat in stanzas:

1. 'I ask thee, O Gotama of great understanding, How is a Sâvaka (disciple) to act to be a good one? is it the one who goes from his house to the wilderness, or the followers with a house? (375)

2. 'For thou knowest the doings of this world and that of the gods, and the final end; there is nobody like thee seeing the subtle meaning (of things); they call thee the excellent Buddha. (376)

3. 'Knowing all knowledge thou hast revealed the Dhamma, having compassion on creatures; thou hast removed the veil (of the world), thou art all-seeing, thou shinest spotless in all the world. (377)

4. 'The king of elephants, Erâvana by name, hearing that thou wert *G*ina (the Conqueror), came to thy presence, and having conversed with thee he went away delighted, after listening (to thee, and saying), "Very good!" (378)

5. 'Also king Vessavana Kuvera came to ask thee about the Dhamma; him, too, thou, O wise man, answeredst when asked, and he also after listening was delighted. (379)

6. 'All these disputatious Titthiyas and Â*g*îvikas and Niga*nth*as do not any of them overcome thee in understanding, as a man standing (does not overcome) the one that is walking quickly. (380)

7. 'All these disputatious Brâhma*n*as, and there are even some old Brâhma*n*as, all are bound by thy opinion, and others also that are considered disputants. (381)

8. This subtle and pleasant Dhamma that has been well proclaimed by thee, O Bhagavat, and which we all long to hear, do thou, O thou best of Buddhas, speak to us when asked. (382)

9. 'Let all these Bhikkhus and also Upâsakas that have sat down to listen, hear the Dhamma learnt (anubuddha) by the stainless (Buddha), as the gods (hear) the well-spoken (words) of Vâsava.' (383)

10. Bhagavat: 'Listen to me, O Bhikkhus, I will teach you the Dhamma that destroys sin, do ye keep it, all of you; let him who looks for what is salutary, the thoughtful, cultivate the mode of life suitable for Pabba*g*itas. (384)

11. 'Let not the Bhikkhu walk about at a wrong time, let him go to the village for alms at the right time; for ties ensnare the one that goes

at a wrong time, therefore Buddhas do not go at a wrong time. (385)

12. 'Form, sound, taste, smell, and touch which intoxicate creatures, having subdued the desire for (all) these things (dhammas), let him in due time go in for his breakfast. (386)

13. 'And let the Bhikkhu, after having obtained his food at the right time and returned, sit down alone and privately; reflecting within himself let him not turn his mind to outward things, (but be) self-collected. (387)

14. 'If he speak with a Sâvaka or with anybody else, or with a Bhikkhu, let him talk about the excellent Dhamma, (but let him) not (utter) slander, nor blaming words against others. (388)

15. 'For some utter language contradicting others[1]; those narrow-minded ones we do not praise. Ties from here and there ensnare them, and they send their mind far away in that (dispute). (389)

16. 'Let a Sâvaka of him with the excellent understanding (Buddha), after hearing the Dhamma taught by Sugata, discriminately seek for food, a monastery, a bed and a chair, and water for taking away the dirt of his clothes. (390)

17. 'But without clinging to these things, to food, to bed and chair, to water for taking away the dirt of his clothes, let a Bhikkhu be like a waterdrop on a lotus. (391)

18. 'A householder's work I will also tell you, how a Sâvaka is to act to be a good one; for that complete Bhikkhu-dhamma cannot be carried out by one who is taken up by (worldly) occupations. (392)

[1] Vâda*m* hi eke pa*t*iseniyanti = virugg*h*anti yugg*h*itukâmâ hutvâ senâya pa*t*imukha*m* ga*kkh*antâ viya honti. Commentator.

19. 'Let him not kill, nor cause to be killed any living being, nor let him approve of others killing, after having refrained from hurting all creatures, both those that are strong and those that tremble in the world. (393)

20. 'Then let the Sâvaka abstain from (taking) anything in any place that has not been given (to him), knowing (it to belong to another), let him not cause any one to take, nor approve of those that take, let him avoid all (sort of) theft. (394)

21. 'Let the wise man avoid an unchaste life as a burning heap of coals; not being able to live a life of chastity, let him not transgress with another man's wife. (395)

22. 'Let no one speak falsely to another in the hall of justice or in the hall of the assembly, let him not cause (any one) to speak (falsely), nor approve of those that speak (falsely), let him avoid all (sort of) untruth. (396)

23. 'Let the householder who approves of this Dhamma, not give himself to intoxicating drinks; let him not cause others to drink, nor approve of those that drink, knowing it to end in madness. (397)

24. 'For through intoxication the stupid commit sins and make other people intoxicated; let him avoid this seat of sin, this madness, this folly, delightful to the stupid. (398)

25. 'Let him not kill any living being, let him not take what has not been given (to him), let him not speak falsely, and let him not drink intoxicating drinks, let him refrain from unchaste sexual intercourse, and let him not at night eat untimely food. (399)

26. 'Let him not wear wreaths nor use perfumes, let him lie on a couch spread on the earth:—this they

call the eightfold abstinence (uposatha), proclaimed by Buddha, who has overcome pain. (400)

27. 'Then having with a believing mind kept abstinence (uposatha) on the fourteenth, fifteenth, and the eighth days of the half-month, and (having kept) the complete Pâ*t*ihârakapakkha[1] consisting of eight parts, (401)

28. 'And then in the morning, after having kept abstinence, let a wise man with a believing mind, gladdening the assembly of Bhikkhus with food and drink, make distributions according to his ability. (402)

29. 'Let him dutifully maintain his parents, and practise an honourable trade; the householder who observes this strenuously goes to the gods by name Sayampabhas.' (403)

Dhammikasutta is ended.

*K*ûlavagga is ended.

---

[1] Compare T. W. Rhys Davids, Buddhism, p. 141.

III. MAHÂVAGGA.

1. PABBA*GG*ÂSUTTA.

King Bimbisâra feeling interested in Buddha tries to tempt him with wealth, but is mildly rebuked by Buddha. (See a free translation in Rhys Davids' Buddhism, 1896, p. 99.)

1. I will praise an ascetic life such as the clearly-seeing (Buddha) led, such as he thinking (over it) approved of as an ascetic life. (404)

2. 'This house-life is pain, the seat of impurity,' and 'an ascetic life is an open-air life,' so considering he embraced an ascetic life. (405)

3. Leading an ascetic life, he avoided with his body sinful deeds, and having (also) abandoned sin in words, he cleansed his life. (406)

4. Buddha went to Râ*g*agaha, he entered the Giribba*g*a in Magadha for alms with a profusion of excellent signs. (407)

5. Bimbisâra standing in his palace saw him, and seeing him endowed with these signs, he spoke these words: (408)

6. 'Attend ye to this man, he is handsome, great, clean, he is both endowed with good conduct, and he does not look before him further than a yuga (the distance of a plough). (409)

7. 'With downcast eyes, thoughtful, this one is not like those of low caste; let the king's messengers run off, (and ask): "Where is the Bhikkhu going?"' (410)

8. The king's messengers followed after (him, and

said): 'Where is the Bhikkhu going, where will he reside? (411)

9. 'Going begging from house to house, watching the door (of the senses), well restrained, he quickly filled his bowl, conscious, thoughtful. (412)

10. 'Wandering about in search of alms, having gone out of town, the Muni repaired to (the mountain) Pa*nd*ava; it must be there he lives.' (413)

11. Seeing that he had entered his dwelling, the messengers then sat down, and one messenger having returned announced it to the king. (414)

12. 'This Bhikkhu, O great king, is sitting on the east side of Pa*nd*ava, like a tiger, like a bull, like a lion in a mountain cave.' (415)

13. Having heard the messenger's words, the Khattiya in a fine chariot hastening went out to the Pa*nd*ava mountain. (416)

14. Having gone as far as the ground was practicable for a chariot, the Khattiya, after alighting from the chariot, and approaching on foot, having come up (to him), seated himself. (417)

15. Having sat down the king then exchanged the usual ceremonious greetings with him, and after the complimentary talk he spoke these words: (418)

16. 'Thou art both young and delicate, a lad in his first youth, possessed of a fine complexion, like a high-born Khattiya. (419)

17. 'I will ornament the army-house, and at the head of the assembly of chiefs (nâga) give (thee) wealth; enjoy it and tell me thy birth, when asked.' (420)

18. Buddha: 'Just beside Himavanta, O king, there lives a people endowed with the power of wealth, the inhabitants of Kosala. (421)

19. 'They are Âdi*kk*as by family, Sâkiyas by birth; from that family I have wandered out, not longing for sensual pleasures. (422)

20. 'Seeing misery in sensual pleasures, and considering the forsaking of the world as happiness, I will go and exert myself; in this my mind delights.' (423)

Pabba*gg*âsutta is ended.

2. PADHÂNASUTTA.

Mâra tries to tempt Buddha, but disappointed is obliged to withdraw. Comp. Gospel of St. Matthew iv.

1. To me, whose mind was intent upon exertion near the river Nera*ñg*arâ, having exerted myself, and given myself to meditation for the sake of acquiring Nibbâna (yogakkhema), (424)

2. Came Namu*k*i speaking words full of compassion: 'Thou art lean, ill-favoured, death is in thy neighbourhood. (425)

3. 'A thousandth part of thee (is the property) of death, (only) one part (belongs to) life; living life, O thou venerable one, is better; living thou wilt be able to do good works. (426)

4. 'When thou livest a religious life, and feedest the sacrificial fire, manifold good works are woven to thee; what dost thou want with exertion? (427)

5. 'Difficult is the way of exertion, difficult to pass, difficult to enter upon; saying these verses Mâra stood near Buddha. (428)

6. To Mâra thus speaking Bhagavat said this: 'O thou friend of the indolent, thou wicked one, for what purpose hast thou come here? (429)

7. 'Even the least good work is of no use to me; and what good works are required, Mâra ought to tell. (430)

8. 'I have faith and power, and understanding is found in me; while thus exerting myself, why do you ask me to live[1]? (431)

9. 'This (burning) wind will dry up even the currents of the rivers; should it not by degrees dry up my blood, while I am exerting myself? (432)

10. 'While the blood is drying up, the bile and the phlegm are dried up; while the flesh is wasting away, the mind gets more tranquil, and my attention, understanding, and meditation get more steadfast[2]. (433)

11. 'While I am living thus, after having felt the extreme sensations, my mind does not look for sensual pleasures; behold a being's purity. (434)

12. 'Lust thy first army is called, discontent thy second, thy third is called hunger and thirst, thy fourth craving. (435)

13. 'Thy fifth is called sloth and drowsiness, thy sixth cowardice, thy seventh doubt, thy eighth hypocrisy and stupor, (436)

14. 'Gain, fame, honour, and what celebrity has been falsely obtained; and he who exalts himself and despises others. (437)

15. 'This, O Namu*k*i, is thine, the black one's,

---

[1] Eva*m* ma*m* pahitattam pi
Ki*m* *g*îvam anupu*kkh*asi.

[2] Lohite sussamânamhi
Pitta*m* semha*ñ* *k*a sussati,
Ma*m*sesu khîyamânesu
Bhiyyo *k*itta*m* pasîdati
Bhiyyo sati *k*a pa*ññ*â *k*a
Samâdhi mama ti*tth*ati.

fighting army; none but a hero conquers it, and after conquering it obtains joy[1]. (438)

16. 'I myself (having conquered) wear Muñga-grass. Woe upon life in this world! death in battle is better for me than that I should live defeated. (439)

17. 'Plunged into this world some Samanas and Brâhmanas are not seen, and they do not know the way in which the virtuous walk. (440)

18. 'Seeing on all sides an army arrayed, and Mâra on his elephant, I am going out to do battle, that he may not drive me away from my place. (441)

19. 'This army of thine, which the world of men and gods cannot conquer, I will crush with understanding as (one crushes) an unbaked earthen pot with a stone[2]. (442)

20. 'Having made my thought subject to me and my attention firm, I shall wander about from kingdom to kingdom, training disciples extensively. (443)

21. 'They (will be) zealous and energetic, executing my orders, (the orders) of one free from lust, and they will go (to the place) where, having gone, they will not mourn.' (444)

22. Mâra: 'For seven years I followed Bhagavat step by step; I found no fault in the perfectly enlightened, thoughtful (Buddha). (445)

23. 'The crow hovered round the rock that looked

---

[1] Saṅgâmâvakarâ anivattino purisâ attano anivattanakabhâvam ñâpanattham sîse vâ dhage vâ âvudhe vâ muñgatinam bandhanti tam ayam pi pariharati-kkeva mam dhârehi tava senâ parâgit' assa. Commentator.

[2] Yam te tam na-ppasahati
Senam loko sadevake
Tam te paññâya gakkhâmi*
Âmam pattam va amhanâ.

* Instead of gakkhâmi I read bhañgâmi. B[a] has vekkhâpi, B[i] vegghâmi.

like (a lump of) fat: "Do we here find something soft, is it something sweet?" (446)

24. 'Having obtained nothing sweet there, the crow went away from that spot. Thus like the crow approaching the rock, being disgusted, we shall go away from Gotama[1].' (447)

25. While overcome with sorrow the string of his lute slipped down; then that evil-minded Yakkha disappeared there. (448)

Padhânasutta is ended.

3. SUBHÂSITASUTTA.

On well-spoken language.

So it was heard by me:

At one time Bhagavat dwelt at Sâvatthî in *G*etavana. Bhagavat said this: 'O Bhikkhus, the speech that is provided with four requisites is well-spoken, not ill-spoken, both faultless and blameless to the wise.'

'Which four?'

'O Bhikkhus, the Bhikkhu speaks well-spoken (language), not ill-spoken; he speaks what is right (dhamma), not what is unrighteous (adhamma); he speaks what is pleasing, not what is unpleasing; he speaks what is true, not what is false. O Bhikkhus, the speech that is provided with these four requisites, is well-spoken, not ill-spoken, both faultless

---

[1] Kâko va selam âsa*gg*a*
Nibbi*gg*âpema Gotama*m*†.

* C[b] C[k] âva*gg*a, B[a] assa*gg*a, B[i] âssa*gg*a. † Instead of Gotama*m* I read Gotamâ.

and blameless to the wise.' This said Bhagavat. When Sugata had said this, then the Master spoke the following:

1. 'Well-spoken language the just call the principal (thing); let one speak what is right (dhamma), not what is unrighteous (adhamma), that is the second; let one speak what is pleasing, not what is unpleasing, that is the third; let one speak what is true, not what is false, that is the fourth.' (449)

Then the venerable Vaṅgîsa, rising from his seat, throwing his robe over one shoulder and bending his joined hands towards Bhagavat, said this: 'It occurs to me, O Sugata!'

'Let it occur to thee, O Vaṅgîsa!' said Bhagavat.

Then the venerable Vaṅgîsa, standing before Bhagavat, praised him with appropriate stanzas:

2. 'Let one say such words by which he does not pain himself, nor hurt others; such words are truly well-spoken. (450)

3. 'Let one speak pleasing words which are received joyfully (by all), and which (saying) he, without committing sins, speaks what is pleasing to others. (451)

4. 'Truth verily is immortal speech, this is a true saying; in what is true, in what is good, and in what is right, the just stand firm, so they say. (452)

5. 'The words which Buddha speaks, which are sure to bring about extinction and put an end to pain, such (words) are truly the best.' (453)

Subhâsitasutta is ended.

4. SUNDARIKABHÂRADVÂ*G*ASUTTA.

Buddha shows to Sundarikabhâradvâ*g*a on whom to bestow oblations, and the Brâhma*n*a is finally converted.

So it was heard by me:

At one time Bhagavat dwelt in Kosala on the bank of the river Sundarikâ. And during that time the Brâhma*n*a Sundarikabhâradvâ*g*a made offerings to the fire and worshipped the fire. Then the Brâhma*n*a Sundarikabhâradvâ*g*a, having made offerings to the fire and worshipped the fire, and having risen from his seat, looked about him on all sides towards the four quarters of the globe, saying: 'Who is to enjoy the rest of this oblation?' The Brâhma*n*a Sundarikabhâradvâ*g*a saw Bhagavat sitting not far off at the root of a tree, wrapped up head and body; and seeing him he, after taking the rest of the oblation with his left hand and the waterpot with his right hand, went up to Bhagavat. Then Bhagavat, on hearing the footsteps of Sundarikabhâradvâ*g*a, the Brâhma*n*a, uncovered his head. Then the Brâhma*n*a Sundarikabhâradvâ*g*a thought: 'This man is shaved, this man is a shaveling,' and he wished to return again from there. Then this came to the mind of Sundarikabhâradvâ*g*a, the Brâhma*n*a: 'Some Brâhma*n*as also here are shaved, I think I shall go up and ask him about his descent.' Then the Brâhma*n*a Sundarikabhâradvâ*g*a went up to Bhagavat, and having gone up he said this: 'Of what family art thou?'

Then Bhagavat answered Sundarikabhâradvâ*g*a, the Brâhma*n*a, in stanzas:

1. 'No Brâhma*n*a am I, nor a king's son, nor any

Vessa; having thoroughly observed the class of common people, I wander about the world reflectingly, possessing nothing. (454)

2. 'Dressed in a saṅghâ*t*i[1] and houseless I wander about, with my hair cut off, calm, not intermixing with people in this world. Thou askest me an unseasonable question about (my) family, O Brâhma*n*a!' (455)

3. Sundarikabhâradvâ*g*a: 'Sir, Brâhma*n*as together with Brâhma*n*as ask truly, Art thou a Brâhma*n*a?'

Bhagavat: 'If thou sayest, I am a Brâhma*n*a, and callest me no Brâhma*n*a, then I ask thee about the Sâvitti that consists of three padas and twenty-four syllables[2].' (456)

4. Sundarikabhâradvâ*g*a: 'For what (reason) did the Isis, men, Khattiyas, Brâhma*n*as make offerings to the gods abundantly in this world?'

Bhagavat: 'He who, perfect and accomplished at the time of offering, obtains the ear of one or the other (god), he will succeed, so I say.' (457)

5. 'Surely his offering will bear fruit,'—so said the Brâhma*n*a,—'because we saw such an accomplished man; for by not seeing such as you, somebody else will enjoy the oblation.' (458)

6. Bhagavat: 'Therefore, O Brâhma*n*a, as you have come here to ask for something, ask; perhaps thou mightest here find one that is calm, without anger, free from pain, free from desire, one with a good understanding.' (459)

---

[1] See Rhys Davids, Buddhism, p. 166.

[2] Ta*m* Sâvitti*m* pu*kkh*âmi
Tipada*m* *k*atuvîsatakkhara*m*.
(Rig-veda III, 62, 10.)

7. Sundarikabhâradvâga: 'I delight in offering, O Gotama, I desire to make an offering, but I do not understand it; do thou instruct me, tell me in what case the offering succeeds.' (460)

8. Bhagavat: 'Therefore, O Brâhmana, lend me thy ear, I will teach thee the Dhamma. (461)

9. 'Do not ask about descent, but ask about conduct; from wood, it is true, fire is born; (likewise) a firm Muni, although belonging to a low family, may become noble, when restrained (from sinning) by humility. (462)

10. 'He who is subdued by truth, endowed with temperance, accomplished, leading a religious life, on such a one in due time people should bestow oblations; let the Brâhmana who has good works in view, offer. (463)

11. 'Those who, after leaving sensual pleasures, wander about houseless, well restrained, being like a straight shuttle, on such in due time people should bestow oblations; let the Brâhmana who has good works in view, offer. (464)

12. 'Those whose passions are gone, whose senses are well composed, who are liberated like the moon out of the grasp of Râhu, on such in due time people should bestow oblations; let the Brâhmana who has good works in view, offer. (465)

13. 'Those who wander about in the world without clinging (to anything), always thoughtful, having left selfishness, on such in due time people should bestow oblations; let the Brâhmana who has good works in view, offer. (466)

14. 'He who, after leaving sensual pleasures, wanders about victorious, he who knows the end of birth and death, who is perfectly happy (parinib-

buta), calm like a deep water, Tathâgata deserves the oblation. (467)

15. 'Just with the just and far from the unjust[1], Tathâgata is possessed of infinite understanding; undefiled both in this world and in the other, Tathâgata deserves the oblation. (468)

16. 'He in whom there lives no deceit, no arrogance, he who is free from cupidity, free from selfishness, free from desire, who has banished anger, who is calm, the Brâhma*n*a who has removed the taint of grief, Tathâgata deserves the oblation. (469)

17. 'He who has banished (every) resting-place of the mind, he for whom there is no grasping, he who covets nothing either in this world or in the other, Tathâgata deserves the oblation[2]. (470)

18. 'He who is composed, who has crossed over the stream (of existence) and knows the Dhamma by (taking) the highest view (of it), he whose passions are destroyed, who is wearing the last body, Tathâgata deserves the oblation. (471)

19. 'He whose passion for existence and whose harsh talk are destroyed, are perished, (and therefore) exist not, he the accomplished and in every respect liberated Tathâgata deserves the oblation. (472)

20. 'He who has shaken off all ties, for whom there are no ties, who amongst arrogant beings is free from arrogance, having penetrated pain together with its domain and subject, Tathâgata deserves the oblation. (473)

21. 'He who, without giving himself up to desire, sees seclusion (i. e. Nibbâna), who has overcome the view that is to be taught by others, to whom there

[1] Samo samehi visamehi dûre.

[2] Comp. Dhp. v. 20.

are no objects of sense whatever, Tathâgata deserves the oblation[1]. (474)

22. 'He to whom all Dhammas of every description, after he has penetrated them, are destroyed, are perished, (and therefore) exist not, he who is calm, liberated in the destruction of attachment (i. e. Nibbâna), Tathâgata deserves the oblation. (475)

23. 'He who sees the destruction of bond and birth, who has totally evaded the path of passion, (who is) pure, faultless, spotless, undepraved, Tathâgata deserves the oblation. (476)

24. 'He who does not measure himself by himself, who is composed, upright, firm, without desire, free from harshness (akhila), free from doubt, Tathâgata deserves the oblation. (477)

25. 'He to whom there is no cause of folly, who has a supernatural insight in all Dhammas, who wears the last body, and who has acquired perfect enlightenment, the highest, the blessed, (for him) thus a Yakkha's purification (takes place)[2].' (478)

26. Sundarikabhâradvâ*g*a: 'May my offering be a true offering, because I met with such an accomplished one; Brahman is my witness, may Bhagavat accept me, may Bhagavat enjoy my oblation.' (479)

27. Bhagavat: 'What is obtained by stanzas is not to be enjoyed by me, this is not the custom of the clearly-seeing, O Brâhma*n*a; Buddhas reject what is obtained by stanzas. While the Dhamma

---

[1] Âsa*m* anissâya vivekadassî
Paravediya*m** di*tth*im upâtivatto
Âramma*n*â yassa na santi ke*k*i, &c.

[2] Comp. Kalahavivâdasutta, v. 14.

* Paravediyan ti parehi *ñ*âpetabba*m*. Commentator.

exists, O Brâhma*n*a, this is the practice (of the Buddhas). (480)

28. 'With other food and drink must thou serve one that is perfect, a great Isi, whose passions are destroyed, and whose misbehaviour has ceased, for this is a field for one who looks for good works[1].' (481)

29. Sundarikabhâradvâ*g*a: 'Good, O Bhagavat, then I should like to know, who will enjoy a gift from one like me, and whom I shall seek at the time of sacrifice (as one worthy of offerings) after having accepted thy doctrine.' (482)

30. Bhagavat: 'Whosoever has no quarrels, whose mind is untroubled, and who has freed himself from lusts, whose sloth is driven away, (483)

31. 'Whosoever conquers his sins, knows birth and death, the Muni who is endowed with wisdom[2], such a one who has attained to offering, (484)

32. 'Him you should worship and honour with food and drink, putting away frowning; so the gifts will prosper.' (485)

33. Sundarikabhâradvâ*g*a: 'Thou Buddha deservest the oblation, (thou art) the best field for good works, the object of offering to all the world; what is given to thee will bear great fruit.' (486)

Then the Brâhma*n*a Sundarikabhâradvâ*g*a said this to Bhagavat: 'It is excellent, O venerable Gotama! It is excellent, O venerable Gotama! As one raises what has been overthrown, or reveals what has been hidden, or tells the way to him who has gone astray, or holds out an oil lamp in the dark that those who have eyes may see the objects, even so by the venerable Gotama in manifold ways the

[1] Comp. Kasibhâradvâ*g*asutta, v. 7.

[2] Moneyyasampanna*m* = pa*ññ*âsampanna*m*. Commentator.

Dhamma has been illustrated; I take refuge in the venerable Gotama, in the Dhamma, and in the Assembly of Bhikkhus; I wish to receive the robe and the orders from the venerable Gotama.'

The Brâhma*n*a Sundarikabhâradvâ*g*a received the pabba*gg*â from Bhagavat, and he received also the upasampadâ; and the venerable Bhâradvâ*g*a, having lately received the upasampadâ, leading a solitary, retired, strenuous, ardent, energetic life, lived after having in a short time in this existence by his own understanding ascertained and possessed himself of that highest perfection of a religious life for the sake of which men of good family rightly wander away from their houses to a houseless state. 'Birth had been destroyed, a religious life had been led, what was to be done had been done, there was nothing else (to be done) for this existence,' so he perceived, and the venerable Bhâradvâ*g*a became one of the arahats.

Sundarikabhâradvâ*g*asutta is ended.

---

5. MÂGHASUTTA.

Buddha on being asked tells Mâgha of those worthy of offerings and the blessing of offering.

So it was heard by me:

At one time Bhagavat dwelt at Râ*g*agaha, in the mountain (called) the Vulture's Peak (Gi*ggh*akû*t*a).

Then the young man Mâgha went to Bhagavat, and having gone to him he talked pleasantly with him, and after having had some pleasant, remarkable conversation with him he sat down apart; sitting down apart the young man Mâgha spoke this to Bhagavat:

'O venerable Gotama, I am a liberal giver, bountiful, suitable to beg of; justly I seek for riches, and having sought for riches justly, I give out of the justly obtained and justly acquired riches to one, to two, to three, to four, to five, to six, to seven, to eight, to nine, to ten, to twenty, to thirty, to forty, to fifty, to a hundred, I give still more. (I should like to know), O venerable Gotama, whether I, while so giving, so offering, produce much good.'

'Certainly, O young man, dost thou in so offering produce much good; he, O young man, who is a liberal giver, bountiful, suitable to beg of, and who justly seeks for riches, and having sought for riches justly, gives out of his justly obtained and justly acquired riches to one, to two, to three, to four, to five, to six, to seven, to eight, to nine, to ten, to twenty, to thirty, to forty, to fifty, to a hundred, and gives still more, produces much good.'

Then the young man Mâgha addressed Bhagavat in stanzas:

1. 'I ask the venerable Gotama, the bountiful,'—so said the young man Mâgha,—'wearing the yellow robe, wandering about houseless:' 'He who is a householder, suitable to beg of, a donor, who, desirous of good, offers having what is good in view, and giving to others in this world food and drink,—where (i.e. on whom bestowed) will the oblation of such an offerer prosper?' (487)

2. 'He who is a householder, suitable to beg of, a donor, O Mâgha,'—so said Bhagavat,—'who, desirous of good, offers having what is good in view, and giving to others in this world food and drink, such a one will prosper with those worthy of offerings.' (488)

3. 'He who is a householder, suitable to beg of, a donor,'—so said the young man,—'who, desirous of good, offers having what is good in view, and giving to others in this world food and drink,—tell me (I being such a one), O Bhagavat, of those worthy of offerings.' (489)

4. Bhagavat: 'Those indeed who wander about in the world without clinging to anything and without possessing anything, perfect, self-restrained, on such in due time people should bestow oblations; let the Brâhma*n*a who has good (works) in view, offer. (490)

5. 'Those who have cut through all bonds and fetters, who are subdued, liberated, free from pain, and free from desire, on such in due time people should bestow oblations; let the Brâhma*n*a who has good (works) in view, offer. (491)

6. 'Those who are released from all bonds, who are subdued, liberated, free from pain, and free from desire, on such in due time people should bestow oblations; let the Brâhma*n*a who has good (works) in view, offer. (492)

7. 'Those who, having forsaken both passion and hatred and folly, have destroyed their desires and lead a religious life, on such in due time people should bestow oblations; let the Brâhma*n*a who has good (works) in view, offer[1]. (493)

8. 'Those in whom there lives no deceit, no arrogance, who are free from cupidity, free from selfishness, free from desire, on such in due time people should bestow oblations; let the Brâhma*n*a who has good (works) in view, offer. (494)

9. 'Those indeed who without being lost in craving,

---

[1] Comp. Dhp. v. 20.

after crossing the stream (of existence), wander about free from selfishness, on such in due time people should bestow oblations; let the Brâhma*n*a who has good (works) in view, offer. (495)

10. 'Those in whom there is no craving for anything in the world, nor for existence after existence here or in the other world, on such in due time people should bestow oblations; let the Brâhma*n*a who has good (works) in view, offer. (496)

11. 'Those who, after leaving sensual pleasures, wander about houseless, well restrained, being like a straight shuttle, on such in due time people should bestow oblations; let the Brâhma*n*a who has good (works) in view, offer. (497)

12. 'Those whose passions are gone, whose senses are well composed, who are liberated like the moon out of the grasp of Râhu, on such in due time people should bestow oblations; let the Brâhma*n*a who has good (works) in view, offer. (498)

13. 'Those who are calm, whose passions are gone, who are without anger, and for whom there is no transmigration after having left here, on such in due time people should bestow oblations; let the Brâhma*n*a who has good (works) in view, offer. (499)

14. 'Those who, after leaving birth and death altogether, have conquered all doubt, on such in due time people should bestow oblations; let the Brâhma*n*a who has good (works) in view, offer. (500)

15. 'Those who wander about in the world with themselves for a light, not possessed of anything, in every respect liberated, on such in due time people should bestow oblations; let the Brâhma*n*a who has good (works) in view, offer. (501)

16. 'Those who in this world rightly understand

this: "This is the last (birth), there is no re-birth," on such in due time people should bestow oblations; let the Brâhma*n*a who has good (works) in view, offer. (502)

17. 'He who is accomplished, and delights in meditation, thoughtful, possessed of thorough enlightenment, a refuge for many, on such a one in due time people should bestow oblations; let the Brâhma*n*a who has good (works) in view, offer.' (503)

18. 'Certainly my question was not in vain, Bhagavat has told me of those worthy of offerings; for thou truly knowest this in this world, as surely to thee this Dhamma is known. (504)

19. 'He who is a householder, suitable to beg of, a donor,'—so said the young man Mâgha,—'who, desirous of good, offers having what is good in view, and giving to others in this world food and drink,—tell me (I being such a one), O Bhagavat, of the blessing of offering.' (505)

20. 'Offer, O Mâgha,'—so said Bhagavat,—'and while offering make calm thy mind in all things; the object of the one that offers is the oblation, standing fast in this he leaves sin behind. (506)

21. 'Such a one whose passion is gone will repress hatred, cultivating an unbounded friendly mind; continually strenuous night and day he will spread infinite goodness through all regions.' (507)

22. Mâgha: 'Who prospers? who is liberated and who is bound? In which way can one by himself go to Brahmaloka? Tell this to me who does not know, O Muni, when asked. Bhagavat is indeed my witness that Brahman is seen by me to-day, for thou art to us equal to Brahman, this is the truth; how can one attain Brahmaloka, O thou glorious one?' (508)

23. 'He who offers the threefold blessing of oblation, O Mâgha,'—so said Bhagavat,—'such a one will prosper with those worthy of offerings; so, having offered properly, he who is suitable to beg of attains Brahmaloka, so I say.' (509)

This having been said, Mâgha the young man spoke as follows to Bhagavat: 'Excellent, O venerable Gotama! Excellent, O venerable Gotama! As one raises what has been overthrown, or reveals what has been hidden, or tells the way to him who has gone astray, or holds out an oil lamp in the dark that those who have eyes may see the objects, even so by the venerable Gotama in manifold ways the Dhamma has been illustrated; I take refuge in the venerable Gotama and in the Dhamma and in the Assembly of Bhikkhus. Let the venerable Gotama accept me as an upâsaka (a follower, me), who henceforth for all my life have taken refuge (in him).'

Mâghasutta is ended.

---

6. SABHIYASUTTA.

Sabhiya, the Paribbâ*g*aka, goes to the six famous teachers of his time to have his questions answered, but not having his doubts solved, he repairs to Gotama and asks him how one is to behave to become a Brâhma*n*a, a Sama*n*a, a Nahâtaka, a Khetta*g*ina, a Kusala, a Pa*nd*ita, a Muni, a Vedagû, an Anuvidita, a Dhîra, an Â*g*âniya, a Sottiya, an Ariya, a *K*ara*n*avat, a Paribbâ*g*aka. Bhagavat answers his questions, and Sabhiya finally receives the robe and the orders from Buddha.

So it was heard by me:

At one time Bhagavat dwelt at Râ*g*agaha, in Ve*l*uvana, in Kalandakanivâpa. And at that time questions were recited to Sabhiya, the Paribbâ*g*aka (wandering mendicant), by a deity who had in a former birth been a relation of his: 'He who, O Sabhiya, be it a Sama*n*a or a Brâhma*n*a, explains these questions to thee when asked, near him thou shouldst live a religious life.'

Then Sabhiya, the Paribbâ*g*aka, having learnt the questions from that deity, went to whatever Sama*n*as and Brâhma*n*as there were that had an assembly (of Bhikkhus), a crowd (of followers), and were well-known teachers, famous leaders, considered excellent by the multitude, as Pûra*n*a-Kassapa, Makkhali-Gosâla, A*g*ita-Kesakambali, Pakudha-Ka*kk*âyana, Sa*ñg*aya-Bela*tth*iputta, and Niga*nth*a-Nâtaputta. Those he went to, and after going to them, he asked the questions. They, being asked the questions by Sabhiya, the Paribbâ*g*aka, did not succeed (in answering them), and not succeeding they showed wrath and hatred and discontent, and they also in return put questions to Sabhiya, the Paribbâ*g*aka.

Then this came to the mind of Sabhiya, the Paribbâ*g*aka: 'Whatever Sama*n*as and Brâhma*n*as there are that have an assembly (of Bhikkhus), a crowd (of followers), and are well-known teachers, famous leaders, considered excellent by the multitude, as Pûra*n*a-Kassapa, Makkhali-Gosâla, A*g*ita-Kesakambali, Pakudha-Ka*kk*âyana, Sa*ñg*aya-Bela*tth*iputta, and Niga*nth*a-Nâtaputta, they, being asked questions by me, did not succeed (in answering them), and not succeeding they showed wrath and hatred and discontent, and they also in return put questions to me in this matter; surely I think I shall go back to what I have left, and enjoy sensual pleasures.

Then this came to the mind of Sabhiya, the Paribbâ*g*aka: 'This Sama*n*a Gotama has both an assembly (of Bhikkhus) and a crowd (of followers), and is a well-known teacher, a famous leader, considered excellent by the multitude, surely I think I shall go to Samana Gotama and ask these questions.' Then this came to the mind of Sabhiya, the Paribbâgaka: 'Whatever Samanas and Brâhmanas there are that are decayed, old, aged, advanced in years, having reached old age, experienced elders, long ordained, having assemblies (of Bhikkhus), crowds (of followers), being teachers well known, famous leaders, considered excellent by the multitude, as Pûrana-Kassapa, Makkhali-Gosâla, Agita-Kesakambali, Pakudha-Kakkâyana, Sañgaya-Belatthiputta, and Nigantha-Nâtaputta, they, being asked questions by me, did not succeed (in answering them), and not succeeding they showed wrath and hatred and discontent, and they also in return put questions to me in this matter; (I should like to know) whether Samana Gotama being asked these questions will be able to explain them to me, for Samana Gotama is both young by birth and new in ascetic life.'

Then this came to the mind of Sabhiya, the Paribbâgaka: 'Samana Gotama is not to be slighted because he is young; even if the Samana is young, yet he is mighty and powerful; surely I think I shall go to Samana Gotama and ask these questions.' Then Sabhiya, the Paribbâgaka, went on a journey to Râgagaha, and wandering on his journey in regular order he came to Râgagaha, Veluvana, Kalandakanivâpa, to Bhagavat, and having come to Bhagavat he talked pleasantly with him, and after having had some pleasant and remarkable conversation with him he sat down apart; sitting down apart

Sabhiya, the Paribbâ*g*aka, spoke to Bhagavat in stanzas:

1. 'Anxious and doubtful I have come,'—so said Sabhiya,—'longing to ask questions. Do thou put an end to these (doubts when) asked these questions by me, in regular order, and rightly explain them to me.' (510)

2. 'Thou hast come from afar, O Sabhiya,'—so said Bhagavat,—'longing to ask questions; I shall put an end to those (doubts when) asked those questions by thee, in regular order, and rightly I shall explain them to thee. (511)

3. 'Ask me, O Sabhiya, a question; whatsoever thou wishest in thy mind that question I (will explain, and) put an end to (thy doubt).' (512)

Then this came to the mind of Sabhiya, the Paribbâ*g*aka: 'It is marvellous, it is wonderful indeed, the reception which I did not get from other Sama*n*as and Brâhma*n*as has been given me by Gotama,' so saying he glad, rejoicing, delighted, and highly elated asked Bhagavat a question:

4. 'What should a man (necessarily) have obtained that people may call him a Bhikkhu?'—so said Sabhiya,—'how may they call him compassionate, and how subdued? how can he be called enlightened (buddha)? Asked (about this) do thou, Bhagavat, explain it to me.' (513)

5. 'He who by the path he has himself made, O Sabhiya,'—so said Bhagavat,—'has attained to perfect happiness, who has conquered doubt, who lives after having left behind both misfortune and fortune[1], who has destroyed re-birth, he is a Bhikkhu. (514)

[1] Vipatti sampatti hâni vu*ddh*i. Commentator.

6. 'Always resigned and attentive, he will not hurt any one in all the world, the Samana who has crossed the stream (of existence, and is) untroubled; for whom there are no desires (ussada), he is compassionate. (515)

7. 'He whose senses are trained internally and externally in all the world, he who after penetrating this and the other world longs for death, being trained, he is subdued. (516)

8. 'Whosoever, after having considered all times (kappa), the revolution (samsâra), both the vanishing and re-appearance (of beings), is free from defilement, free from sin, is pure, and has obtained destruction of birth, him they call enlightened (buddha).' (517)

Then Sabhiya, the Paribbâgaka, having approved of and rejoiced at the words of Bhagavat, glad, rejoicing, delighted, highly elated, asked Bhagavat another question:

9. 'What should a man (necessarily) have obtained that people may call him a Brâhmana?'—so said Sabhiya,—'and how (may they call him) a Samana? and how a Nahâtaka? how can he be called a Nâga? Asked (about this) do thou, Bhagavat, explain it to me.' (518)

10. 'He who, after removing all sins, O Sabhiya,' —so said Bhagavat,—'is immaculate, well composed, firm-minded, perfect after crossing the Samsâra, such an independent one is called a Brâhmana. (519)

11. 'He who is calm, having left behind good and evil, free from defilement, having understood this and the other world, and conquered birth and death, such a one is called a Samana by being so[1].' (520)

---

[1] Samano tâdi pavukkate tathattâ.

12. 'Whosoever, after having washed away all sins internally and externally in all the world, does not enter time (kappa) amongst gods and men who are subject to time, him they call a Nahâtaka (cleansed)[1]. (521)

13. 'He who does not commit any crime in the world, who, after abandoning all bonds and fetters, clings to nothing, being liberated, such a one is called a Nâga (sinless) by being so[2].' (522)

Then Sabhiya, the Paribbâ*g*aka, having approved of and rejoiced at the words of Bhagavat, glad, rejoicing, delighted, highly elated, further asked Bhagavat a question:

14. 'Whom do the Buddhas call a Khetta*g*ina?'—so said Sabhiya,—'how (can they call any one) a Kusala? and how a Pa*nd*ita? how can he be called a Muni? Asked (about this) do thou, Bhagavat, explain it to me.' (523)

15. 'He who, after examining all regions, O Sabhiya,'—so said Bhagavat,—'the divine and the human, and Brahman's region, is delivered from the radical bond of all regions, such a one is called a Khetta*g*ina (he who has conquered the regions) by being so. (524)

16. 'He who, after examining all treasures, the divine and the human, and Brahman's treasure, is delivered from the radical bond of all treasures, such a one is called a Kusala (happy) by being so. (525)

---

[1] Devamanussesu kappiyesu
Kappan n' eti tam âhu nahâtako.

[2] Âgu*m* na karoti ki*ñk*i loke
Sabbasa*m*yoge visa*gg*a bandhanâni
Sabbattha na sa*gg*atî vimutto
Nâgo tâdi pavu*kk*ate tathattâ.

But compare Pabba*gg*âsutta 17, Mâgandiyasutta 11, &c.

17. 'He who, after examining both kinds of senses, internally and externally, is endowed with a clear understanding and has conquered evil and good (ka*n*hasukka), such a one is called a Pa*nd*ita (wise) by being so. (526)

18. 'He who, having understood the Dhamma of the just and the unjust, internally and externally, in all the world, is to be worshipped by gods and men, he, after breaking through the net of ties, is called a Muni (sage).' (527)

Then Sabhiya, the Paribbâ*g*aka, having approved of and rejoiced at the words of Bhagavat, glad, rejoicing, delighted, highly elated, further asked Bhagavat a question:

19. 'What should one (necessarily) have obtained that people may call him Vedagû?'—so said Sabhiya,—'and how (may they call him) Anuvidita? and how Viriyavat? How does one become Â*g*âniya? Asked (about this) do thou, O Bhagavat, explain it to me.' (528)

20. 'He who, having conquered all sensations, O Sabhiya,'—so said Bhagavat,—'which are (known) to Sama*n*as and to Brâhma*n*as, is free from passion for all sensations, he is Vedagû (having passed sensation) after conquering all sensation. (529)

21. 'He who, having seen the delusion of name and form [1], internally and externally, the root of sickness, and is delivered from the radical bond of all sickness, such a one is called Anuvidita (well-informed) by being so. (530)

22. 'He who is disgusted in this world with all sins, is strong after conquering the pain of hell, is

[1] Anuvi*kk*a papa*ñk*anâmarûpa*m*.

strong and powerful, such a one is called Dhîra (= viriyavat, firm) by being so. (531)

23. 'He whose bonds are cut off internally and externally, the root of ties[1], who is delivered from the radical bond of all ties, such a one is called Âgâniya (high-bred) by being so.' (532)

Then Sabhiya, the Paribbâgaka, having approved of and rejoiced at the words of Bhagavat, glad, rejoicing, delighted, highly elated, further asked Bhagavat a question:

24. 'What should a man (necessarily) have obtained that people may call him a Sottiya?'—so said Sabhiya,—'how (may they call him) an Ariya? and how a *K*ara*n*avat? how may he become a Paribbâgaka? Asked (about this) do thou, O Bhagavat, explain it to me.' (533)

25. 'Whosoever, after having heard and understood every Dhamma in the world, O Sabhiya,'—so said Bhagavat,—'whatsoever is wrong and whatsoever is blameless, is victorious, free from doubt, liberated, free from pain in every respect, him they call a Sottiya (learned in the revelation). (534)

26. 'Whosoever, after having cut off passions and desires, is wise and does not (again) enter the womb, having driven away the threefold sign, the mud (of lust), and who does not (again) enter time (kappa), him they call an Ariya (noble). (535)

27. 'He who in this world, after having attained the (highest) gain in the *K*ara*n*as, is skilful, has always understood the Dhamma, clings to nothing, is liberated, and for whom there are no passions, he is a *K*ara*n*avat (endowed with the observances). (536)

[1] Yass' assu lutâni bandhanâni
Aggha*tt*a*m* bahiddhâ *k*a sangamûla*m*.

28. 'Whosoever abstains from the action that has a painful result, above and below and across and in the middle, who wanders with understanding, who has put an end to deceit, arrogance, cupidity and anger, name and form, him they call a Paribbâgaka (a wandering mendicant) who has attained the (highest) gain.' (537)

Then Sabhiya, the Paribbâgaka, having approved of and rejoiced at the words of Bhagavat, glad, rejoicing, delighted, highly elated, having risen from his seat, and having put his upper robe upon one shoulder, bending his joined hands towards Bhagavat, praised Bhagavat face to face in appropriate stanzas:

29. 'Having conquered the three and sixty (philosophical) views referring to the disputations of the Samanas, thou hast crossed over the darkness of the stream[1]. (?) (538)

30. 'Thou hast passed to the end of and beyond pain, thou art a saint, perfectly enlightened, I consider thee one that has destroyed his passions, thou art glorious, thoughtful, of great understanding, O thou who puts an end to pain, thou hast carried me across. (539)

31. 'Because thou sawest my longing, and carriedst me across my doubt, adoration be to thee, O Muni, who hast attained the (highest) gain in the ways of wisdom; O thou who art a true kinsman of the Âdikkas, thou art compassionate. (540)

32. 'The doubt I had before thou hast cleared away for me, O thou clearly-seeing; surely thou art a Muni, perfectly enlightened, there is no obstacle for thee. (541)

[1] Yâni ka tîni yâni ka satthi
Samanappavâdasitâni bhûripañña
Saññakkhara saññanissitâni (?)
Osaranâni vineyya oghatam' agâ.

33. 'And all thy troubles are scattered and cut off, thou art calm, subdued, firm, truthful. (542)

34. 'All gods and both Nârada and Pabbata rejoice at thee, the chief of the sinless (nâganâga), the great hero, when thou art speaking. (543)

35. 'Adoration be to thee, O noble man, adoration be to thee, O thou best of men; in the world of men and gods there is no man equal to thee. (544)

36. 'Thou art Buddha, thou art the Master, thou art the Muni that conquers Mâra; after having cut off desire thou hast crossed over and hast carried across this generation. (545)

37. 'The elements of existence (upadhi) are overcome by thee, the passions are destroyed by thee, thou art a lion, free from desire, thou hast left behind fear and terror. (546)

38. 'As a beautiful lotus does not adhere to the water, so thou dost not cling to good and evil, to either; stretch forth thy feet, O hero, Sabhiya worships the Master's (feet).' (547)

Then Sabhiya, the Paribbâ*g*aka, stooping with his head to Bhagavat's feet, said this to Bhagavat:

'It is excellent, O venerable! It is excellent, O venerable! As one raises what has been overthrown, or reveals what has been hidden, or tells the way to him who has gone astray, or holds out an oil lamp in the dark that those who have eyes may see the objects, even so by the venerable Gotama in manifold ways the Dhamma has been illustrated; I take refuge in the venerable Gotama, in the Dhamma, and in the Assembly of Bhikkhus; I wish to receive the robe and the orders from the venerable Bhagavat.

'He who, O Sabhiya, formerly belonging to

another creed (aññatitthiyapubba), wishes to be adopted into this religion (dhammavinaya), and wishes to receive the robe and the orders, he serves for four months; after the lapse of four months Bhikkhus who have appeased their thoughts will give him the robe and the orders to become a Bhikkhu, (for) I also in this matter acknowledge a difference of persons.'

'If, O venerable, those that formerly belonged to another creed and wish to be adopted into this religion and to receive the robe and the orders, serve for four months, and after the lapse of four months Bhikkhus who have appeased their thoughts give them the robe and the orders that they may become Bhikkhus, I will serve for four years, and after the lapse of four years Bhikkhus who have appeased their thoughts shall give (me) the robe and the orders that I may become a Bhikkhu.'

Sabhiya, the Paribbâ*g*aka, received the robe and the orders from Bhagavat, and the venerable Sabhiya, having lately received the upasampadâ, leading a solitary, retired, strenuous, ardent, energetic life, lived after having in a short time in this existence by his own understanding ascertained and possessed himself of that highest perfection of a religious life for the sake of which men of good family rightly wander away from their houses to a houseless state. 'Birth had been destroyed, a religious life had been led, what was to be done had been done, there was nothing else (to be done) for this existence,' so he perceived, and the venerable Sabhiya became one of the saints.

Sabhiyasutta is ended.

7. SELASUTTA.

Kenya, the *Gaṭila*, invites Buddha with his assembly to take his meals with him on the morrow. Sela, the Brâhmana, arrived at that place with his three hundred young men; seeing the preparations he asks what is going on, and is answered that Buddha is expected the next day. On hearing the word 'Buddha,' Sela asks where Buddha lives, goes to him, converses with him, and is converted; so are his followers.

So it was heard by me:

At one time Bhagavat wandering about in Aṅguttarâpa, with a large assembly of Bhikkhus, with 1250 Bhikkhus, went to Âpana, a town in Aṅguttarâpa.

And Keniya, the ascetic, with matted hair (*gaṭila*) heard the following: 'The Samana, the venerable Gotama, the Sakya son, gone out from the family of the Sakyas, wandering about in Aṅguttarâpa with a large assembly of Bhikkhus, with 1250 Bhikkhus, has reached Âpana, and the following good praising words met the venerable Gotama: "And so he is Bhagavat, the venerable, the perfectly enlightened, endowed with science and works (viggâkarana), the happy, knowing the world, the incomparable, the charioteer of men that are to be subdued, the master, the enlightened of gods and men, the glorious; he teaches this world and the world of gods, of Mâras, of Brahmans, and beings comprising Samanas and Brâhmanas, gods and men, having himself known and seen them face to face; he teaches the Dhamma (which is) good in the beginning, in the middle, and in the end, is full of meaning and rich in words, quite complete; he teaches a perfectly pure religious life, and good is the sight of such saints."'

Then Keniya, the *Gaṭila*, went (to the place) where

Bhagavat was, and having gone there he talked pleasantly with him, and after having had some pleasant and remarkable conversation (with him) he sat down apart; and while Keniya, the *Gatila*, was sitting down apart, Bhagavat, by religious talk, taught, advised, roused, and delighted him. Then Keniya, the *Gatila*, having been taught, advised, roused, and delighted by Bhagavat through religious talk, said this to Bhagavat:

'Let the venerable Gotama accept my food to-morrow, together with the assembly of Bhikkhus.'

This having been said, Bhagavat answered Keniya, the *Gatila*: 'Large, O Keniya, is the assembly of Bhikkhus, one thousand two hundred and fifty Bhikkhus, and thou art intimate with the Brâhmanas.'

A second time Keniya, the *Gatila*, said this to Bhagavat: 'Although, O venerable Gotama, the assembly of Bhikkhus is large, one thousand two hundred and fifty Bhikkhus, and I am intimate with the Brâhmanas, let the venerable Gotama accept my food to-morrow, together with the assembly of Bhikkhus.'

A second time Bhagavat said this to Keniya, the *Gatila*: 'Large, O Keniya, is the assembly of Bhikkhus, one thousand two hundred and fifty Bhikkhus, and thou art intimate with the Brâhmanas.'

A third time Keniya, the *Gatila*, said this to Bhagavat: 'Although, O venerable Gotama, the assembly of Bhikkhus is large, one thousand two hundred and fifty Bhikkhus, and I am intimate with the Brâhmanas, yet let the venerable Gotama accept my food to-morrow, together with the assembly of Bhikkhus.' Bhagavat assented by being silent.

Then Keniya, the *Gaṭila*, having learnt the assent of Bhagavat, after rising from his seat went to his hermitage, and having gone there he addressed his friends and servants, his relatives and kinsmen (as follows): 'Let my venerable friends and servants, relatives and kinsmen hear me;—the Samana Gotama has been invited by me to (take his) food (with me) to-morrow, together with the assembly of Bhikkhus: wherefore you must render me bodily service.'

'Surely, O venerable one,' so saying the friends and servants, relatives and kinsmen of Keniya, the *Gaṭila*, complying with his request, some of them dug fireplaces, some chopped firewood, some washed the vessels, some placed waterpots, some prepared seats. Keniya, the *Gaṭila*, on the other hand, himself provided a circular pavilion.

At that time the Brâhmana Sela lived at Âpana, perfect in the three Vedas, vocabulary, Keṭubha, etymology, Itihâsa as the fifth (Veda), versed in metre, a grammarian, one not deficient in popular controversy and the signs of a great man, he taught three hundred young men the hymns[1]. At that time Keniya, the *Gaṭila*, was intimate with the Brâhmana Sela. Then the Brâhmana Sela surrounded by three hundred young men, walking on foot, arrived at the place where the hermitage of Keniya, the *Gaṭila*, was. And the Brâhmana Sela saw the *Gaṭilas* in Keniya's hermitage, some of them digging fireplaces, some chopping firewood, some washing the vessels, some placing waterpots, some

[1] Tena kho pana samayena Selo brâhmano Âpane paṭivasati tinnam vedânam pâragû sanighanduke*ṭ*ubhânam sâkkharappabhedânam itihâsapañkamânam padako veyyâkarano lokâyatamahâpurisalakkhanesu anavayo tîni mânavakasatâni mante vâketi.

preparing seats, and Ke*n*iya, the *Ga*t*i*la, on the other hand, himself providing a circular pavilion; seeing Ke*n*iya, the *Ga*t*i*la, he said this: 'Is the venerable Ke*n*iya to celebrate the marriage of a son or the marriage of a daughter, or is there a great sacrifice at hand, or has Bimbisâra, the king of Magadha, who has a large body of troops, been invited for to-morrow, together with his army?'

'I am not to celebrate the marriage of a son or the marriage of a daughter, nor has Bimbisâra, the king of Magadha, who has a large body of troops, been invited for to-morrow, together with his army, yet a great sacrifice of mine is at hand. The Sama*n*a Gotama, the Sakya son, gone out from the Sakya family, wandering about in Aṅguttarâpa with a large assembly of Bhikkhus, one thousand two hundred and fifty Bhikkhus, has reached Âpa*n*a, and the following good praising words met the venerable Gotama: "And so he is Bhagavat, the venerable, the perfectly enlightened, endowed with science and works (vi*gg*â*k*ara*n*a), the happy, knowing the world, the incomparable, the charioteer of men that are to be subdued, the master, the enlightened of gods and men, the glorious, he has been invited by me for to-morrow, together with the assembly of Bhikkhus."'

'Didst thou say that he is a Buddha, O venerable Ke*n*iya?'

'Yes, I say, O venerable Sela, that he is a Buddha.'

'Didst thou say that he is a Buddha, O venerable Ke*n*iya?'

'Yes, I say, O venerable Sela, that he is a Buddha.'

Then this occurred to the Brâhma*n*a Sela: 'This sound "Buddha" is (indeed) rare, but in our hymns are to be found the thirty-two signs of a great man, and for a great man endowed with these there are two conditions and no more: if he lives in a house he is a king, a universal (king), a just religious king, a lord of the four-cornered (earth), a conqueror, one who has obtained the security of his people (and) is possessed of the seven gems. These are his seven gems, namely, the wheel gem, the elephant gem, the horse gem, the pearl gem, the woman gem, the householder gem, and the chief gem as the seventh. He has more than a thousand sons, heroes, possessing great bodily strength and crushing foreign armies; he having conquered this ocean-girt earth without a rod and without a weapon, but by justice, lives (in a house). But if, on the other hand, he goes out from (his) house to the houseless state, he becomes a saint, a perfectly enlightened, one who has removed the veil in the world. And where, O venerable Ke*n*iya, dwells now that venerable Gotama, the saint and the perfectly enlightened?'

This having been said, Ke*n*iya, the *Gat*ila, stretching out his right arm, spoke as follows to the Brâhma*n*a Sela: 'There, where yon blue forest line is, O venerable Sela.'

Then the Brâhma*n*a Sela together with (his) three hundred young men went to the place where Bhagavat was. Then the Brâhma*n*a Sela addressed those young men: 'Come ye, venerable ones, with but little noise, walking step by step, for Bhagavats are difficult of access, walking alone like lions, and when I speak to the venerable Sama*n*a Gotama, do ye not utter interrupting words, but wait ye venerable ones, for the end of my speech.'

Then the Brâhma*n*a Sela went to the place where

Bhagavat was, and having gone there he talked pleasantly with Bhagavat, and after having had some pleasant and remarkable conversation with him he sat down apart, and while sitting down apart Sela, the Brâhma*n*a, looked for the thirty-two signs of a great man on the body of Bhagavat. And the Brâhma*n*a Sela saw the thirty-two signs of a great man on the body of Bhagavat with the exception of two; in respect to two of the signs of a great man he had doubts, he hesitated, he was not satisfied, he was not assured as to the member being enclosed in a membrane and as to his having a large tongue.

Then this occurred to Bhagavat: 'This Brâhma*n*a Sela sees in me the thirty-two signs of a great man with the exception of two, in respect to two of the signs of a great man he has doubts, he hesitates, he is not satisfied, he is not assured as to the member being enclosed in a membrane, and as to my having a large tongue.' Then Bhagavat created such a miraculous creature that the Brâhma*n*a Sela might see Bhagavat's member enclosed in a membrane. Then Bhagavat having put out his tongue touched and stroked both his ears, touched and stroked both nostrils, and the whole circumference of his forehead he covered with his tongue.

Then this occurred to the Brâhma*n*a Sela: 'The Sama*n*a Gotama is endowed with the thirty-two signs of a great man, with them all, not with (only) some of them, and yet I do not know whether he is a Buddha or not; I have heard old and aged Brâhma*n*as, teachers and their previous teachers, say that those who are saints and perfectly enlightened manifest themselves when their praise is uttered. I think I shall praise the Sama*n*a Gotama face to face in suitable stanzas.' Then the Brâhma*n*a Sela praised Bhagavat face to face in suitable stanzas :

1. 'Thou hast a perfect body, thou art resplendent, well-born, of beautiful aspect, thou hast a golden colour, O Bhagavat, thou hast very white teeth, thou art strong. (548)

2. 'All the signs that are for a well-born man, they are on thy body, the signs of a great man. (549)

3. 'Thou hast a bright eye, a handsome countenance, thou art great, straight, majestic, thou shinest like a sun in the midst of the assembly of the Sama*n*as. (550)

4. 'Thou art a Bhikkhu of a lovely appearance, thou hast a skin like gold; what is the use of being a Sama*n*a to thee who art possessed of the highest beauty? (551)

5. 'Thou deservest to be a king, a king of universal kings, a ruler of the four-cornered (earth), a conqueror, a lord of the jambu grove (i. e. India). (552)

6. 'Khattiyas and wealthy kings are devoted to thee; rule, O Gotama, as a king of kings, a leader of men.' (553)

7. 'I am a king, O Sela,'—so said Bhagavat,—an incomparable, religious king (dhammarâ*g*an), with justice (dhammena) I turn the wheel, a wheel that is irresistible[1].' (554)

8. 'Thou acknowledgest thyself (to be) perfectly enlightened (sambuddha),'—so said Sela, the Brâhma*n*a,—'an incomparable, religious king; "with justice I turn the wheel," so thou sayest, O Gotama. (555)

---

[1] Compare Gospel of St. John xviii. 37.

9. 'Who is thy general, (who is thy) disciple, (who is) the successor of the master, who is to turn after thee the wheel of religion turned (by thee)?' (556)

10. 'The wheel turned by me, O Sela,'—so said Bhagavat,—'the incomparable wheel of religion, Sâriputta is to turn after (me), he taking after Tathâgata. (557)

11. 'What is to be known is known (by me), what is to be cultivated is cultivated (by me), what is to be left is left by me, therefore I am a Buddha, O Brâhma*n*a. (558)

12. 'Subdue thy doubt about me, have faith (in me), O Brâhma*n*a, difficult (to obtain) is the sight of Buddhas repeatedly. (559)

13. 'Of those whose manifestation is difficult for you (to obtain) in the world repeatedly, I am, O Brâhma*n*a, a perfectly enlightened, an incomparable physician, (560)

14. 'Most eminent, matchless, a crusher of Mâra's army; having subjected all enemies I rejoice secure on every side.' (561)

15. Sela: 'O venerable ones, pay attention to this: as the clearly-seeing (Buddha) says, (so it is): he is a physician, a great hero, and roars like a lion in the forest. (562)

16. 'Who, having seen him, the most eminent, the matchless, the crusher of Mâra's army, is not appeased, even if he be of black origin (ka*n*hâbhi-*g*âtika). (563)

17. 'He who likes me, let him follow after (me), he who does not like me, let him go away; I shall at once take the orders in the presence of him of excellent understanding (i. e. Buddha).' (564)

18. The followers of Sela: 'If this doctrine of the perfectly enlightened pleases thee, we also shall take the orders in the presence of him of excellent understanding.' (565)

19. Sela, these three hundred Brâhma*n*as ask with clasped hands (to be admitted into the order): 'we want to cultivate a religious life, O Bhagavat, in thy presence.' (566)

20. 'A religious life is well taught (by me),—O Sela,' so said Bhagavat,—'an instantaneous, an immediate (life), in which it is not in vain to become an ascetic to one who learns in earnest[1].' (567)

Then the Brâhma*n*a Sela together with his assembly took the robe and the orders in the presence of Bhagavat.

Then Ke*n*iya, the *Gat*ila, by the expiration of that night, having provided in his hermitage nice hard food and soft food, let Bhagavat know the time (of the meal): 'It is time, O venerable Gotama, the meal is prepared.' Then Bhagavat in the morning, having put on his raiment and taken his bowl and robes, went to the *Gat*ila Ke*n*iya's hermitage, and having gone there he sat down on the prepared seat, together with the assembly of Bhikkhus. Then Ke*n*iya, the *Gat*ila, satisfied and served with his own hands the assembly of Bhikkhus, with Buddha at their head, with nice hard food and soft food. Then Ke*n*iya, the *Gat*ila, having gone up to Bhagavat who had finished eating and had taken his hand out of the bowl, took a low seat and sat down apart, and while Ke*n*iya, the *Gat*ila, was sitting down apart, Bhagavat delighted him with these stanzas:

21. 'The principal thing in sacrifice is the sacred fire, the principal thing amongst the hymns is the Sâ-

vitti[1], the king is the principal amongst men, and the sea the principal amongst waters (nadîna*m*[2]). (568)

22. 'Amongst the stars the moon is the principal thing, the sun is the principal thing amongst the burning[3] (objects), amongst those that wish for good works and make offerings the assembly (sa*m*gha) indeed is the principal.' (569)

Then Bhagavat, having delighted Ke*n*iya, the *Gat*ila, with these stanzas, rose from (his) seat and went away.

Then the venerable Sela together with his assembly leading a solitary, retired, strenuous, ardent, energetic life, lived after having in a short time in this existence by his own understanding ascertained and possessed himself of that highest perfection of a religious life for the sake of which men of good family rightly wander away from their houses to a houseless state; 'birth (had been) destroyed, a religious life (had been) led, what was to be done (had been) done, there was nothing else (to be done) for this existence,' so he perceived, and the venerable Sela together with his assembly became one of the saints.

Then the venerable Sela together with his assembly went to Bhagavat, and having gone (to him) he put his upper robe on one shoulder, and bending his joined hands towards Bhagavat he addressed him in stanzas:

23. 'Because we took refuge in thee on the eighth day previous to this, O thou clearly-seeing, in seven nights, O Bhagavat, we have been trained in thy doctrine. (570)

[1] Sâvittî *kh*andaso mukha*m*. [2] Comp. Nâlakasutta, v. 42.
[3] Âdi*kk*o tapata*m* mukha*m*.

24. 'Thou art Buddha, thou art the Master, thou art the Muni that conquered Mâra, thou hast, after cutting off the affections, crossed over (the stream of existence) and taken over these beings. (571)

25. 'The elements of existence (upadhi) have been overcome by thee, the passions have been destroyed by thee, thou art a lion not seizing on anything, thou hast left behind fear and danger. (572)

26. 'These three hundred Bhikkhus stand here with clasped hands; stretch out thy feet, O hero, let the Nâgas worship the Master's feet.' (573)

Selasutta is ended.

8. SALLASUTTA.

Life is short, all mortals are subject to death, but knowing the terms of the world the wise do not grieve, and those who have left sorrow will be blessed.—Text in the Dasaratha-*G*âtaka, p. 34.

1. Without a cause and unknown is the life of mortals in this world, troubled and brief, and combined with pain. (574)

2. For there is not any means by which those that have been born can avoid dying; after reaching old age there is death, of such a nature are living beings. (575)

3. As ripe fruits are early in danger of falling, so mortals when born are always in danger of death. (576)

4. As all earthen vessels made by the potter end in being broken, so is the life of mortals. (577)

5. Both young and grown-up men, both those who are fools and those who are wise men, all fall into the power of death, all are subject to death. (578)

6. Of those who, overcome by death, go to the other world, a father does not save his son, nor relatives their relations. (579)

7. Mark! while relatives are looking on and lamenting greatly, one by one of the mortals is carried off, like an ox that is going to be killed. (580)

8. So the world is afflicted with death and decay, therefore the wise do not grieve, knowing the terms of the world. (581)

9. For him, whose way thou dost not know, either when he is coming or when he is going, not seeing both ends, thou grievest in vain. (582)

10. If he who grieves gains anything, (although he is only) a fool hurting himself, let the wise man do the same. (583)

11. Not from weeping nor from grieving will any one obtain peace of mind; (on the contrary), the greater his pain will be, and his body will suffer. (584)

12. He will be lean and pale, hurting himself by himself, (and yet) the dead are not kept alive [1], lamentation (therefore) is of no avail. (585)

13. He who does not leave grief behind, goes (only) deeper into pain; bewailing the dead he falls into the power of grief. (586)

14. Look at others passing away, men that go (to what they deserve) according to their deeds, beings trembling already here, after falling into the power of death. (587)

15. In whatever manner people think (it will come to pass), different from that it becomes, so great is the disappointment [2] (in this world); see, (such are) the terms of the world. (588)

[1] Na yâpenti na ta*m* tesâ*m* upakârâya hoti. Commentator.

[2] Etâdiso vinâbhâvo.

16. Even if a man lives a hundred years or even more, he is at last separated from the company of his relatives, and leaves life in this world. (589)

17. Therefore let one, hearing (the words of) the saint, subdue his lamentation; seeing the one that has passed away and is dead, (let him say): 'He will not be found by me (any more).' (590)

18. As a house on fire is extinguished by water, so also the wise, sensible, learned, clever man rapidly drives away sorrow that has arisen, as the wind a tuft of cotton. (591)

19. He who seeks his own happiness should draw out his arrow (which is) his lamentation, and complaint, and grief. (592)

20. He who has drawn out the arrow and is not dependent (on anything), he, having obtained peace of mind, (and) having overcome all sorrow, will become free from sorrow, and blessed (nibbuta). (593)

Sallasutta is ended.

---

9. VÂSE*TTH*ASUTTA.

A dispute arose between two young men, Bhâradvâ*g*a and Vâse*tth*a, the former contending man to be a Brâhma*n*a by birth, the latter by deeds. They agreed to go and ask Sama*n*a Gotama, and he answered that man is a Brâhma*n*a by his work only. The two young men are converted.—Text (from Ma*gg*h*imanikâya) and translation in Alwis's Buddhist Nirvâ*n*a, p. 103.

So it was heard by me:

At one time Bhagavat dwelt at I*kkh*âna*m*kala, in the I*kkh*âna*m*kala forest. At that time many distinguished, wealthy Brâhma*n*as lived at I*kkh*âna*m*kala, as the Brâhma*n*a *K*a*m*kin, the Brâhma*n*a

Târukkha, the Brâhma*n*a Pokkharasâti, the Brâhma*n*a *G*ânusso*n*i, the Brâhma*n*a Todeyya, and other distinguished, wealthy Brâhma*n*as.

Then this dialogue arose between the young men Vâse*tth*a and Bhâradvâ*g*a while walking about:

'How does one become a Brâhma*n*a?'

The young man Bhâradvâ*g*a said: 'When one is noble by birth on both sides, on the mother's and on the father's side, of pure conception up to the seventh generation of ancestors, not discarded and not reproached in point of birth, in this way one is a Brâhma*n*a.'

The young man Vâse*tth*a said: 'When one is virtuous and endowed with (holy) works, in this way he is a Brâhma*n*a.'

Neither could the young man Bhâradvâ*g*a convince the young man Vâse*tth*a, nor could the young man Vâse*tth*a convince the young man Bhâradvâ*g*a. Then the young man Vâse*tth*a addressed the young man Bhâradvâ*g*a: 'O Bhâradvâ*g*a, this Sama*n*a Gotama, the Sakya son, gone out from the Sakya family, dwells at I*kkh*âna*m*kala, in the forest of I*kkh*âna*m*kala, and the following good praising words met the venerable Gotama: "And so he is Bhagavat, the venerable, the enlightened, the glorious, let us go, O venerable Bhâradvâ*g*a, let us go (to the place) where the Sama*n*a Gotama is, and having gone there let us ask the Sama*n*a Gotama about this matter, and as the Sama*n*a Gotama replies so will we understand it."'

'Very well, O venerable one;' so the young man Bhâradvâ*g*a answered the young man Vâse*tth*a.

Then the young men Vâse*tth*a and Bhâradvâ*g*a went (to the place) where Bhagavat was, and having gone, they talked pleasantly with Bhagavat, and after having had some pleasant and remarkable conversation (with him) they sat down apart. Sitting down apart the young man Vâse*tth*a addressed Bhagavat in stanzas:

1. 'We are accepted and acknowledged masters of the three Vedas, I am (a pupil) of Pokkharasâti, and this young man is (the pupil) of Târukkha. (594)

2. 'We are accomplished in all the knowledge propounded by those who are acquainted with the three Vedas, we are padakas (versed in the metre), veyyâkara*n*as (grammarians?), and equal to our teachers in recitation (*g*appa)[1]. (595)

3. 'We have a controversy regarding (the distinctions of) birth, O Gotama! Bhâradvâ*g*a says, one is a Brâhma*n*a by birth, and I say, by deeds; know this, O thou clearly-seeing! (596)

4. 'We are both unable to convince each other, (therefore) we have come to ask thee (who art) celebrated as perfectly enlightened. (597)

5. 'As people adoring the full moon worship (her) with uplifted clasped hands, so (they worship) Gotama in the world. (598)

6. 'We ask Gotama who has come as an eye to the world: Is a man a Brâhma*n*a by birth, or is he so by deeds? Tell us who do not know, that we may know a Brâhma*n*a.' (599)

7. 'I will explain to you, O Vâse*tth*a,'—so said Bhagavat,—'in due order the exact distinction of

[1] Tevi*gg*âna*m** yad akkhâta*m*
Tatra kevalino 'smase,
Padak' asmâ veyyâkara*n*â
*G*appe† â*k*ariyasâdisâ.

* Tevi*gg*âna*m* = tivedâna*m*. Commentator; but compare v. 63.
† *G*appe = vede. Commentator.

living beings according to species, for their species are manifold. (600)

8. 'Know ye the grass and the trees, although they do not exhibit (it), the marks that constitute species are for them, and (their) species are manifold. (601)

9. 'Then (know ye) the worms, and the moths, and the different sorts of ants, the marks that constitute species are for them, and (their) species are manifold. (602)

10. 'Know ye also the four-footed (animals), small and great, the marks that constitute species are for them, and (their) species are manifold. (603)

11. 'Know ye also the serpents, the long-backed snakes, the marks that constitute species are for them, and (their) species are manifold. (604)

12. 'Then know ye also the fish which range in the water, the marks that constitute species are for them, and (their) species are manifold. (605)

13. 'Then know ye also the birds that are borne along on wings and move through the air, the marks that constitute species are for them, and (their) species are manifold. (606)

14. 'As in these species the marks that constitute species are abundant, so in men the marks that constitute species are not abundant. (607)

15. 'Not as regards their hair, head, ears, eyes, mouth, nose, lips, or brows, (608)

16. 'Nor as regards their neck, shoulders, belly, back, hip, breast, female organ, sexual intercourse, (609)

17. 'Nor as regards their hands, feet, palms, nails, calves, thighs, colour, or voice are there marks that constitute species as in other species. (610)

18. 'Difference there is in beings endowed with

bodies, but amongst men this is not the case, the difference amongst men is nominal (only)[1]. (611)

19. 'For whoever amongst men lives by cow-keeping,—know this, O Vâse*tth*a,—he is a husbandman, not a Brâhma*n*a. (612)

20. 'And whoever amongst men lives by different mechanical arts,—know this, O Vâse*tth*a,—he is an artisan, not a Brâhma*n*a. (613)

21. 'And whoever amongst men lives by trade,—know this, O Vâse*tth*a,—he is a merchant, not a Brâhma*n*a. (614)

22. 'And whoever amongst men lives by serving others,—know this, O Vâse*tth*a,—he is a servant, not a Brâhma*n*a. (615)

23. 'And whoever amongst men lives by theft,—know this, O Vâse*tth*a,—he is a thief, not a Brâhma*n*a. (616)

24. 'And whoever amongst men lives by archery,—know this, O Vâse*tth*a,—he is a soldier, not a Brâhma*n*a. (617)

25. 'And whoever amongst men lives by performing household ceremonials,—know this, O Vâse*tth*a,—he is a sacrificer, not a Brâhma*n*a. (618)

26. 'And whoever amongst men possesses villages and countries,—know this, O Vâse*tth*a,—he is a king, not a Brâhma*n*a. (619)

27. 'And I do not call one a Brâhma*n*a on account of his birth or of his origin from (a particular) mother; he may be called bhovâdi, and he may be wealthy, (but) the one who is possessed of nothing

[1] Pa*kk*atta*m* sasariresu,
Manussesv-eta*m* na viggati,
Vokâra*ñ* *k*a manussesu
Samaññâya pavu*kk*ati.

and seizes upon nothing, him I call a Brâhma*n*a[1]. (620)

28. 'Whosoever, after cutting all bonds, does not tremble, has shaken off (all) ties and is liberated, him I call a Brâhma*n*a. (621)

29. 'The man who, after cutting the strap (i. e. enmity), the thong (i. e. attachment), and the rope (i. e. scepticism) with all that pertains to it, has destroyed (all) obstacles (i. e. ignorance), the enlightened (buddha), him I call a Brâhma*n*a. (622)

30. 'Whosoever, being innocent, endures reproach, blows, and bonds, the man who is strong in (his) endurance and has for his army this strength, him I call a Brâhma*n*a. (623)

31. 'The man who is free from anger, endowed with (holy) works, virtuous, without desire, subdued, and wearing the last body, him I call a Brâhma*n*a. (624)

32. 'The man who, like water on a lotus leaf, or a mustard seed on the point of a needle, does not cling to sensual pleasures, him I call a Brâhma*n*a. (625)

33. 'The man who knows in this world the destruction of his pain, who has laid aside (his) burden, and is liberated, him I call a Brâhma*n*a. (626)

34. 'The man who has a profound understanding, who is wise, who knows the true way and the wrong way, who has attained the highest good, him I call a Brâhma*n*a. (627)

35. 'The man who does not mix with householders nor with the houseless, who wanders about without a house, and who has few wants, him I call a Brâhma*n*a. (628)

36. 'Whosoever, after refraining from hurting

[1] Comp. Dhp. v. 396, &c.

(living) creatures, (both) those that tremble and those that are strong, does not kill or cause to be killed, him I call a Brâhma*n*a. (629)

37. 'The man who is not hostile amongst the hostile, who is peaceful amongst the violent, not seizing (upon anything) amongst those that seize (upon everything), him I call a Brâhma*n*a. (630)

38. 'The man whose passion and hatred, arrogance and hypocrisy have dropt like a mustard seed from the point of a needle, him I call a Brâhma*n*a. (631)

39. 'The man that utters true speech, instructive and free from harshness, by which he does not offend any one, him I call a Brâhma*n*a. (632)

40. 'Whosoever in the world does not take what has not been given (to him), be it long or short, small or large, good or bad, him I call a Brâhma*n*a. (633)

41. 'The man who has no desire for this world or the next, who is desireless and liberated, him I call a Brâhma*n*a. (634)

42. 'The man who has no desire, who through his knowledge is free from doubt, and has attained the depth of immortality, him I call a Brâhma*n*a. (635)

43. 'Whosoever in this world has overcome good and evil, both ties, who is free from grief and defilement, and is pure, him I call a Brâhma*n*a. (636)

44. 'The man that is stainless like the moon, pure, serene, and undisturbed, who has destroyed joy, him I call a Brâhma*n*a. (637)

45. 'Whosoever has passed over this quagmire difficult to pass, (who has passed over) revolution (sa*m*sâra) and folly, who has crossed over, who has reached the other shore, who is meditative, free from desire and doubt, calm without seizing (upon anything), him I call a Brâhma*n*a. (638)

46. 'Whosoever in this world, after abandoning sensual pleasures, wanders about houseless, and has destroyed the existence of sensual pleasures (kâmabhava), him I call a Brâhma*n*a. (639)

47. 'Whosoever in this world, after abandoning craving, wanders about houseless, and has destroyed the existence of desire (ta*n*hâbhava), him I call a Brâhma*n*a. (640)

48. 'Whosoever, after leaving human attachment (yoga), has overcome divine attachment, and is liberated from all attachment, him I call a Brâhma*n*a. (641)

49. 'The man that, after leaving pleasure and disgust, is calm and free from the elements of existence (nirupadhi), who is a hero, and has conquered all the world, him I call a Brâhma*n*a. (642)

50. 'Whosoever knows wholly the vanishing and reappearance of beings, does not cling to (anything), is happy (sugata), and enlightened, him I call a Brâhma*n*a. (643)

51. 'The man whose way neither gods nor Gandhabbas nor men know, and whose passions are destroyed, who is a saint, him I call a Brâhma*n*a. (644)

52. 'The man for whom there is nothing, neither before nor after nor in the middle, who possesses nothing, and does not seize (upon anything), him I call a Brâhma*n*a. (645)

53. 'The (man that is undaunted like a) bull, who is eminent, a hero, a great sage (mahesi), victorious, free from desire, purified, enlightened, him I call a Brâhma*n*a. (646)

54. 'The man who knows his former dwellings, who sees both heaven and hell, and has reached the destruction of births, him I call a Brâhma*n*a. (647)

55. 'For what has been designated as "name" and "family" in the world is only a term, what has been designated here and there is understood by common consent. (648)

56. 'Adhered to for a long time are the views of the ignorant, the ignorant tell us, one is a Brâhma*n*a by birth. (649)

57. 'Not by birth is one a Brâhma*n*a, nor is one by birth no Brâhma*n*a; by work (kammanâ) one is a Brâhma*n*a, by work one is no Brâhma*n*a. (650)

58. 'By work one is a husbandman, by work one is an artisan, by work one is a merchant, by work one is a servant. (651)

59. 'By work one is a thief, by work one is a soldier, by work one is a sacrificer, by work one is a king. (652)

60. 'So the wise, who see the cause of things and understand the result of work, know this work as it really is. (653)

61. 'By work the world exists, by work mankind exists, beings are bound by work as the linch-pin of the rolling cart (keeps the wheel on). (654)

62. 'By penance, by a religious life, by self-restraint, and by temperance, by this one is a Brâhma*n*a, such a one (they call) the best Brâhma*n*a. (655)

63. 'He who is endowed with the threefold knowledge, is calm, and has destroyed regeneration,—know this, O Vâse*tth*a,—he is to the wise Brahman and Sakka.' (656)

This having been said, the young men Vâse*tth*a and Bhâradvâ*g*a spoke to Bhagavat as follows:

'It is excellent, O venerable Gotama! It is excellent, O venerable Gotama! As one raises what has been overthrown, or reveals what has been hidden, or tells the way to him who has gone astray, or holds out an oil lamp in the dark that those who have eyes may see the objects, even so by the venerable Gotama in manifold ways the Dhamma has been illustrated; we take refuge in the venerable Gotama, in the Dhamma, and in the Assembly of Bhikkhus; may the venerable Gotama receive us as followers (upâsaka), who from this day for life have taken refuge (in him).'

Vâse*tth*asutta is ended.

---

10. KOKÂLIYASUTTA.

Kokâliya abuses Sâriputta and Moggallâna to Buddha; therefore as soon as he has left Buddha, he is struck with boils, dies and goes to the Paduma hell, whereupon Buddha describes to the Bhikkhus the punishment of backbiters in hell.

So it was heard by me:

At one time Bhagavat dwelt at Sâvatthî, in *G*etavana, in the park of Anâthapi*nd*ika. Then the Bhikkhu Kokâliya approached Bhagavat, and after having approached and saluted Bhagavat he sat down apart; sitting down apart the Bhikkhu Kokâliya said this to Bhagavat: 'O thou venerable one, Sâriputta and Moggallâna have evil desires, they have fallen into the power of evil desires.'

When this had been said, Bhagavat spoke to the Bhikkhu Kokâliya as follows: '(Do) not (say) so, Kokâliya; (do) not (say) so, Kokâliya; appease, O Kokâliya, (thy) mind in regard to Sâriputta and Moggallâna: Sâriputta and Moggallâna are amiable[1].'

---

[1] Pesalâ ti piyasîlâ. Commentator.

A second time the Bhikkhu Kokâliya said this to Bhagavat: 'Although thou, O venerable Bhagavat, (appearest) to me (to be) faithful and trustworthy, yet Sâriputta and Moggallâna have evil desires, they have fallen into the power of evil desires.'

A second time Bhagavat said this to the Bhikkhu Kokâliya: '(Do) not (say) so, Kokâliya; (do) not (say) so, Kokâliya; áppease, O Kokâliya, (thy) mind in regard to Sâriputta and Moggallâna: Sâriputta and Moggallâna are amiable.'

A third time the Bhikkhu Kokâliya said this to Bhagavat: 'Although thou, O venerable Bhagavat, (appearest) to me (to be) faithful and trustworthy, yet Sâriputta and Moggallâna have evil desires, Sâriputta and Moggallâna have fallen into the power of evil desires.'

A third time Bhagavat said this to the Bhikkhu Kokâliya: '(Do) not (say) so, Kokâliya; (do) not (say) so, Kokâliya; appease, O Kokâliya, (thy) mind in regard to Sâriputta and Moggallâna: Sâriputta and Moggallâna are amiable.'

Then the Bhikkhu Kokâliya, after having risen from his seat and saluted Bhagavat and walked round him towards the right, went away; and when he had been gone a short time, all his body was struck with boils as large as mustard seeds; after being only as large as mustard seeds, they became as large as kidney beans; after being only as large as kidney beans, they became as large as chick peas; after being only as large as chick peas, they became as large as a Kola*tth*i egg (?); after being only as large as a Kola*tth*i egg, they became as large as the jujube fruit; after being only as large as the jujube fruit, they became as large as the fruit of the emblic myrobalan; after being only as large as the fruit of the emblic myrobalan, they became as large as the unripe beluva fruit; after being only as large as the unripe beluva fruit, they became as large as a billi fruit (?); after being as large as a billi fruit, they broke, and matter and blood flowed out. Then the Bhikkhu Kokâliya died of that disease, and when he had died the Bhikkhu Kokâliya went to the Paduma hell, having shown a hostile mind against Sâriputta and Moggallâna. Then when the night had passed Brahman Sahampati of a beautiful appearance, having lit up all *G*etavana, approached Bhagavat, and having approached and saluted Bhagavat, he stood apart, and standing apart Brahman Sahampati said this to Bhagavat: 'O thou venerable one, Kokâliya, the Bhikkhu, is dead; and after death, O thou venerable one, the Bhikkhu Kokâliya is gone to the Paduma hell, having shown a hostile mind against Sâriputta and Moggallâna.'

This said Brahman Sahampati, and after saying this and saluting Bhagavat, and walking round him towards the right, he disappeared there.

Then Bhagavat, after the expiration of that night, addressed the Bhikkhus thus: 'Last night, O Bhikkhus, when the night had (nearly) passed, Brahman Sahampati of a beautiful appearance, having lit up all *G*etavana, approached Bhagavat, and having approached and saluted Bhagavat, he stood apart, and standing apart Brahman Sahampati said this to Bhagavat: "O thou venerable one, Kokâliya, the Bhikkhu, is dead; and after death, O thou venerable one, the Bhikkhu Kokâliya is gone to the Paduma hell, having shown a hostile mind against Sâriputta and Moggallâna." This said Brahman Sahampati, O

Bhikkhus, and having said this and saluted me, and walked round me towards the right, he disappeared there.'

When this had been said, a Bhikkhu asked Bhagavat: 'How long is the rate of life, O venerable one, in the Paduma hell?'

'Long, O Bhikkhu, is the rate of life in the Paduma hell, it is not easy to calculate either (by saying) so many years or so many hundreds of years or so many thousands of years or so many hundred thousands of years.'

'But it is possible, I suppose, to make a comparison, O thou venerable one?'

'It is possible, O Bhikkhu;' so saying, Bhagavat spoke (as follows): 'Even as, O Bhikkhu, (if there were) a Kosala load of sesamum seed containing twenty khâris, and a man after the lapse of every hundred years were to take from it one sesamum seed at a time, then that Kosala load of sesamum seed, containing twenty khâris, would, O Bhikkhu, sooner by this means dwindle away and be used up than one Abbuda hell; and even as are twenty Abbuda hells, O Bhikkhu, so is one Nirabbuda hell; and even as are twenty Nirabbuda hells, O Bhikkhu, so is one Ababa hell; and even as are twenty Ababa hells, O Bhikkhu, so is one Ahaha hell; and even as are twenty Ahaha hells, O Bhikkhu, so is one A*t*a*t*a hell; and even as are twenty A*t*a*t*a hells, O Bhikkhu, so is one Kumuda hell; and even as are twenty Kumuda hells, O Bhikkhu, so is one Sogandhika hell; and even as are twenty Sogandhika hells, O Bhikkhu, so is one Uppalaka hell; and even as are twenty Uppalaka hells, O Bhikkhu, so is one Pu*nd*arîka hell; and even as are twenty

Pu*nd*arîka hells, O Bhikkhu, so is one Paduma hell; and to the Paduma hell, O Bhikkhu, the Bhikkhu Kokâliya is gone, having shown a hostile mind against Sâriputta and Moggallâna.' This said Bhagavat, and having said this Sugata, the Master, furthermore spoke as follows:

1. 'To (every) man that is born, an axe is born in his mouth, by which the fool cuts himself, when speaking bad language. (657)

2. 'He who praises him who is to be blamed, or blames him who is to be praised, gathers up sin in his mouth, and through that (sin) he will not find any joy. (658)

3. 'Trifling is the sin that (consists in) losing riches by dice; this is a greater sin that corrupts the mind against Sugatas. (659)

4. 'Out of the one hundred thousand Nirabbudas (he goes) to thirty-six, and to five Abbudas; because he blames an Ariya he goes to hell, having employed his speech and mind badly. (660)

5. 'He who speaks falsely goes to hell, or he who having done something says, "I have not done it;" both these after death become equal, in another world (they are both) men guilty of a mean deed[1]. (661)

6. 'He who offends an offenceless man, a pure man, free from sin, such a fool the evil (deed) reverts against, like fine dust thrown against the wind[2]. (662)

7. 'He who is given to the quality of covetousness, such a one censures others in his speech, (being himself) unbelieving, stingy, wanting in affability, niggardly, given to backbiting. (663)

[1] Comp. Dhp. v. 306. [2] Comp. Dhp. v. 125.

8. 'O thou foul-mouthed, false, ignoble, blasting, wicked, evil-doing, low, sinful, base-born man, do not be garrulous in this world, (else) thou wilt be an inhabitant of hell[1]. (664)

9. 'Thou spreadest pollution to the misfortune (of others), thou revilest the just, committing sin (yourself), and having done many evil deeds thou wilt go to the pool (of hell) for a long time. (665)

10. 'For one's deeds are not lost, they will surely come (back to you), (their) master will meet with them, the fool who commits sin will feel the pain in himself in the other world[2]. (666)

11. 'To the place where one is struck with iron rods, to the iron stake with sharp edges he goes; then there is (for him) food as appropriate, resembling a red-hot ball of iron. (667)

12. 'For those who have anything to say (there) do not say fine things, they do not approach (with pleasing faces); they do not find refuge (from their sufferings), they lie on spread embers, they enter a blazing pyre. (668)

13. 'Covering (them) with a net they kill (them) there with iron hammers; they go to dense darkness[3], for that is spread out like the body of the earth. (669)

14. 'Then (they enter) an iron pot, they enter a blazing pyre, for they are boiled in those (iron pots) for a long time, jumping up and down in the pyre. (670)

---

[1] Mukhadugga vibhûta-m-anariya
Bhûnahu* pâpaka dukkatakâri.

[2] Comp. Revelation xiv. 13.

[3] Andha*m* va Timisa*m* âyanti.

* Bhûnahu bhûtihanaka vuddhinâsaka. Commentator.

15. 'Then he who commits sin is surely boiled in a mixture of matter and blood; whatever quarter he inhabits, he becomes rotten there from coming in contact (with matter and blood). (671)

16. 'He who commits sin will surely be boiled in the water, the dwelling-place of worms; there it is not (possible) to get to the shore, for the jars (are) even all round. (672)

17. 'Again they enter the sharp Asipattavana with mangled limbs; having seized the tongue with a hook, the different watchmen (of hell) kill (them). (673)

18. 'Then they enter Vetara*n*î, that is difficult to cross and has got streams of razors with sharp edges; there the fools fall in, the evil-doers after having done evil. (674)

19. 'There black, mottled flocks of ravens eat them who are weeping, and dogs, jackals, great vultures, falcons, crows tear (them). (675)

20. 'Miserable indeed is the life here (in hell) which the man sees that commits sin. Therefore should a man in this world for the rest of his life be strenuous, and not indolent. (676)

21. 'Those loads of sesamum seed which are carried in Paduma hell have been counted by the wise, they are five nahutas of ko*t*is and twelve hundred ko*t*is besides [1]. (677)

22. 'As long as hells are called painful in this world, so long people will have to live there for a long time; therefore amongst those who have pure, amiable, and good qualities one should always guard speech and mind.' (678)

Kokâliyasutta is ended.

[1] That is 512,000 000,000.

11. NÂLAKASUTTA.

The Isi Asita, also called Ka*n*hasiri, on seeing the gods rejoicing, asks the cause of it, and having heard that Buddha has been born, he descends from Tusita heaven. When the Sakyas showed the child to him, he received it joyfully and prophesied about it. Buddha explains to Nâlaka, the sister's son of Asita, the highest state of wisdom.—Compare Lalita-vistara, Adhyâya VII; Asita and Buddha, or the Indian Simeon, by J. Muir, in the Indian Antiquary, Sept. 1878.

Vatthugâthâ.

1. The Isi Asita saw in (their) resting-places during the day the joyful, delighted flocks of the Tidasa gods, and the gods in bright clothes, always highly praising Inda, after taking their clothes and waving them. (679)

2. Seeing the gods with pleased minds, delighted, and showing his respect, he said this on that occasion: 'Why is the assembly of the gods so exceedingly pleased, why do they take their clothes and wave them? (680)

3. 'When there was an encounter with the Asuras, a victory for the gods, and the Asuras were defeated, then there was not such a rejoicing. What wonderful (thing) have the gods seen that they are so delighted? (681)

4. 'They shout and sing and make music, they throw (about their) arms and dance; I ask you, the inhabitants of the tops of (mount) Meru, remove my doubt quickly, O venerable ones!' (682)

5. 'The Bodhisatta, the excellent pearl, the incomparable, is born for the good and for a blessing in the world of men, in the town of the Sakyas, in

the country of Lumbinî. Therefore we are glad and exceedingly pleased. (683)

6. 'He, the most excellent of all beings, the pre-eminent man, the bull of men, the most excellent of all creatures will turn the wheel (of the Dhamma) in the forest called after the Isis, (he who is) like the roaring lion, the strong lord of beasts.' (684)

7. Having heard that noise he descended from (the heaven of) Tusita. Then he went to Suddhodana's palace, and having sat down there he said this to the Sakyas: 'Where is the prince? I wish to see (him).' (685)

8. Then the Sakyas showed to (the Isi), called Asita, the child, the prince who was like shining gold, manufactured by a very skilful (smith) in the mouth of a forge, and beaming in glory and having a beautiful appearance. (686)

9. Seeing the prince shining like fire, bright like the bull of stars wandering in the sky, like the burning sun in autumn, free from clouds, he joyfully obtained great delight. (687)

10. The gods held in the sky a parasol with a thousand circles and numerous branches, yaks' tails with golden sticks were fanned, but those who held the yaks' tails and the parasol were not seen. (688)

11. The Isi with the matted hair, by name Ka*n*hasiri, on seeing the yellow blankets (shining) like a golden coin, and the white parasol held over his head, received him delighted and happy. (689)

12. And having received the bull of the Sakyas, he who was wishing to receive him and knew the signs and the hymns, with pleased thoughts raised his voice, saying: 'Without superior is this, the most excellent of men.' (690)

13. Then remembering his own migration he was displeased and shed tears; seeing this the Sakyas asked the weeping Isi, whether there would be any obstacle in the prince's path. (691)

14. Seeing the Sakyas displeased the Isi said: 'I do not remember anything (that will be) unlucky for the prince, there will be no obstacles at all for him, for this is no inferior (person). Be without anxiety. (692)

15. 'This prince will reach the summit of perfect enlightenment, he will turn the wheel of the Dhamma, he who sees what is exceedingly pure (i. e. Nibbâna), this (prince) feels for the welfare of the multitude, and his religion[1] will be widely spread. (693)

16. 'My life here will shortly be at an end, in the middle (of his life) there will be death for me; I shall not hear the Dhamma of the incomparable one; therefore I am afflicted, unfortunate, and suffering.' (694)

17. Having afforded the Sakyas great joy he went out from the interior of the palace to lead a religious life; but taking pity on his sister's son, he induced him to embrace the Dhamma of the incomparable one. (695)

18. 'When thou hearest from others the sound "Buddha," (or) "he who has acquired perfect enlightenment walks the way of the Dhamma," then going there and enquiring about the particulars, lead a religious life with that Bhagavat.' (696)

19. Instructed by him, the friendly-minded, by one who saw in the future what is exceedingly pure (i. e. Nibbâna), he, Nâlaka, with a heap of

---

[1] Brahma*k*ariya*m* = sâsana*m*. Commentator.

gathered-up good works, and with guarded senses dwelt (with him), looking forward to *G*ina (i. e. Buddha). (697)

20. Hearing the noise, while the excellent *G*ina turned the wheel (of the Dhamma), and going and seeing the bull of the Isis, he, after being converted, asked the eminent Muni about the best wisdom, when the time of Asita's order had come. (698)

The Vatthugâthâs are ended.

21. 'These words of Asita are acknowledged true (by me), therefore we ask thee, O Gotama, who art perfect in all things (dhamma). (699)

22. 'O Muni, to me who am houseless, and who wish to embrace a Bhikkhu's life, explain when asked the highest state, the state of wisdom (moneyya).' (700)

23. 'I will declare to thee the state of wisdom,' —so said Bhagavat,—'difficult to carry out, and difficult to obtain; come, I will explain it to thee, stand fast, be firm. (701)

24. 'Let a man cultivate equanimity: which is (both) reviled and praised in the village, let him take care not to corrupt his mind, let him live calm, and without pride. (702)

25. 'Various (objects) disappear, like a flame of fire in the wood; women tempt the Muni, let them not tempt him. (703)

26. 'Let him be disgusted with sexual intercourse, having left behind sensual pleasures of all kinds, being inoffensive and dispassionate towards living creatures, towards anything that is feeble or strong. (704)

27. 'As I am so are these, as these are so am

I, identifying himself with others, let him not kill nor cause (any one) to kill[1]. (705)

28. 'Having abandoned desire and covetousness let him act as one that sees clearly where a common man sticks, let him cross over this hell. (706)

29. 'Let him be with an empty stomach, taking little food, let him have few wants and not be covetous; not being consumed by desire he will without desire be happy. (707)

30. 'Let the Muni, after going about for alms, repair to the outskirts of the wood, let him go and sit down near the root of a tree. (708)

31. 'Applying himself to meditation, and being wise, let him find his pleasure in the outskirts of the wood, let him meditate at the root of a tree enjoying himself. (709)

32. 'Then when night is passing away let him repair to the outskirts of the village, let him not delight in being invited nor in what is brought away from the village. (710)

33. 'Let not the Muni, after going to the village, walk about to the houses in haste; cutting off (all) talk while seeking food, let him not utter any coherent speech. (711)

34. '"What I have obtained that is good," "I did not get (anything that is) good," so thinking in both cases he returns to the tree unchanged[2]. (712)

35. 'Wandering about with his alms-bowl in his hand, considered dumb without being dumb, let him not disregard a little gift, let him not despise the giver. (713)

[1] Comp. Dhp. v. 129.

[2] Tâdi = nibbikâro. Commentator.

36. 'Various are the practices illustrated by the Samana, they do not go twice to the other shore, this (is) not once thought. (?) (714)

37. 'For whom there is no desire, for the Bhikkhu who has cut off the stream (of existence) and abandoned all kinds of work, there is no pain. (715)

38. 'I will declare to thee the state of wisdom,'—so said Bhagavat,—'let one be like the edge of a razor, having struck his palate with his tongue, let him be restrained in (regard to his) stomach. (716)

39. 'Let his mind be free from attachment, let him not think much (about worldly affairs), let him be without defilement, independent, and devoted to a religious life. (717)

40. 'For the sake of a solitary life and for the sake of the service that is to be carried out by Samanas, let him learn, solitariness is called wisdom; alone indeed he will find pleasure. (718)

41. 'Then he will shine through the ten regions, having heard the voice of the wise, of the meditating, of those that have abandoned sensual pleasures, let my adherent then still more devote himself to modesty and belief. (719)

42. 'Understand this from the waters in chasms and cracks: noisy go the small waters, silent goes the vast ocean. (720)

43. 'What is deficient that makes a noise, what is full that is calm; the fool is like a half-(filled) water-pot, the wise is like a full pool. (721)

44. 'When the Samana speaks much that is possessed of good sense, he teaches the Dhamma while knowing it, while knowing it he speaks much. (722)

45. 'But he who while knowing it is self-restrained, and while knowing it does not speak much, such a

Muni deserves wisdom (mona), such a Muni has attained to wisdom (mona).' (723)

Nâlakasutta is ended.

---

12. DVAYATÂNUPASSANÂSUTTA.

All pain in the world arises from upadhi, avi*gg*â, sa*m*khârâ, vi*ññ*â*n*a, phassa, vedanâ, ta*n*hâ, upâdâna, ârambha, âhâra, i*ñg*ita, nissaya, rûpa, mosadhamma, sukha.

So it was heard by me:

At one time Bhagavat dwelt at Sâvatthî in Pubbârâma, Migâramâtar's mansion. At that time Bhagavat on the Uposatha day[1], on the fifteenth, it being full moon, in the evening was sitting in the open air, surrounded by the assembly of Bhikkhus. Then Bhagavat surveying the silent assembly of Bhikkhus addressed them (as follows):

'Whichever Dhammas there are, O Bhikkhus, good, noble, liberating, leading to perfect enlightenment,—what is the use to you of listening to these good, noble, liberating Dhammas, leading to perfect enlightenment? If, O Bhikkhus, there should be people that ask so, they shall be answered thus: Yes, for the right understanding of the two Dhammas.' 'Which two do you mean?' '(I mean), "this is pain, this is the origin of pain," this is one consideration, "this is the destruction of pain, this is the way leading to the destruction of pain," this is the second consideration; thus, O Bhikkhus, by the Bhikkhu that considers the Dyad duly[2], is stre-

---

[1] See Rhys Davids, Buddhism, p. 140.

[2] . . . kâ upanisâ savanâyâ 'ti iti *k*e bhikkhave pu*kkh*itâro assu te

nuous, ardent, resolute, of two fruits one fruit is to be expected: in this world perfect knowledge, or, if any of the (five) attributes still remain, the state of an Anâgâmin (one that does not return).' This said Bhagavat, (and) when Sugata had said this, the Master further spoke:

1. 'Those who do not understand pain and the origin of pain, and where pain wholly and totally is stopped, and do not know the way that leads to the cessation of pain, (724)

2. 'They, deprived of the emancipation of thought and the emancipation of knowledge, are unable to put an end (to sa*m*sâra), they will verily continue to undergo birth and decay. (725)

3. 'And those who understand pain and the origin of pain, and where pain wholly and totally is stopped, and who know the way that leads to the cessation of pain, (726)

4. 'They, endowed with the emancipation of thought and the emancipation of knowledge, are able to put an end (to sa*m*sâra), they will not undergo birth and decay. (727)

'"Should there be a perfect consideration of the Dyad in another way," if, O Bhikkhus, there are people that ask so, they shall be told, there is, and how there is: "Whatever pain arises is all in consequence of the upadhis (elements of existence)," this is one consideration, "but from the complete destruction of the upadhis, through absence of pas-

evam assu va*k*anîyâ: yâvad eva dvayatâna*m* dhammâna*m* yathâbhûta*m* *ñ*â*n*âyâ 'ti, ki*ñk*a dvayata*m* vadetha? 'ida*m* dukkha*m*, aya*m* dukkhasamudayo' ti ayam ekânupassanâ, 'aya*m* dukkhanirodho, aya*m* dukkhanirodhagâminî pa*t*ipadâ' ti aya*m* dutiyânupassanâ; eva*m* sammâdvayatânupassino . . .

sion, there is no origin of pain," this is the second consideration; thus, O Bhikkhus, by the Bhikkhu that considers the Dyad duly, that is strenuous, ardent, resolute, of two fruits one fruit is to be expected: in this world perfect knowledge, or, if any of the (five) attributes still remain, the state of an Anâgâmin (one that does not return).' This said Bhagavat, (and) when Sugata had said this, the Master further spoke:

5. 'Whatever pains there are in the world, of many kinds, they arise having their cause in the upadhis; he who being ignorant creates upadhi, that fool again undergoes pain; therefore being wise do not create upadhi, considering what is the birth and origin of pain. (728)

'"Should there be a perfect consideration of the Dyad in another way," if, O Bhikkhus, there are people that ask so, they shall be told, there is, and how there is: "Whatever pain arises is all in consequence of aviggâ (ignorance)," this is one consideration, "but from the complete destruction of aviggâ, through absence of passion, there is no origin of pain," this is the second consideration; thus, O Bhikkhus, by the Bhikkhu that considers the Dyad duly, that is strenuous, ardent, resolute, of two fruits one fruit is to be expected: in this world perfect knowledge, or, if any of the (five) attributes still remain, the state of an Anâgâmin (one that does not return).' This said Bhagavat, (and) when Sugata had said this, the Master further spoke:

6. Those who again and again go to samsâra with birth and death, to existence in this way or in that way,—that is the state of aviggâ. (729)

7. 'For this aviggâ is the great folly by which

this (existence) has been traversed long, but those beings who resort to knowledge do not go to re-birth. (730)

'"Should there be a perfect consideration of the Dyad in another way," if, O Bhikkhus, there are people that ask so, they shall be told, there is, and how there is: "Whatever pain arises is all in consequence of the sa*m*khâras (matter)," this is one consideration, "but from the complete destruction of the sa*m*khâras, through absence of passion, there is no origin of pain," this is the second consideration; thus, O Bhikkhus, by the Bhikkhu that considers the Dyad duly, that is strenuous, ardent, resolute, of two fruits one fruit is to be expected: in this world perfect knowledge, or, if any of the (five) attributes still remain, the state of an Anâgâmin (one that does not return).' This said Bhagavat, (and) when Sugata had said this, the Master further spoke:

8. 'Whatever pain arises is all in consequence of the sa*m*khâras, by the destruction of the sa*m*khâras there will be no origin of pain. (731)

9. 'Looking upon this pain that springs from the sa*m*khâras as misery, from the cessation of all the sa*m*khâras, and from the destruction of consciousness will arise the destruction of pain, having understood this exactly, (732)

10. 'The wise who have true views and are accomplished, having understood (all things) completely, and having conquered all association with Mâra, do not go to re-birth. (733)

'"Should there be a perfect consideration of the Dyad in another way," if, O Bhikkhus, there are people that ask so, they shall be told, there is, and how there is: "Whatever pain arises is all in consequence of *viññâna* (consciousness)," this is one consideration, "but from the complete destruction of viññâna, through absence of passion, there is no origin of pain," this is the second consideration; thus, O Bhikkhus, by the Bhikkhu that considers the Dyad duly, that is strenuous, ardent, resolute, of two fruits one fruit is to be expected: in this world perfect knowledge, or, if any of the (five) attributes still remain, the state of an Anâgâmin (one that does not return).' This said Bhagavat, (and) when Sugata had said this, the Master further spoke:

11. 'Whatever pain arises is all in consequence of viññâna, by the destruction of viññâna there is no origin of pain. (734)

12. 'Looking upon this pain that springs from viññâna as misery, from the cessation of viññâna a Bhikkhu free from desire (will be) perfectly happy (parinibbuta). (735)

'"Should there be a perfect consideration of the Dyad in another way," if, O Bhikkhus, there are people that ask so, they shall be told, there is, and how there is: "Whatever pain arises is all in consequence of *phassa* (touch)," this is one consideration, "but from the complete destruction of phassa, through absence of passion, there is no origin of pain," this is the second consideration; thus, O Bhikkhus, by the Bhikkhu that considers the Dyad duly, that is strenuous, ardent, resolute, of two fruits one fruit is to be expected: in this world perfect knowledge, or, if any of the (five) attributes still remain, the state of an Anâgâmin (one that does not return).' This said Bhagavat, (and) when Sugata had said this, the Master further spoke:

13. 'For those who are ruined by phassa, who follow the stream of existence, who have entered a bad way, the destruction of bonds is far off. (736)

14. 'But those who, having fully understood phassa, knowingly have taken delight in cessation, they verily from the destruction of phassa[1], and being free from desire, are perfectly happy. (737)

'"Should there be a perfect consideration of the Dyad in another way," if, O Bhikkhus, there are people that ask so, they shall be told, there is, and how there is: "Whatever pain arises is all in consequence of the vedanâs (sensations)," this is one consideration, "but from the complete destruction of the vedanâs, through absence of passion, there is no origin of pain," this is the second consideration; thus, O Bhikkhus, by the Bhikkhu that considers the Dyad duly, that is strenuous, ardent, resolute, of two fruits one fruit is to be expected: in this world perfect knowledge, or, if any of the (five) attributes still remain, the state of an Anâgâmin (one that does not return).' This said Bhagavat, (and) when Sugata had said this, the Master further spoke:

15. 'Pleasure or pain, together with want of pleasure and want of pain, whatever is perceived internally and externally, (738)

16. 'Looking upon this as pain, having touched what is perishable and fragile, seeing the decay (of everything), the Bhikkhu is disgusted, having

[1] Phassanirodha. Commentator.

from the perishing of the vedanâs become free from desire, and perfectly happy[1]. (739)

'"Should there be a perfect consideration of the Dyad in another way," if, O Bhikkhus, there are people that ask so, they shall be told, there is, and how there is: "Whatever pain arises is all in consequence of ta*n*hâ (craving)," this is one consideration, "but from the complete destruction of ta*n*hâ, through absence of passion, there is no origin of pain," this is the second consideration; thus, O Bhikkhus, by the Bhikkhu that considers the Dyad duly, that is strenuous, ardent, resolute, of two fruits one fruit is to be expected: in this world perfect knowledge, or, if any of the (five) attributes still remain, the state of an Anâgâmin (one that does not return).' This said Bhagavat, (and) when Sugata had said this, the Master further spoke:

17. 'A man accompanied by ta*n*hâ, for a long time transmigrating into existence in this way or that way, does not overcome transmigration (sa*m*sâra). (740)

18. 'Looking upon this as misery, this origin of the pain of ta*n*hâ, let the Bhikkhu free from ta*n*hâ, not seizing (upon anything), thoughtful, wander about. (741)

'"Should there be a perfect consideration of the Dyad in another way," if, O Bhikkhus, there are people that ask so, they shall be told, there is, and how there is: "Whatever pain arises is all in consequence of the upâdânas (the seizures)," this is one consideration, "but from the complete destruc-

[1] Mosadhamman ti nassanadhamma*m* palokinan ti *g*arâmara*n*ehi palu*gg*anadhamma*m*. Commentator; see my Glossary.

tion of the upâdânas, through absence of passion, there is no origin of pain," this is the second consideration; thus, O Bhikkhus, by the Bhikkhu that considers the Dyad duly, that is strenuous, ardent, resolute, of two fruits one fruit is to be expected: in this world perfect knowledge, or, if any of the (five) attributes still remain, the state of an Anâgâmin (one that does not return).' This said Bhagavat, (and) when Sugata had said this, the Master further spoke:

19. 'The existence is in consequence of the upâdânas; he who has come into existence goes to pain, he who has been born is to die, this is the origin of pain. (742)

20. 'Therefore from the destruction of the upâdânas the wise with perfect knowledge, having seen (what causes) the destruction of birth, do not go to re-birth. (743)

'"Should there be a perfect consideration of the Dyad in another way," if, O Bhikkhus, there are people that ask so, they shall be told, there is, and how there is: "Whatever pain arises is all in consequence of the ârambhas (exertions)," this is one consideration, "but from the complete destruction of the ârambhas, through absence of passion, there is no origin of pain," this is the second consideration; thus, O Bhikkhus, by the Bhikkhu that considers the Dyad duly, that is strenuous, ardent, resolute, of two fruits one fruit is to be expected: in this world perfect knowledge, or, if any of the (five) attributes still remain, the state of an Anâgâmin (one that does not return).' This said Bhagavat, (and) when Sugata had said this, the Master further spoke:

21. 'Whatever pain arises is all in consequence of the ârambhas, by the destruction of the ârambhas there is no origin of pain[1]. (744)

22, 23. 'Looking upon this pain that springs from the ârambhas as misery, having abandoned all the ârambhas, birth and transmigration have been crossed over by the Bhikkhu who is liberated in non-exertion, who has cut off the craving for existence, and whose mind is calm; there is for him no re-birth. (745, 746)

'"Should there be a perfect consideration of the Dyad in another way," if, O Bhikkhus, there are people that ask so, they shall be told, there is, and how there is: "Whatever pain arises is all in consequence of the âhâras (food?)," this is one consideration, "but from the complete destruction of the âhâras, through absence of passion, there is no origin of pain," this is the second consideration; thus, O Bhikkhus, by the Bhikkhu that considers the Dyad duly, that is strenuous, ardent, resolute, of two fruits one fruit is to be expected: in this world perfect knowledge, or, if any of the (five) attributes still remain, the state of an Anâgâmin (one that does not return).' This said Bhagavat, (and) when Sugata had said this, the Master further spoke:

24. 'Whatever pain arises is all in consequence of the âhâras, by the destruction of the âhâras there is no origin of pain. (747)

25. 'Looking upon this pain that springs from the âhâras as misery, having seen the result of all âhâras, not resorting to all âhâras, (748)

[1] Ârambhapa*kk*ayâ ti Kammapayuttaviriyappa*kk*ayâ anârambhe vimuttino ti anârambhe nibbâne vimuttassa . . . âhârappa*kk*ayâ ti kammasampayuttâhârupa*kk*ayâ. Commentator.

26. 'Having seen that health is from the destruction of desire, he that serves discriminatingly and stands fast in the Dhamma cannot be reckoned as existing, being accomplished[1]. (749)

'"Should there be a perfect consideration of the Dyad in another way," if, O Bhikkhus, there are people that ask so, they shall be told, there is, and how there is: "Whatever pain arises is all in consequence of the *iñgitas* (commotions)," this is one consideration, "but from the complete destruction of the *iñgitas*, through absence of passion, there is no origin of pain," this is the second consideration; thus, O Bhikkhus, by the Bhikkhu that considers the Dyad duly, that is strenuous, ardent, resolute, of two fruits one fruit is to be expected: in this world perfect knowledge, or, if any of the (five) attributes still remain, the state of an Anâgâmin (one that does not return).' This said Bhagavat, (and) when Sugata had said this, the Master further spoke:

27. 'Whatever pain arises is all in consequence of the *iñgitas*, by the destruction of the *iñgitas* there is no origin of pain. (750)

28. 'Looking upon this pain that springs from the *iñgitas* as misery, and therefore having abandoned the *iñgitas* and having stopped the *samkhâras*, let the Bhikkhu free from desire and not seizing (upon anything), thoughtful, wander about. (751)

'"Should there be a perfect consideration of the Dyad in another way," if, O Bhikkhus, there are people that ask so, they shall be told, there is, and how there is: "For the *nissita* (dependent) there is vacillation," this is one consideration, "the inde-

[1] Sa*m*kha*m* nôpeti vedagû.

pendent (man) does not vacillate," this is the second consideration; thus, O Bhikkhus, by the Bhikkhu that considers the Dyad duly, that is strenuous, ardent, resolute, of two fruits one fruit is to be expected: in this world perfect knowledge, or, if any of the (five) attributes still remain, the state of an Anâgâmin (one that does not return).' This said Bhagavat, (and) when Sugata had said this, the Master further spoke:

29. 'The independent (man) does not vacillate, and the dependent (man) seizing upon existence in one way or in another, does not overcome sa*m*sâra. (752)

30. 'Looking upon this as misery (and seeing) great danger in things you depend upon, let a Bhikkhu wander about independent, not seizing (upon anything), thoughtful. (753)

'"Should there be a perfect consideration of the Dyad in another way," if, O Bhikkhus, there are people that ask so, they shall be told, there is, and how there is: "The formless (beings), O Bhikkhus, are calmer than the rûpas (for ruppa, i. e. form-possessing)," this is one consideration, "cessation is calmer than the formless," this is another consideration; thus, O Bhikkhus, by the Bhikkhu that considers the Dyad duly, that is strenuous, ardent, resolute, of two fruits one fruit is to be expected: in this world perfect knowledge, or, if any of the (five) attributes still remain, the state of an Anâgâmin (one that does not return).' This said Bhagavat, (and) when Sugata had said this, the Master further spoke:

31. 'Those beings who are possessed of form, and those who dwell in the formless (world), not knowing cessation, have to go to re-birth. (754)

32. 'But those who, having fully comprehended the forms, stand fast in the formless (worlds), those who are liberated in the cessation, such beings leave death behind. (755)

'"Should there be a perfect consideration of the Dyad in another way," if, O Bhikkhus, there are people that ask so, they shall be told, there is, and how there is: "What has been considered true by the world of men, together with the gods, Mâra, Brahman, and amongst the Sama*n*as, Brâhma*n*as, gods, and men, that has by the noble through their perfect knowledge been well seen to be really false," this is one consideration; "what, O Bhikkhus, has been considered false by the world of men, together with the gods, Mâra, Brahman, and amongst the Sama*n*as, Brâhma*n*as, gods, and men, that has by the noble through their perfect knowledge been well seen to be really true," this is another consideration. Thus, O Bhikkhus, by the Bhikkhu that considers the Dyad duly, that is strenuous, ardent, resolute, of two fruits one fruit is to be expected: in this world perfect knowledge, or, if any of the (five) attributes still remain, the state of an Anâgâmin (one that does not return).' This said Bhagavat, (and) when Sugata had said this, the Master further spoke:

33. 'Seeing the real in the unreal, the world of men and gods dwelling in name and form[1], he thinks: "This is true." (756)

34. 'Whichever way they think (it), it becomes otherwise, for it is perishable to him, and what is perishable is wretched. (?) (757)

---

[1] Nâmarûpasmi*m*, 'individuality.'

35. 'What is not perishable, the Nibbâna, that the noble conceive as true, they verily from the comprehension of truth are free from desire (and) perfectly happy. (758)

'"Should there be a perfect consideration of the Dyad in another way," if, O Bhikkhus, there are people that ask so, they shall be told, there is, and how there is: "What, O Bhikkhus, has been considered pleasure by the world of men, gods, Mâra, Brahman, and amongst the Sama*n*as, Brâhma*n*as, gods, and men, that has by the noble by (their) perfect knowledge been well seen to be really pain," this is one consideration; "what, O Bhikkhus, has been considered pain by the world of men, gods, Mâra, Brahman, and amongst the Sama*n*as, Brâhma*n*as, gods, and men, that has by the noble by their perfect knowledge been well seen to be really pleasure," this is the second consideration. Thus, O Bhikkhus, by the Bhikkhu who considers the Dyad duly, who is strenuous, ardent, resolute, of two fruits one fruit is to be expected: in this world perfect knowledge, or, if any of the (five) attributes still remain, the state of an Anâgâmin (one who does not return).' This said Bhagavat, (and) when Sugata had said so, the Master further spoke:

36. 'Form, sound, taste, smell, and touch are all wished for, pleasing and charming (things) as long as they last, so it is said. (759)

37. 'By you, by the world of men and gods these (things) are deemed a pleasure, but when they cease it is deemed pain by them. (760)

38. 'By the noble the cessation of the existing body is regarded as pleasure; this is the opposite of (what) the wise in all the world (hold). (761)

39. 'What fools say is pleasure that the noble say is pain, what fools say is pain that the noble know as pleasure:—see here is a thing difficult to understand, here the ignorant are confounded. (762)

40. 'For those that are enveloped there is gloom, for those that do not see there is darkness, and for the good it is manifest, for those that see there is light; (even being) near, those that are ignorant of the way and the Dhamma, do not discern (anything). (763)

41. 'By those that are overcome by the passions of existence, by those that follow the stream of existence, by those that have entered the realm of Mâra, this Dhamma is not perfectly understood. (764)

42. 'Who except the noble deserve the well understood state (of Nibbâna)? Having perfectly conceived this state, those free from passion are completely extinguished.' (765)

This spoke Bhagavat. Glad those Bhikkhus rejoiced at the words of Bhagavat. While this explanation was being given, the minds of sixty Bhikkhus, not seizing (upon anything), were liberated.

Dvayatânupassanâsutta is ended.

Mahâvagga, the third.

IV. A*TTH*AKAVAGGA.

---

1. KÂMASUTTA.

Sensual pleasures are to be avoided.

1. If he who desires sensual pleasures is successful, he certainly becomes glad-minded, having obtained what a mortal wishes for. (766)

2. But if those sensual pleasures fail the person who desires and wishes (for them), he will suffer, pierced by the arrow (of pain). (767)

3. He who avoids sensual pleasures as (he would avoid treading upon) the head of a snake with his foot, such a one, being thoughtful (sato), will conquer this desire. (768)

4. He who covets extensively (such) pleasures (as these), fields, goods, or gold, cows and horses, servants, women, relations, (769)

5. Sins will overpower him, dangers will crush him, and pain will follow him as water (pours into) a broken ship. (770)

6. Therefore let one always be thoughtful, and avoid pleasures; having abandoned them, let him cross the stream, after baling out the ship, and go to the other shore. (771)

Kâmasutta is ended.

2. GUHATTHAKASUTTA.

Let no one cling to existence and sensual pleasures.

1. A man that lives adhering to the cave (i.e. the body), who is covered with much (sin), and sunk into delusion, such a one is far from seclusion, for the sensual pleasures in the world are not easy to abandon. (772)

2. Those whose wishes are their motives, those who are linked to the pleasures of the world, they are difficult to liberate, for they cannot be liberated by others, looking for what is after or what is before, coveting these and former sensual pleasures. (773)

3. Those who are greedy of, given to, and infatuated by sensual pleasures, those who are niggardly, they, having entered upon what is wicked, wail when they are subjected to pain, saying: 'What will become of us, when we die away from here?' (774)

4. Therefore let a man here[1] learn, whatever he knows as wicked in the world, let him not for the sake of that (?) practise (what is) wicked[2]; for short is this life, say the wise. (775)

5. I see in the world this trembling race given to desire for existences; they are wretched men who lament in the mouth of death, not being free from the craving for reiterated existences. (776)

6. Look upon those men trembling in selfishness, like fish in a stream nearly dried up, with little water; seeing this, let one wander about unselfish, without forming any attachment to existences. (777)

---

[1] Idheva = imasmi*m* yeva sâsane. Commentator.

[2] *N*a tassa hetu visama*m* *k*areyya.

7. Having subdued his wish for both ends , having fully understood touch without being greedy, not doing what he has himself blamed, the wise (man) does not cling to what is seen and heard. (778)

8. Having understood name[2], let the Muni cross over the stream, not defiled by any grasping; having pulled out the arrow (of passion), wandering about strenuous, he does not wish for this world or the other. (779)

Guha*tth*akasutta is ended.

---

3. DU*TTH*A*TTH*AKASUTTA.

The Muni undergoes no censure, for he has shaken off all systems of philosophy, and is therefore independent.

1. Verily, some wicked-minded people censure, and also just-minded people censure, but the Muni does not undergo the censure that has arisen; therefore there is not a discontented (khila) Muni anywhere. (780)

2. How can he who is led by his wishes and possessed by his inclinations overcome his own (false) view? Doing his own doings let him talk according to his understanding. (781)

3. The person who, without being asked, praises his own virtue and (holy) works to others, him the good call ignoble, one who praises himself[3]. (782)

---

[1] Comp. Sallasutta, v. 9.

[2] Sa*ññ*a*m*=nâmarûpa*m*. Commentator.

[3] Yo âtumâna*m* sayam eva pâvâ=yo eva*m* attâna*m* sayam eva vadati. Commentator.

4. But the Bhikkhu who is calm and of a happy mind, 'so I am,' thus not praising himself for his virtues, him the good call noble, one for whom there are no desires anywhere in the world[1]. (783)

5. He whose Dhammas are (arbitrarily) formed and fabricated, placed in front, and confused, because he sees in himself a good result, is therefore given to (the view which is called) kuppa-pa*t*i*kk*a-santi. (?) (784)

6. For the dogmas of philosophy are not easy to overcome, amongst the Dhammas (now this and now that) is adopted after consideration; therefore a man rejects and adopts (now this and now that) Dhamma amongst the dogmas[2]. (785)

7. For him who has shaken off (sin) there is nowhere in the world any prejudiced view of the different existences; he who has shaken off (sin), after leaving deceit and arrogance behind, which (way) should he go, he (is) independent[3]. (786)

8. But he who is dependent undergoes censure amongst the Dhammas; with what (name) and how should one name him who is independent? For by him there is nothing grasped or rejected, he has in this world shaken off every (philosophical) view[4] (787)

Du*tth*a*tth*akasutta is ended.

[1] Yass' ussadâ n' atthi kuhi*ñk*i loke.

[2] Comp. Parama*tth*akasutta, v. 6.

[3] Yo panâyam sabbadi*tth*igatâdidosadhunatâya pa*ññ*âya samannâgatattâ dhono tassa dhonassa.

[4] Upayo ti ta*n*hâdi*tth*inissito. Commentator.

4. SUDDHAṬṬHAKASUTTA.

No one is purified by philosophy, those devoted to philosophy run from one teacher to another, but the wise are not led by passion, and do not embrace anything in the world as the highest.

1. I see a pure, most excellent, sound man, by his views a man's purification takes place, holding this opinion, and having seen this view to be the highest, he goes back to knowledge, thinking to see what is pure. (788)

2. If a man's purification takes place by (his philosophical) views, or he by knowledge leaves pain behind, then he is purified by another (way than the ariyamagga, i. e. the noble way), together with his upadhis, on account of his views he tells him to say so[1]. (789)

3. But the Brâhmaṇa who does not cling to what has been seen, or heard, to virtue and (holy) works, or to what has been thought, to what is good and to what is evil, and who leaves behind what has been grasped, without doing anything in this world, he does not acknowledge that purification comes from another. (790)

4. Having left (their) former (teacher) they go to another, following their desires they do not break asunder their ties; they grasp, they let go like a monkey letting go (one) branch to catch hold of (another). (791)

5. Having himself undertaken some (holy) works he goes to various (things) led by his senses, but a man of great understanding, a wise man who by

---

[1] Diṭṭhihi naṃ pâva tathâ vadânaṃ. Comp. Garâsutta, v. 10; Pasûrasutta, v. 7.

his wisdom has understood the Dhamma, does not go to various (occupations). (792)

6. He being secluded[1] amongst all the Dhammas, whatever has been seen, heard, or thought—how should any one in this world be able to alter him, the seeing one, who wanders openly? (793)

7. They do not form (any view), they do not prefer (anything), they do not say, 'I am infinitely pure;' having cut the tied knot of attachment, they do not long for (anything) anywhere in the world. (794)

8. He is a Brâhma*n*a that has conquered (sin); by him there is nothing embraced after knowing and seeing it; he is not affected by any kind of passion; there is nothing grasped by him as the highest in this world. (795)

Suddha*tth*akasutta is ended.

---

5. PARAMA*TTH*AKASUTTA.

One should not give oneself to philosophical disputations; a Brâhma*n*a who does not adopt any system of philosophy, is unchangeable, has reached Nibbâna.

1. What one person, abiding by the (philosophical) views, saying, 'This is the most excellent, considers the highest in the world, everything different from that he says is wretched, therefore he has not overcome dispute[2]. (796)

2. Because he sees in himself a good result, with regard to what has been seen (or) heard, virtue

---

[1] Mârasena*m* vinâsetvâ *th*itabhâvena visenibhûto. Commentator.

[2] Properly, 'others (are) wretched.'

and (holy) works, or what has been thought, therefore, having embraced that, he looks upon everything else as bad. (797)

3. The expert call just that a tie dependent upon which one looks upon anything else as bad. Therefore let a Bhikkhu not depend upon what is seen, heard, or thought, or upon virtue and (holy) works. (798)

4. Let him not form any (philosophical) view in this world, either by knowledge or by virtue and (holy) works, let him not represent himself equal (to others), nor think himself either low or distinguished. (799)

5. Having left what has been grasped, not seizing upon anything he does not depend even on knowledge. He does not associate with those that are taken up by different things, he does not return to any (philosophical) view. (800)

6. For whom there is here no desire for both ends, for reiterated existence either here or in another world, for him there are no resting-places (of the mind) embraced after investigation amongst the doctrines (dhammesu). (801)

7. In him there is not the least prejudiced idea with regard to what has been seen, heard, or thought; how could any one in this world alter such a Brâhma*n*a who does not adopt any view? (802)

8. They do not form (any view), they do not prefer (anything), the Dhammas are not chosen by them, a Brâhma*n*a is not dependent upon virtue and (holy) works; having gone to the other shore, such a one does not return. (803)

Parama*tth*akasutta is ended.

6. GARÂSUTTA.

From selfishness come grief and avarice. The Bhikkhu who has turned away from the world and wanders about houseless, is independent, and does not wish for purification through another.

1. Short indeed is this life, within a hundred years one dies, and if any one lives longer, then he dies of old age. (804)

2. People grieve from selfishness, perpetual cares kill them, this (world) is full of disappointment; seeing this, let one not live in a house[1]. (805)

3. That even of which a man thinks 'this is mine' is left behind by death: knowing this, let not the wise (man) turn himself to worldliness (while being my) follower. (806)

4. As a man awakened does not see what he has met with in his sleep, so also he does not see the beloved person that has passed away and is dead. (807)

5. Both seen and heard are the persons whose particular name is mentioned, but only the name remains undecayed of the person that has passed away. (808)

6. The greedy in their selfishness do not leave sorrow, lamentation, and avarice; therefore the Munis leaving greediness wandered about seeing security (i. e. Nibbâna) (809)

7. For a Bhikkhu, who wanders about unattached and cultivates the mind of a recluse, they say it is proper that he does not show himself (again) in existence[2]. (810)

---

[1] Reading with Ckb him*s*anti ni*kk*â pariggahâ.

[2] Bi has vivitta-.

8. Under all circumstances the independent Muni does not please nor displease (any one); sorrow and avarice do not stick to him (as little) as water to a leaf. (811)

9. As a drop of water does not stick to a lotus, as water does not stick to a lotus, so a Muni does not cling to anything, namely, to what is seen or heard or thought. (812)

10. He who has shaken off (sin) does not therefore think (much of anything) because it has been seen or heard or thought; he does not wish for purification through another, for he is not pleased nor displeased (with anything)[1]. (813)

*G*arâsutta is ended.

7. TISSAMETTEYYASUTTA.

Sexual intercourse should be avoided.

1. 'Tell me, O venerable one,'—so said the venerable Tissa Metteyya,—'the defeat of him who is given to sexual intercourse; hearing thy precepts we will learn in seclusion.' (814)

2. 'The precepts of him who is given to sexual intercourse, O Metteyya,'—so said Bhagavat,—'are lost, and he employs himself wrongly, this is what is ignoble in him. (815)

3. 'He who, having formerly wandered alone, gives himself up to sexual intercourse, him they call in the world a low, common fellow, like a rolling chariot. (816)

[1] Comp. Suddha*tth*akasutta, v. 2.

4. 'What honour and renown he had before, that is lost for him; having seen this let him learn to give up sexual intercourse. (817)

5. 'He who overcome by his thoughts meditates like a miser, such a one, having heard the (blaming) voice of others, becomes discontented. (818)

6. 'Then he makes weapons (i.e. commits evil deeds) urged by the doctrines of others, he is very greedy, and sinks into falsehood. (819)

7. 'Designated "wise" he has entered upon a solitary life, then having given himself up to sexual intercourse, he (being) a fool suffers pain. (820)

8. 'Looking upon this as misery let the Muni from first to last in the world firmly keep to his solitary life, let him not give himself up to sexual intercourse. (821)

9. 'Let him learn seclusion, this is the highest for noble men, but let him not therefore think himself the best, although he is verily near Nibbâna. (822)

10. 'The Muni who wanders void (of desire), not coveting sensual pleasures, and who has crossed the stream, him the creatures that are tied in sensual pleasures envy.' (823)

Tissametteyyasutta is ended.

---

8. PASÛRASUTTA.

Disputants brand each other as fools, they wish for praise, but being repulsed they become discontented; one is not purified by dispute, but by keeping to Buddha, who has shaken off all sin.

1. Here they maintain 'purity,' in other doctrines (dhamma) they do not allow purity; what they have

devoted themselves to, that they call good, and they enter extensively upon the single truths. (824)

2. Those wishing for dispute, having plunged into the assembly, brand each other as fools mutually, they go to others and pick a quarrel, wishing for praise and calling themselves (the only) expert. (825)

3. Engaged in dispute in the middle of the assembly, wishing for praise he lays about on all sides; but when his dispute has been repulsed he becomes discontented, at the blame he gets angry he who sought for the faults (of others). (826)

4. Because those who have tested his questions say that his dispute is lost and repulsed, he laments and grieves having lost his disputes; 'he has conquered me,' so saying he wails. (827)

5. These disputes have arisen amongst the Sama*n*as, in these (disputes) there is (dealt) blow (and) stroke; having seen this, let him leave off disputing, for there is no other advantage to obtain from getting praise. (828)

6. Or he is praised there, having cleared up the dispute in the middle of the assembly; therefore he will laugh and be elated, having won that case as he had a mind to. (829)

7. That which is his exaltation will also be the field of his defeat, still he talks proudly and arrogantly; seeing this, let no one dispute, for the expert do not say that purification (takes place) by that[1]. (830)

8. As a hero nourished by kingly food goes about roaring, wishing for an adversary—where he (i. e. the philosopher, Di*tth*igatika) is, go thou there, O

[1] Comp. Suddha*tth*akasutta, v. 2.

hero; formerly there was nothing like this to fight against. (831)

9. Those who, having embraced a (certain philosophical) view, dispute and maintain 'this only (is) true,' to them say thou when a dispute has arisen, 'Here is no opponent[1] for thee.' (832)

10. Those who wander about after having secluded themselves, without opposing view to view—what (opposition) wilt thou meet with amongst those, O Pasûra, by whom nothing in this world is grasped as the best? (833)

11. Then thou wentest to reflection thinking in thy mind over the (different philosophical) views; thou hast gone into the yoke with him who has shaken off (all sin), but thou wilt not be able to proceed together (with him). (834)

Pasûrasutta is ended.

---

9. MÂGANDIYASUTTA.

A dialogue between Mâgandiya and Buddha. The former offers Buddha his daughter for a wife, but Buddha refuses her. Mâgandiya says that purity comes from philosophy, Buddha from 'inward peace.' The Muni is a confessor of peace, he does not dispute, he is free from marks.

1. Buddha: 'Even seeing Ta*n*hâ, Arati, and Ragâ (the daughters of Mâra), there was not the least wish (in me) for sexual intercourse. What is this (thy daughter's body but a thing) full of water and excrement? I do not even want to touch it with my foot.' (835)

---

[1] Pa*t*isenikattâ ti pa*t*ilomakârako. Commentator.

2. Mâgandiya: 'If thou dost not want such a pearl, a woman desired by many kings, what view, virtue, and (holy) works, (mode of) life, re-birth dost thou profess?' (836)

3. '"This I say," so (I do now declare), after investigation there is nothing amongst the doctrines which such a one (as I would) embrace, O Mâgandiya,' —so said Bhagavat,—'and seeing (misery) in the (philosophical) views, without adopting (any of them), searching (for truth) I saw "inward peace."' (837)

4. 'All the (philosophical) resolutions[1] that have been formed,'—so said Mâgandiya,—'those indeed thou explainest without adopting (any of them); the notion "inward peace" which (thou mentionest), how is this explained by the wise?' (838)

5. 'Not by (any philosophical) opinion, not by tradition, not by knowledge, O Mâgandiya,'—so said Bhagavat,—'not by virtue and (holy) works can any one say that purity exists; nor by absence of (philosophical) opinion, by absence of tradition, by absence of knowledge, by absence of virtue and (holy) works either; having abandoned these without adopting (anything else), let him, calm and independent, not desire existence.' (839)

6. 'If one cannot say by (any philosophical) opinion, or by tradition, or by knowledge,'—so said Mâgandiya,—'or by virtue and (holy) works that purity exists, nor by absence of (philosophical) opinion, by absence of tradition, by absence of knowledge, by absence of virtue and (holy) works, then I consider the doctrine foolish, for by (philosophical) opinions some return to purity.' (840)

[1] Vini*kkh*aya, placita?

7. 'And asking on account of (thy philosophical) opinion, O Mâgandiya,'—so said Bhagavat,—'thou hast gone to infatuation in what thou hast embraced, and of this (inward peace) thou hast not the least idea, therefore thou holdest it foolish. (841)

8. 'He who thinks himself equal (to others), or distinguished, or low, he for that very reason disputes; but he who is unmoved under those three conditions, for him (the notions) "equal" and "distinguished" do not exist. (842)

9. 'The Brâhma*n*a for whom (the notions) "equal" and "unequal" do not exist, would he say, "This is true?" Or with whom should he dispute, saying, "This is false?" With whom should he enter into dispute? (843)

10. 'Having left his house, wandering about houseless, not making acquaintances in the village, free from lust, not desiring (any future existence), let the Muni not get into quarrelsome talk with people. (844)

11. 'Let not an eminent man (nâga) dispute after having embraced those (views) separated from which he (formerly) wandered in the world; as the thorny lotus elambu*g*a is undefiled by water and mud, so the Muni, the confessor of peace, free from greed, does not cling to sensual pleasures and the world. (845)

12. 'An accomplished man does not by (a philosophical) view, or by thinking become arrogant, for he is not of that sort; not by (holy) works, nor by tradition is he to be led, he is not led into any of the resting-places (of the mind). (846)

13. 'For him who is free from marks there are no ties, to him who is delivered by understanding

there are no follies; (but those) who grasped after marks and (philosophical) views, they wander about in the world annoying (people).' (847)

Mâgandiyasutta is ended.

---

10. PURÂBHEDASUTTA.

Definition of a calm Muni.

1. 'With what view and with what virtue is one called calm, tell me that, O Gotama, (when) asked about the best man?' (848)

2. 'He whose craving is departed before the dissolution (of his body),'—so said Bhagavat,—'who does not depend upon beginning and end, nor reckons upon the middle, by him there is nothing preferred. (849)

3. 'He who is free from anger, free from trembling, free from boasting, free from misbehaviour, he who speaks wisely, he who is not elated, he is indeed a Muni who has restrained his speech. (850)

4. 'Without desire for the future he does not grieve for the past, he sees seclusion in the phassas (touch), and he is not led by (any philosophical) views. (851)

5. 'He is unattached, not deceitful, not covetous, not envious, not impudent, not contemptuous, and not given to slander. (852)

6. 'Without desire for pleasant things and not given to conceit, and being gentle, intelligent, not credulous, he is not displeased (with anything). (853)

7. 'Not from love of gain does he learn, and

he does not get angry on account of loss, and untroubled by craving he has no greed for sweet things. (854)

8. 'Equable (upekhaka), always thoughtful, he does not think himself equal (to others)[1] in the world, nor distinguished, nor low: for him there are no desires (ussada). (855)

9. 'The man in whom there is nothing upon which he depends, who is independent, having understood the Dhamma, in whom there is no craving for coming into existence or leaving existence, (856)

10. 'Him I call calm, not looking for sensual pleasures; for him there are no ties, he has overcome desire. (857)

11. 'For him there are no sons, cattle, fields, wealth, nothing grasped or rejected is to be found in him. (858)

12. 'That fault of which common people and Sama*n*as and Brâhma*n*as say that he is possessed, is not possessed by him, therefore he is not moved by their talk. (859)

13. 'Free from covetousness, without avarice, the Muni does not reckon himself amongst the distinguished, nor amongst the plain, nor amongst the low, he does not enter time, being delivered from time. (860)

14. 'He for whom there is nothing in the world (which he may call) his own, who does not grieve over what is no more, and does not walk amongst the Dhammas (after his wish), he is called calm[2].' (861)

Purâbhedasutta is ended.

---

[1] Compare Tuva*t*akasutta, v. 4; Attada*nd*asutta, v. 20.

[2] Comp. infra, Attada*nd*asutta, v. 16, and Dhp. v. 367.

11. KALAHAVIVÂDASUTTA.

The origin of contentions, disputes, &c. &c.

1. 'Whence (do spring up) contentions and disputes, lamentation and sorrow together with envy; and arrogance and conceit together with slander, whence do these spring up? pray, tell me this.' (862)

2. 'From dear (objects) spring up contentions and disputes, lamentation and sorrow together with envy; arrogance and conceit together with slander; contentions and disputes are joined with envy, and there is slander in the disputes arisen.' (863)

3. 'The dear (objects) in the world whence do they originate, and (whence) the covetousness that prevails in the world, and desire and fulfilment whence do they originate, which are (of consequence) for the future state of a man[1]?' (864)

4. 'From wish[2] originate the dear (objects) in the world, and the covetousness that prevails in the world, and desire and fulfilment originate from it, which are (of consequence) for the future state of a man.' (865)

5. 'From what has wish in the world its origin, and resolutions[3] whence do they spring, anger and falsehood and doubt, and the Dhammas which are made known by the Sama*n*a (Gotama)?' (866)

6. 'What they call pleasure and displeasure in the world, by that wish springs up; having seen decay and origin in (all) bodies[4], a person forms (his) resolutions in the world. (867)

---

[1] Ye samparâyâya narassa honti.
[2] *Kh*anda.
[3] Vini*kkh*aya.
[4] Rûpesu disvâ vibhava*m* bhava*ñ k*a.

7. 'Anger and falsehood and doubt, these Dhammas are a couple[1]; let the doubtful learn in the way of knowledge, knowingly the Dhammas have been proclaimed by the Samana.' (868)

8. 'Pleasure and displeasure, whence have they their origin, for want of what do these not arise? This notion which (thou mentionest), viz. "decay and origin," tell me from what does this arise.' (869)

9. 'Pleasure and displeasure have their origin from phassa (touch), when there is no touch they do not arise. This notion which (thou mentionest), viz. "decay and origin," this I tell thee has its origin from this.' (870)

10. 'From what has phassa its origin in the world, and from what does grasping spring up? For want of what is there no egotism, by the cessation of what do the touches not touch?' (871)

11. 'On account of name and form the touches (exist), grasping has its origin in wish; by the cessation of wishes there is no egotism, by the cessation of form the touches do not touch.' (872)

12. 'How is one to be constituted that (his) form may cease to exist, and how do joy and pain cease to exist? Tell me this, how it ceases, that we should like to know, such was my mind?' (873)

13. 'Let one not be with a natural consciousness, nor with a mad consciousness, nor without consciousness, nor with (his) consciousness gone; for him who is thus constituted form ceases to exist, for what is called delusion has its origin in consciousness.' (?) (874)

---

[1] Te pi kodhâdayo dhammâ sâtâsâtadvaye sante eva pahonti uppaggantı. Commentator.

14. 'What we have asked thee thou hast explained unto us; we will ask thee another question, answer us that: Do not some (who are considered) wise in this world tell us that the principal (thing) is the purification of the yakkha, or do they say something different from this[1]?' (875)

15. 'Thus some (who are considered) wise in this world say that the principal (thing) is the purification of the yakkha; but some of them say samaya[2] (annihilation), the expert say (that the highest purity lies) in anupâdisesa (none of the five attributes remaining). (876)

16. 'And having known these to be dependent, the investigating Muni, having known the things we depend upon, and after knowing them being liberated, does not enter into dispute, the wise (man) does not go to reiterated existence.' (877)

Kalahavivâdasutta is ended.

---

12. *K*ÛLAVIYÛHASUTTA.

A description of disputing philosophers. The different schools of philosophy contradict each other, they proclaim different truths, but the truth is only one. As long as the disputations are going on, so long will there be strife in the world.

1. Abiding by their own views, some (people), having got into contest, assert themselves to be the (only) expert (saying), '(He) who understands this, he knows the Dhamma; he who reviles this, he is not perfect.' (878)

---

[1] Comp. Sundarikabhâradvâ*g*asutta, v. 25.

[2] U*kkh*eda*m*. Commentator.

2. So having got into contest they dispute: 'The opponent (is) a fool, an ignorant (person),' so they say. Which one of these, pray, is the true doctrine (vâda)? for all these assert themselves (to be the only) expert. (879)

3. He who does not acknowledge an opponent's doctrine (dhamma), he is a fool, a beast, one of poor understanding, all are fools with a very poor understanding; all these abide by their (own) views. (880)

4. They are surely purified by their own view, they are of a pure understanding, expert, thoughtful, amongst them there is no one of poor understanding, their view is quite perfect! (881)

5. I do not say, 'This is the reality,' which fools say mutually to each other; they made their own views the truth, therefore they hold others to be fools. (882)

6. What some say is the truth, the reality, that others say is void, false, so having disagreed they dispute. Why do not the Samanas say one (and the same thing)? (883)

7. For the truth is one, there is not a second, about which one intelligent man might dispute with another intelligent man; (but) they themselves proclaim different truths, therefore the Samanas do not say one (and the same thing). (884)

8. Why do the disputants that assert themselves (to be the only) expert, proclaim different truths? Have many different truths been heard of, or do they (only) follow (their own) reasoning? (885)

9. There are not many different truths in the world, no eternal ones except consciousness; but having reasoned on the (philosophical) views they proclaim a double Dhamma, truth and falsehood. (886)

10. In regard to what has been seen, or heard, virtue and (holy) works, or what has been thought, and on account of these (views) looking (upon others) with contempt, standing in (their) resolutions joyful, they say that the opponent is a fool and an ignorant person. (?) (887)

11. Because he holds another (to be) a fool, therefore he calls himself expert, in his own opinion he is one that tells what is propitious, others he blames, so he said. (?) (888)

12. He is full of his overbearing (philosophical) view, mad with pride, thinking himself perfect, he is in his own opinion anointed with the spirit (of genius), for his (philosophical) view is quite complete. (889)

13. If he according to another's report is low, then (he says) the other is also of a low understanding, and if he himself is accomplished and wise, there is not any fool amongst the Sama*n*as[1]. (890)

14. 'Those who preach a doctrine (dhamma) different from this, fall short of purity and are imperfect,' so the Titthiyas say repeatedly, for they are inflamed by passion for their own (philosophical) views. (891)

15. Here they maintain purity, in other doctrines (dhamma) they do not allow purity; so the Titthiyas, entering extensively (upon details), say that in their own way there is something firm. (892)

16. And saying that there is something firm in his own way he holds his opponent to be a fool; thus he himself brings on strife, calling his opponent a fool and impure (asuddhadhamma). (893)

17. Standing in (his) resolution, having himself

[1] So pi ten' eva. Commentator. Ved. tva (?).

measured (teachers, &c.), he still more enters into dispute in the world; but having left all resolutions nobody will excite strife in the world. (894)

*K*ûlaviyûhasutta is ended.

13. MAHÂVIYÛHASUTTA.

Philosophers cannot lead to purity, they only praise themselves and stigmatise others. But a Brâhma*n*a has overcome all dispute, he is indifferent to learning, he is appeased.

1. Those who abiding in the (philosophical) views dispute, saying, 'This is the truth,' they all incur blame, and they also obtain praise in this matter. (895)

2. This is little, not enough to (bring about) tranquillity, I say there are two fruits of dispute; having seen this let no one dispute, understanding Khema (i.e. Nibbâna) to be the place where there is no dispute. (896)

3. The opinions that have arisen amongst people, all these the wise man does not embrace; he is independent. Should he who is not pleased with what has been seen and heard resort to dependency[1]? (?) (897)

4. Those who consider virtue the highest of all, say that purity is associated with restraint; having taken upon themselves a (holy) work they serve. Let us learn in this (view), then, his (the Master's) purity; wishing for existence they assert themselves to be the only expert. (898)

5. If he falls off from virtue and (holy) works, he trembles, having missed (his) work; he laments, he

[1] Khantim, so all the MSS.

prays for purity in this world, as one who has lost his caravan or wandered away from his house. (899)

6. Having left virtue and (holy) works altogether, and both wrong and blameless work, not praying for purity or impurity, he wanders abstaining (from both purity and impurity), without having embraced peace. (900)

7. By means of penance, or anything disliked, or what has been seen, or heard, or thought, going upwards they wail for what is pure, without being free from craving for reiterated existence. (901)

8. For him who wishes (for something there always are) desires[1], and trembling in (the midst of his) plans; he for whom there is no death and no re-birth, how can he tremble or desire anything? (902)

9. What some call the highest Dhamma, that others again call wretched; which one of these, pray, is the true doctrine (vâda)? for all these assert themselves (to be the only) expert. (903)

10. Their own Dhamma they say is perfect, another's Dhamma again they say is wretched; so having disagreed they dispute, they each say their own opinions (are) the truth. (904)

11. If one (becomes) low by another's censure, then there will be no one distinguished amongst the Dhammas; for they all say another's Dhamma (is) low, in their own they say there is something firm. (905)

12. The worshipping of their own Dhamma is as great as their praise of their own ways; all schools would be in the same case, for their purity is individual. (906)

13. There is nothing about a Brâhma*n*a de-

[1] *G*appitâni.

pendent upon others, nothing amongst the Dhammas which he would embrace after investigation; therefore he has overcome the disputes, for he does not regard any other Dhamma as the best. (907)

14. 'I understand, I see likewise this,' so saying, some by (their philosophical) views return to purity. If he saw purity, what then (has been effected) by another's view? Having conquered they say that purity exists by another. (?) (908)

15. A seeing man will see name and form, and having seen he will understand those (things); let him at pleasure see much or little, for the expert do not say that purity exists by that. (909)

16. A dogmatist is no leader to purity, being guided by prejudiced views, saying that good consists in what he is given to, and saying that purity is there, he saw the thing so. (910)

17. A Brâhma*n*a does not enter time, (or) the number (of living beings), (he is) no follower of (philosophical) views, nor a friend of knowledge; and having penetrated the opinions that have arisen amongst people, he is indifferent to learning, while others acquire it. (911)

18. The Muni, having done away with ties here in the world, is no partisan in the disputes that have arisen; appeased amongst the unappeased he is indifferent, not embracing learning, while others acquire it. (912)

19. Having abandoned his former passions, not contracting new ones, not wandering according to his wishes, being no dogmatist, he is delivered from the (philosophical) views, being wise, and he does not cling to the world, neither does he blame himself. (913)

20. Being secluded amongst all the doctrines (dhamma), whatever has been seen, heard, or thought, he is a Muni who has laid down his burden and is liberated, not belonging to time (na kappiyo), not dead, not wishing for anything. So said Bhagavat. (914)

Mahâviyûhasutta is ended.

---

14. TUVAṬAKASUTTA.

How a Bhikkhu attains bliss, what his duties are, and what he is to avoid.

1. 'I ask thee, who art a kinsman of the Âdi*kk*as and a great Isi, about seclusion (viveka) and the state of peace. How is a Bhikkhu, after having seen it, extinguished, not grasping at anything in the world?' (915)

2. 'Let him completely cut off the root of what is called papa*ñk*a[1] (delusion), thinking "I am wisdom;"'—so said Bhagavat,—'all the cravings that arise inwardly, let him learn to subdue them, always being thoughtful. (916)

3. 'Let him learn every Dhamma inwardly or outwardly; let him not therefore be proud, for that is not called bliss by the good. (917)

4. 'Let him not therefore think himself better (than others or) low or equal (to others); questioned by different people, let him not adorn himself[2]. (918)

5. 'Let the Bhikkhu be appeased inwardly, let him not seek peace from any other (quarter); for

---

[1] Avi*gg*âdayo kilesâ. Commentator.

[2] Nâtumâna*m* vikappayan ti*tth*e.

him who is inwardly appeased there is nothing grasped or rejected. (919)

6. 'As in the middle (i.e. depth) of the sea no wave is born, (but as it) remains still[1], so let the Bhikkhu be still[1], without desire, let him not desire anything whatever.' (920)

7. He with open eyes expounded clearly the Dhamma that removes (all) dangers; tell (now) the religious practices; the precepts or contemplation. (921)

8. Bhagavat: 'Let him not be greedy with his eyes, let him keep his ears from the talk of the town, let him not be greedy after sweet things, and let him not desire anything in the world. (922)

9. 'When he is touched by the touch (of illness), let the Bhikkhu not lament, and let him not wish for existence anywhere, and let him not tremble at dangers. (923)

10. 'Having obtained boiled rice and drink, solid food and clothes, let him not store up (these things), and let him not be anxious, if he does not get them. (924)

11. 'Let him be meditative, not prying, let him abstain from misbehaviour[2], let him not be indolent, let the Bhikkhu live in his quiet dwelling. (925)

12. 'Let him not sleep too much, let him apply himself ardently to watching, let him abandon sloth, deceit, laughter, sport, sexual intercourse, and adornment. (926)

13. 'Let him not apply himself to practising (the hymns of) the Âthabba*n*a(-veda), to (the interpretation of) sleep and signs, nor to astrology; let not

[1] *Th*ito. [2] Virame kukku*kk*a*m*.

(my) follower (mâmaka) devote himself to (interpreting) the cry of birds, to causing impregnation, nor to (the art of) medicine. (927)

14. 'Let the Bhikkhu not tremble at blame, nor puff himself up when praised; let him drive off covetousness together with avarice, anger, and slander. (928)

15. 'Let the Bhikkhu not be engaged in purchase and sale, let him not blame others in anything, let him not scold in the village, let him not from love of gain speak to people. (929)

16. 'Let not the Bhikkhu be a boaster, and let him not speak coherent[1] language; let him not learn pride, let him not speak quarrelsome language. (930)

17. 'Let him not be led into falsehood, let him not consciously do wicked things; and with respect to livelihood, understanding, virtue, and (holy) works let him not despise others. (931)

18. 'Having heard much talk from much-talking Samanas let him not irritated answer them with harsh language; for the good do not thwart[2] others. (932)

19. 'Having understood this Dhamma, let the investigating and always thoughtful Bhikkhu learn; having conceived bliss to consist in peace, let him not be indolent in Gotama's commandments. (933)

20 'For he a conqueror unconquered saw the Dhamma visibly, without any traditional instruction[3]; therefore let him learn, heedful in his, Bhagavat's, commandments, and always worshipping.' (934)

Tuvatakasutta is ended.

---

[1] Payuta; comp. Nâlakasutta, v. 33.

[2] Patisenikaronti.

[3] Sakkhi dhammam anîtiham adassî.

15. ATTADANDASUTTA.

Description of an accomplished Muni.

1. From a stick seized fear arises. Look at people killing (each other); I will tell of grief as it is known to me[1]. (935)

2. Seeing people struggling like fish in (a pond with) little water, seeing them obstructed by each other, a fear came over me. (936)

3. The world is completely unsubstantial, all quarters are shaken; wishing for a house for myself I did not see (one) uninhabited. (937)

4. But having seen (all beings) in the end obstructed, discontent arose in me; then I saw in this world an arrow, difficult to see, stuck in the heart. (938)

5. He who has been pierced by this arrow runs through all quarters; but having drawn out that arrow, he will not run, he will sit down (quietly). (939)

6. There (many) studies are gone through; what is tied in the world let him not apply himself to (untie) it; having wholly transfixed desire, let him learn his own extinction (nibbâna). (940)

7. Let the Muni be truthful, without arrogance, undeceitful, free from slander, not angry, let him overcome avarice. (941)

8. Let the man who has turned his mind to Nibbâna conquer sleepiness, drowsiness, and sloth; let him not live together with indolence, let him not indulge in conceit. (942)

[1] The Commentator understands the verse differently. He says, *tam sabbam attadandabhayam gâtam attano dukkaritakâranâ gâtam.*

9. Let him not be led into falsehood, let him not turn his affection to form; let him penetrate arrogance, let him wander abstaining from violence. (943)

10. Let him not delight in what is old, let him not bear with what is new, let him not grieve for what is lost, let him not give himself up to desire[1]. (944)

11. (This desire) I call greed, the great stream, I call (it) precipitation, craving, a trouble, a bog of lust difficult to cross. (945)

12. The Muni who without deviating from truth stands fast on the firm ground (of Nibbâna, being) a Brâhma*n*a, he, having forsaken everything, is indeed called calm. (946)

13. He indeed is wise, he is accomplished, having understood the Dhamma independent (of everything); wandering rightly in the world he does not envy any one here. (947)

14. Whosoever has here overcome lust, a tie difficult to do away with in the world, he does not grieve, he does not covet[2], having cut off the stream, and being without bonds. (948)

15. What is before (thee), lay that aside; let there be nothing behind thee; if thou wilt not grasp after what is in the middle, thou wilt wander calm[3]. (949)

16. The man who has no desire at all for name and form (individuality) and who does not grieve over what is no more, he indeed does not decay in the world[4]. (950)

---

[1] Âkâsa*m* na sito siyâ ti ta*n*ha*m* nissito na bhaveyya. Commentator.

[2] Nâ*gg*h*eti=nâbhi*ggh*ati (read nâbhi*ggh*âyati). Commentator.

[3] Comp. infra, *G*atuka*nn*in's question, v. 4, and Dhammapada, p. 308.

[4] Comp. infra, *G*atuka*nn*in's question, v. 5.

17. He who does not think, 'this is mine' and 'for others there is also something,' he, not having egotism, does not grieve at having nothing. (951)

18. Not being harsh, not greedy, being without desire, and being the same under all circumstances (samo[1]),—that I call a good result, when asked about an undaunted man. (952)

19. For him who is free from desire, for the discerning (man) there is no Sa*m*khâra; abstaining from every sort of effort he sees happiness everywhere. (953)

20. The Muni does not reckon himself amongst the plain, nor amongst the low, nor amongst the distinguished; being calm and free from avarice, he does not grasp after nor reject anything[2]. (954)

Attada*nd*asutta is ended.

---

16. SÂRIPUTTASUTTA.

On Sâriputta asking what a Bhikkhu is to devote himself to, Buddha shows what life he is to lead.

1. 'Neither has before been seen by me,'—so said the venerable Sâriputta,—'nor has any one heard of such a beautifully-speaking master, a teacher arrived from the Tusita heaven. (955)

2. 'As he, the clearly-seeing, appears to the world of men and gods, after having dispelled all darkness, so he wanders alone in the midst (of people). (956)

3. 'To this Buddha, who is independent, unchanged, a guileless teacher, who has arrived (in

[1] =upekhako. Commentator.

[2] Comp. supra, Purâbhedasutta, vv. 15, 20.

the world), I have come supplicatingly with a question[1] from many who are bound in this world. (957)

4. 'To a Bhikkhu who is loath (of the world) and affects an isolated seat, the root of a tree or a cemetery, or (who lives) in the caves of the mountains, (958)

5. 'How many dangers (are there not) in these various dwelling-places at which the Bhikkhu does not tremble in his quiet dwelling[2]! (959)

6. 'How many dangers (are there not) in the world for him who goes to the immortal region[3], (dangers) which the Bhikkhu overcomes in his distant dwelling! (960)

7. 'Which are his words, which are his objects in this world, which are the virtue and (holy) works of the energetic Bhikkhu? (961)

8. 'What study having devoted himself to, intent on one object[4], wise and thoughtful, can he blow off his own filth as the smith (blows off) that of the silver[5]?' (962)

9. 'What is pleasant for him who is disgusted (with birth, &c.), O Sâriputta,'—so said Bhagavat,—'if he cultivates a lonely dwelling-place, and loves perfect enlightenment in accordance with the Dhamma, that I will tell thee as I understand it. (963)

10. 'Let not the wise and thoughtful Bhikkhu wandering on the borders[6] be afraid of the five

---

[1] Atthi pa*ñ*hena âgami*m*=atthiko pa*ñ*hena âgato 'mhîti atthikâna*m* vâ pa*ñ*hena atthi âgamana*ñ* *k*â ti. Commentator.

[2] U*kk*âva*k*esû 'ti hînapanîtesu. Commentator.

[3] Ga*kkh*ato amata*m* disa*m*.

[4] Ekodi=ekagga*k*itto. Commentator.

[5] Comp. Dhp. v. 239.

[6] Pariyanta*k*ârî.

dangers: gad-flies and (all other) flies[1], snakes, contact with (evil) men[2], and quadrupeds. (964)

11. 'Let him not be afraid of adversaries[3], even having seen many dangers from them; further he will overcome other dangers while seeking what is good. (965)

12. 'Touched by sickness and hunger let him endure cold and excessive heat, let him, touched by them in many ways, and being houseless, make strong exertions. (966)

13. 'Let him not commit theft, let him not speak falsely, let him touch friendly what is feeble or strong, what he acknowledges to be the agitation of the mind, let him drive that off as a partisan of Ka*n*ha (i. e. Mâra). (967)

14. 'Let him not fall into the power of anger and arrogance; having dug up the root of these, let him live, and let him overcome both what is pleasant and what is unpleasant. (968)

15. 'Guided by wisdom, taking delight in what is good, let him scatter those dangers, let him overcome discontent in his distant dwelling, let him overcome the four causes of lamentation. (969)

16. 'What shall I eat, or where shall I eat?—he lay indeed uncomfortably (last night)—where shall I lie this night? let the Sekha who wanders about houseless subdue these lamentable doubts. (970)

17. 'Having had in (due) time both food and clothes, let him know moderation in this world for

[1] *D*a*m*sâdhipâtânan ti pingalamakkhikânañ *k*a sesamakkhikânañ *k*a, sesamakkhikâ hi tato adhipatitvâ khâdanti, tasmâ adhipâtâ ti vu*kk*anti. Commentator.

[2] Manussaphassânan ti *k*orâdiphassâna*m*. Commentator.

[3] Paradhammikâna*m*.

the sake of happiness; guarded in these (things) and wandering restrained in the village let him, even (if he be) irritated, not speak harsh words. (971)

18. 'Let him be with down-cast eyes, and not prying, devoted to meditation, very watchful; having acquired equanimity let him with a composed mind cut off the seat of doubt, and misbehaviour. (972)

19. 'Urged on by words (of his teachers) let him be thoughtful and rejoice (at this urging), let him break stubbornness in his fellow-students, let him utter propitious words and not unseasonable, let him not think detractingly of others. (973)

20. 'And then the five impurities in the world, the subjection of which he must learn thoughtfully, —let him overcome passion for form, sound and taste, smell and touch. (974)

21. 'Let the Bhikkhu subdue his wish for these Dhammas and be thoughtful, and with his mind well liberated, then in time he will, reflecting upon Dhamma, and having become intent upon one object, destroy darkness.' So said Bhagavat. (975)

Sâriputtasutta is ended.

A*tth*akavagga, the fourth.

V. PÂRÂYANAVAGGA.

To the Brâhma*n*a Bâvarî, living on the banks of the Godhâvarî, in Assaka's territory, comes another Brâhma*n*a and asks for five hundred pieces of money, but not getting them he curses Bâvarî, saying, 'May thy head on the seventh day hence cleave into seven.' A deity comforts Bâvarî by referring him to Buddha. Then Bâvarî sends his sixteen disciples to Buddha, and each of them asks Buddha a question.

1. VATTHUGÂTHÂ.

1. From the beautiful city of the Kosalas (Sâvatthî) a Brâhma*n*a, well versed in the hymns, went to the South (Dakkhi*n*âpatha) wishing for nothingness[1]. (976)

2. In Assaka's territory, in the neighbourhood of A*l*aka, he dwelt on the banks of the Godhâvarî, (living) on gleanings and fruit. (977)

3. And close by the bank there was a large village, with the income of which he prepared a great sacrifice. (978)

4. Having offered the great sacrifice, he again entered the hermitage. Upon his re-entering, another Brâhma*n*a arrived, (979)

5. With swollen feet[2], trembling, with dirty teeth, and with dust on his head. And he going up

---

[1] Âki*ñk*a*ññ*a.

[2] Uggha*tt*apâdo ti maggakkamanena gha*tt*apâdatalo pa*n*hikâya vâ pa*n*hika*m* gopphakena vâ gopphaka*m* ga*nn*ukena ga*nn*uka*m* âgantvâpi gha*tt*apâdo. Commentator.

to him (i. e. the first Brâhma*n*a) demanded five hundred (pieces of money). (980)

6. Bâvarî, seeing him, bade him be seated, asked him whether he was happy and well, and spoke as follows: (981)

7. 'What gifts I had are all given away by me; pardon me, O Brâhma*n*a, I have no five hundred.' (982)

8. 'If thou wilt not give to me who asks, may thy head on the seventh day cleave into seven.' (983)

9. So after the usual ceremonies this impostor made known his fearful (curse). On hearing these his words Bâvarî became sorrowful. (984)

10. He wasted away taking no food, transfixed by the arrow of grief, but yet his mind delighted in meditation. (985)

11. Seeing Bâvarî struck with horror and sorrowful, the benevolent deity (of that place) approached him and said as follows: (986)

12. 'He does not know (anything about) the head; he is a hypocrite coveting riches; knowledge of the head and head-splitting is not found in him.' (987)

13. 'If the venerable (deity) knows it, then tell me, when asked, all about the head and head-splitting; let us hear thy words.' (988)

14. 'I do not know this; knowledge of it is not found in me; as to the head and head-splitting, this is to be seen by Buddhas (only).' (989)

15. 'Who then, say, in the circumference of the earth knows the head and head-splitting, tell me that, O deity?' (990)

16. 'Formerly went out from Kapilavatthu a ruler of the world, an offspring of the Okkâka king, the Sakya son, the light-giving; (991)

17. 'He is, O Brâhma*n*a, the perfectly Enlightened (Sambuddha); perfect in all things, he has attained the power of all knowledge, sees clearly in everything; he has arrived at the destruction of all things, and is liberated in the destruction of the upadhis[1]. (992)

18. 'He is Buddha, he is Bhagavat in the world, he, the clearly-seeing, teaches the Dhamma; go thou to him and ask, he will explain it to thee.' (993)

19. Having heard the word 'Sambuddha,' Bâvarî rejoiced, his grief became little, and he was filled with great delight. (994)

20. Bâvarî glad, rejoicing, and eager asked the deity: 'In what village or in what town or in what province dwells the chief of the world, that going there we may adore the perfectly Enlightened, the first of men?' (995)

21. 'In Sâvatthî, the town of the Kosalas, dwells *G*ina (the Victorious), of great understanding and excellent wide knowledge, he the Sakya son, unyoked, free from passion, skilled in head-splitting, the bull of men.' (996)

22. Then (Bâvarî) addressed his disciples, Brâhma*n*as, perfect in the hymns: 'Come, youths, I will tell (you something), listen to my words: (997)

23. 'He whose appearance in the world is difficult to be met with often, he is at the present time[2] born in the world and widely renowned as Sambuddha (the perfectly Enlightened); go quickly to Sâvatthî and behold the best of men.' (998)

24. 'How then can we know, on seeing him, that

---

[1] Sabbadhammakkhaya*m* patto (i. e. nibbâna)
Vimutto upadhisa*m*khaye.

[2] Sv-â*gg*a

he is Buddha, O Brâhma*n*a? Tell us who do not know him, by what may we recognise him? (999)

25. 'For in the hymns are to be found the marks of a great man, and thirty-two are disclosed altogether, one by one.' (1000)

26. 'For him on whose limbs these marks of a great man are to be found, there are two ways left, a third does not exist. (1001)

27. 'If he abides in a dwelling, he will subdue this earth without rod (or) sword, he will rule with justice. (1002)

28. 'And if he departs from his dwelling for the wilderness, he becomes the saint, incomparable Sambuddha, who has removed the veil (from the world)[1]. (1003)

29. 'Ask in your mind about my birth and family, my marks, hymns, and my other disciples, the head and head-splitting. (1004)

30. 'If he is Buddha, the clear-sighted, then he will answer by word of mouth the questions you have asked in your mind.' (1005)

31, 32, 33. Having heard Bâvarî's words his disciples, sixteen Brâhma*n*as, A*g*ita, Tissametteyya, Pu*nn*aka, further Mettagû, Dhotaka and Upasîva, and Nanda, further Hemaka, the two Todeyya and Kappa, and the wise *G*atuka*nn*î, Bhadrâvudha and Udaya, and also the Brâhma*n*a Posâla, and the wise Mogharâ*g*an, and the great Isi Piṅgiya, (1006–1008)

34. All of them, having each their host (of pupils), and being themselves widely renowned throughout the world, thinkers delighting in meditation, wise, scented with the perfume of former (good deeds)[2], (1009)

[1] Comp. Lalita-vistara (ed. Calc.), pp. 116, 118.

[2] Pubbavâsanavâsitâ.

35. Having saluted Bâvarî and gone round him towards the right, all with matted hair and bearing hides, departed with their faces turned to the north. (1010)

36. To Pati*tth*âna of A*l*aka first, then to Mâhissatî, and also to U*gg*enî, Gonaddha, Vedisâ, Vanasavhaya, (1011)

37. And also to Kosambî, Sâketa, and Sâvatthî, the most excellent of cities, to Setavya, Kapilavatthu, and the city of Kusinâra, (1012)

38. And to Pâva, the city of wealth, to Vesâlî, the city of Magadha, to Pâsâ*n*aka *K*etiya (the Rock Temple), the lovely, the charming. (1013)

39. As he who is athirst (longs for) the cold water, as the merchant (longs for) gain, as he who is plagued by heat (longs for) shade, so in haste they ascended the mountain. (1014)

40. And Bhagavat at that time attended by the assembly of the Bhikkhus taught the Dhamma to the Bhikkhus, and roared like a lion in the forest. (1015)

41. A*g*ita beheld Sambuddha as the shining (sun) without (burning) rays, as the moon on the fifteenth, having reached her plenitude. (1016)

42. Then observing on his body all the marks in their fulness, standing apart, rejoiced, he asked the questions of his mind:— (1017)

43. 'Tell me about (my master's) birth, tell me about his family together with the marks, tell me about his perfection in the hymns, how many (hymns) does the Brâhma*n*a recite?' (1018)

44. Bhagavat said: 'One hundred and twenty years (is his) age, and by family he is a Bâvarî; three are his marks on the limbs, and in the three Vedas he is perfect. (1019)

45. 'In the marks and in the Itihâsa together with Nigha*nd*u and Ke*t*ubha—he recites five hundred—and in his own Dhamma he has reached perfection.' (1020)

46. A*g*ita thought: 'Explain fully the marks of Bâvarî, O thou best of men, who cuts off desire; let there be no doubt left for us.' (1021)

47. Bhagavat said: 'He covers his face with his tongue, he has a circle of hair between the eyebrows, (his) privy member (is) hidden in a sheath, know this, O young man.' (1022)

48. Not hearing him ask anything, but hearing the questions answered, the multitude reflected overjoyed and with joined hands:— (1023)

49. 'Who, be he a god, or Brahman, or Inda, the husband of Su*g*â, asked in his mind those questions, and to whom did that (speech) reply?' (1024)

50. A*g*ita said: 'The head and head-splitting Bâvarî asked about; explain that, O Bhagavat, remove our doubt, O Isi.' (1025)

51. Bhagavat said: 'Ignorance is the head, know this; knowledge cleaves the head, together with belief, thoughtfulness, meditation, determination, and strength.' (1026)

52. Then with great joy having composed himself the young man put his hide on one shoulder, fell at (Bhagavat's) feet (and saluted him) with his head, (saying): (1027)

53. 'Bâvarî, the Brâhma*n*a, together with his disciples, O thou venerable man, delighted and glad, does homage to thy feet, O thou clearly-seeing.' (1028)

54. Bhagavat said: 'Let Bâvarî, the Brâhma*n*a, be glad together with his disciples! Be thou also glad, live long, O young man! (1029)

55. 'For Bâvarî and for thee, for all there are all (kinds of) doubt; having got an opportunity, ask ye whatever you wish.' (1030)

56. After getting permission from Sambuddha, Agita sitting there with folded hands asked Tathâgata the first question. (1031)

The Vatthugâthâs are ended.

2. AGITAMÂNAVAPUKKHÂ.

1. 'By what is the world shrouded,'—so said the venerable Agita,—'by what does it not shine? What callest thou its pollution, what is its great danger[1]?' (1032)

2. 'With ignorance is the world shrouded, O Agita,'—so said Bhagavat,—'by reason of avarice it does not shine; desire I call its pollution, pain is its great danger.' (1033)

3. 'The streams of desire flow in every direction,'—so said the venerable Agita;—'what dams the streams, say what restrains the streams, by what may the streams be shut off[2]?' (1034)

4. 'Whatever streams there are in the world, O Agita,'—so said Bhagavat,—'thoughtfulness is their dam, thoughtfulness I call the restraint of the streams, by understanding they are shut off.' (1035)

5. 'Both understanding and thoughtfulness,'—so said the venerable Agita,—'and name and shape[3], O venerable man,—asked about this by me, declare by what is this stopped?' (1036)

[1] Cf. Mahâbh. III, 17366; XII, 11030. Kena svid âvrito lokah kena svin na prakâsate, &c.

[2] Comp. Dhp. v. 340.

[3] Nâmarûpañ ka.

6. Buddha: 'This question which thou hast asked, O A*g*ita, that I will explain to thee; (I will explain to thee) by what name and shape[1] are totally stopped; by the cessation of consciousness this is stopped here.' (1037)

7. A*g*ita: 'Those who have examined (all) Dhammas (i.e. the saints), and those who are disciples, (and those who are) common men here, —when thou art asked about their mode of life, declare it unto me, thou who art wise, O venerable man.' (1038)

8. Buddha: 'Let the Bhikkhu not crave for sensual pleasures, let him be calm in mind, let him wander about skilful in all Dhammas, and thoughtful.' (1039)

A*g*itamâ*n*avapu*kkh*â is ended.

3. TISSAMETTEYYAMÂ*N*AVAPU*KKH*Â.

1. 'Who is contented in the world,'—so said the venerable Tissametteyya,—'who is without commotions? Who after knowing both ends does not stick in the middle, as far as his understanding is concerned? Whom dost thou call a great man? Who has overcome desire in this world?' (1040)

2. 'The Bhikkhu who abstains from sensual pleasures, O Metteyya,'—so said Bhagavat,—'who is free from desire, always thoughtful, happy by reflection, he is without commotions, he after knowing both ends does not stick in the middle, as far as his understanding is concerned; him I call a great man; he has overcome craving in this world.' (1041)

Tissametteyyamâ*n*avapu*kkh*â is ended.

[1] Nâma*ñ* *k*a rûpa*ñ* *k*a.

4. PU*NN*AKAMÂ*N*AVAPU*KKH*Â.

1. 'To him who is without desire, who has seen the root (of sin),'—so said the venerable Pu*nn*aka,—'I have come supplicatingly with a question: on account of what did the Isis and men, Khattiyas and Brâhma*n*as, offer sacrifices to the gods abundantly in this world? (about this) I ask thee, O Bhagavat, tell me this.' (1042)

2. 'All these Isis and men, Khattiyas and Brâhma*n*as, O Pu*nn*aka,'—so said Bhagavat,—'who offered sacrifices to the gods abundantly in this world, offered sacrifices, O Pu*nn*aka, after reaching old age, wishing for their present condition.' (1043)

3. 'All these Isis and men, Khattiyas and Brâhma*n*as,'—so said the venerable Pu*nn*aka,—'who offered sacrifices to the gods abundantly in this world, did they, O Bhagavat, indefatigable in the way of offering, cross over both birth and old age, O venerable man? I ask thee, O Bhagavat, tell me this.' (1044)

4. 'They wished for, praised, desired, abandoned (sensual pleasures), O Pu*nn*aka,'—so said Bhagavat,—'they desired sensual pleasures on account of what they reached by them; they, devoted to offering, dyed with the passions of existence, did not cross over birth and old age, so I say.' (1045)

5. 'If they, devoted to offering,'—so said the venerable Pu*nn*aka,—'did not by offering cross over birth and old age, O venerable man, who then in the world of gods and men crossed over birth and old age, O venerable man, I ask thee, O Bhagavat, tell me this?' (1046)

6. 'Having considered everything[1] in the world, O Pu*nn*aka,'—so said Bhagavat,—'he for whom there is no commotion[2] anywhere in the world, who is calm without the smoke of passions, free from woe, free from craving, he crossed over birth and old age, so I say.' (1047)

Pu*nn*akamâ*n*avapu*kkh*â is ended.

---

5. METTAGÛMÂ*N*AVAPU*KKH*Â.

1. 'I ask thee, O Bhagavat, tell me this,'—so said the venerable Mettagû,—'I consider thee accomplished and of a cultivated mind, why are these (creatures), whatsoever they are of many kinds in the world, always subject to pain?' (1048)

2. 'Thou mayest well ask me concerning the origin of pain, O Mettagû,'—so said Bhagavat,—'I will explain that to thee in the way I myself know it: originating in the upadhis pains arise, whatsoever they are, of many kinds in the world. (1049)

3. 'He who being ignorant creates upadhi, that fool again undergoes pain; therefore let not the wise man create upadhi, considering (that this is) the birth and origin of pain.' (1050)

4. Mettagû: 'What we have asked thee thou hast explained to us; another (question) I ask thee, answer that, pray: How do the wise cross the stream, birth and old age, and sorrow and lamenta-

[1] Parovarânîti parâni *k*a orâni *k*a parattabhâvasakattabhâvâdîni parâni *k*a orâni *k*â ti vutta*m* hoti. Commentator.

[2] Read yass' i*ñ*gita*m* n' atthi.

tion? Explain that thoroughly to me, O Muni, for this thing (dhamma) is well known to thee.' (1051)

5. 'I will explain the Dhamma to thee, O Mettagû,'—so said Bhagavat;—'if a man in the visible world, without any traditional instruction, has understood it, and wanders about thoughtful, he may overcome desire in the world.' (1052)

6. Mettagû: 'And I take a delight in that, in the most excellent Dhamma, O great Isi, which if a man has understood, and he wanders about thoughtful, he may overcome desire in the world.' (1053)

7. 'Whatsoever thou knowest, O Mettagû,'—so said Bhagavat,—'(of what is) above, below, across, and in the middle, taking no delight and no rest in these things, let thy mind not dwell on existence. (1054)

8. 'Living so, thoughtful, strenuous, let the Bhikkhu wandering about, after abandoning selfishness, birth, and old age, and sorrow, and lamentation, being a wise man, leave pain in this world.' (1055)

9. Mettagû: 'I delight in these words of the great Isi; well expounded, O Gotama, is (by thee) freedom from upadhi (i.e. Nibbâna). Bhagavat in truth has left pain, for this Dhamma is well known to thee[1]. (1056)

10. 'And those also will certainly leave pain whom thou, O Muni, constantly mayest admonish; therefore I bow down to thee, having come hither, O chief (nâga), may Bhagavat also admonish me constantly.' (1057)

11. Buddha: 'The Brâhma*n*a whom I may ac-

[1] Sukittita*m* Gotama nûpadhikan ti ettha anupadhikan ti nibbâna*m*, ta*m* sandhâya vâ Bhagavanta*m* âlapanto âha sukittita*m*, &c. Commentator.

knowledge as accomplished, possessing nothing, not cleaving to the world of lust, he surely has crossed this stream, and he has crossed over to the other shore, free from harshness (akhila), (and) free from doubt. (1058)

12. 'And he is a wise and accomplished man in this world; having abandoned this cleaving to reiterated existence he is without craving, free from woe, free from longing, he has crossed over birth and old age, so I say.' (1059)

Mettagûmâ*n*avapu*kkh*â is ended.

---

6. DHOTAKAMÂ*N*AVAPU*KKH*Â.

1. 'I ask thee, O Bhagavat, tell me this,'—so said the venerable Dhotaka,—'I long for thy word, O great Isi; may one, having listened to thy utterance, learn his own extinction[1].' (1060)

2. 'Exert thyself then, O Dhotaka,'—so said Bhagavat,—'being wise and thoughtful in this world, let one, having listened to my utterance, learn his own extinction.' (1061)

3. Dhotaka: 'I see in the world of gods and men a Brâhma*n*a wandering about, possessing nothing; therefore I bow down to thee, O thou all-seeing one, free me, O Sakka, from doubts.' (1062)

4. Buddha: 'I shall not go to free any one in the world who is doubtful, O Dhotaka; when thou hast learned the best Dhamma, then thou shalt cross this stream.' (1063)

---

[1] Attano râgâdîna*m* nibbânatthâya adhisîlâdîni sikkheyya. Commentator.

5. Dhotaka: 'Teach (me), O Brâhma*n*a, having compassion (on me), the Dhamma of seclusion (i. e. Nibbâna), that I may understand (it and) that I, without falling into many shapes like the air, may wander calm and independent in this world[1].' (?) (1064)

6. 'I will explain to thee peace[2], O Dhotaka,'—so said Bhagavat;—'if a man in the visible world, without any traditional instruction, has understood it, and wanders about thoughtful, he may overcome desire in the world.' (1065)

7. Dhotaka: 'And I take delight in that, the highest peace[3], O great Isi, which if a man has understood, and he wanders about thoughtful, he may overcome desire in the world.' (1066)

8. 'Whatsoever thou knowest, O Dhotaka,'—so said Bhagavat,—'(of what is) above, below, across, and in the middle, knowing this to be a tie in the world, thou must not thirst for reiterated existence.' (1067)

Dhotakamâ*n*avapu*kkh*â is ended.

7. UPASÎVAMÂ*N*AVAPU*KKH*Â.

1. 'Alone, O Sakka, and without assistance I shall not be able to cross the great stream,'—so said the venerable Upasîva;—'tell me an object, O thou all-seeing one, by means of which one may cross this stream.' (1068)

[1] Nânappakârata*m* anâpa*gg*amâno. Commentator.

[2] Santi*m*.

[3] Santim uttama*m*.

2. 'Having in view nothingness, being thoughtful, O Upasîva,'—so said Bhagavat,—'by the reflection of nothing existing shalt thou cross the stream; having abandoned sensual pleasures, being loath of doubts, thou shalt regard the extinction of craving (i. e. Nibbâna), both day and night.' (1069)

3. Upasîva: 'He whose passion for all sensual pleasures has departed, having resorted to nothingness, after leaving everything else, and being delivered in the highest deliverance by knowledge, will he remain there without proceeding further?' (1070)

4. 'He whose passion for all sensual pleasures has departed, O Upasîva,'—so said Bhagavat,—'having resorted to nothingness after leaving everything else, and being delivered in the highest deliverance by knowledge, he will remain there without proceeding further.' (1071)

5. Upasîva: 'If he remains there without proceeding further for a multitude of years, O thou all-seeing one, (and if) he becomes there tranquil and delivered, will there be consciousness for such a one?' (1072)

6. 'As a flame blown about by the violence of the wind, O Upasîva,'—so said Bhagavat,—'goes out, cannot be reckoned (as existing), even so a Muni, delivered from name and body, disappears, and cannot be reckoned (as existing).' (1073)

7. Upasîva: 'Has he (only) disappeared, or does he not exist (any longer), or is he for ever free from sickness? Explain that thoroughly to me, O Muni, for this Dhamma is well known to thee.' (1074)

8. 'For him who has disappeared there is no form, O Upasîva,—so said Bhagavat,—'that by

which they say he is, exists for him no longer, when all things (dhamma) have been cut off, all (kinds of) dispute are also cut off.' (1075)

Upasîvamâ*n*avapu*kkh*â is ended.

8. NANDAMÂ*N*AVAPU*KKH*Â.

1. 'There are Munis in the world,'—so said the venerable Nanda,—'so people say. How is this (understood) by thee? Do they call him a Muni who is possessed of knowledge or him who is possessed of life?' (1076)

2. Buddha: 'Not because of (any philosophical) view, nor of tradition, nor of knowledge, O Nanda, do the expert call (any one) a Muni; (but) such as wander free from woe, free from desire, after having secluded themselves, those I call Munis.' (1077)

3. 'All these Sama*n*as and Brâhma*n*as,'—so said the venerable Nanda,—'say that purity comes from (philosophical) views, and from tradition, and from virtue and (holy) works, and in many (other) ways. Did they, in the way in which they lived in the world, cross over birth and old age, O venerable man? I ask thee, O Bhagavat, tell me this.' (1078)

4. 'All these Sama*n*as and Brâhma*n*as, O Nanda,' —so said Bhagavat,—'say that purity comes from (philosophical) views, and from tradition, and from virtue and (holy) works, and in many (other) ways; still they did not, in the way in which they lived in the world, cross over birth and old age, so I say.' (1079)

5. 'All these Sama*n*as and Brâhma*n*as,'—so said

the venerable Nanda,—'say that purity comes from (philosophical) views, and from tradition, and from virtue and (holy) works, and in many (other) ways; if thou, O Muni, sayest that such have not crossed the stream, who then in the world of gods and men crossed over birth and old age, O venerable man? I ask thee, O Bhagavat, tell me this.' (1080)

6. 'I do not say that all Samanas and Brâhmanas, O Nanda,'—so said Bhagavat,—'are shrouded by birth and old age; those who, after leaving in this world what has been seen or heard or thought, and all virtue and (holy) works, after leaving everything of various kinds, after penetrating craving, are free from passion, such indeed I call men that have crossed the stream.' (1081)

7. Nanda: 'I delight in these words of the great Isi; well expounded (by thee), O Gotama, is freedom from upadhi (i. e. Nibbâna); those who, after leaving in this world what has been seen or heard or thought, and all virtue and (holy) works, after leaving everything of various kinds, after penetrating craving, are free from passion, such I verily call men that have crossed the stream.' (1082)

Nandamânavapukkhâ is ended.

---

9. HEMAKAMÂNAVAPUKKHÂ.

1. 'Those who before,'—so said the venerable Hemaka,—'explained to me (their doctrine), previously to Gotama's doctrine, saying, "So it was, so it will be," all that (was only) oral tradition, all

that (was only) something that increased (my) doubts[1]. (1083)

2. 'I took no pleasure in that, but tell thou me the Dhamma that destroys craving, O Muni, which if a man has understood, and he wanders about thoughtful, he may cross desire in the world.' (1084)

3. Buddha: 'In this world (much) has been seen, heard, and thought; the destruction of passion and of wish for the dear objects that have been perceived, O Hemaka, is the imperishable state of Nibbâna. (1085)

4. 'Those who, having understood this, are thoughtful, calm, because they have seen the Dhamma, tranquil and divine, such have crossed desire in this world[2].' (1086)

Hemakamâ*n*avapu*kkh*â is ended.

---

10. TODEYYAMÂ*N*AVAPU*KKH*Â.

1. 'He in whom there live no lusts,'—so said the venerable Todeyya,—'to whom there is no craving, and who has overcome doubt, what sort of deliverance is there for him?' (1087)

2. 'He in whom there live no lusts, O Todeyya,'—so said Bhagavat,—'to whom there is no craving, and who has overcome doubt, for him there is no other deliverance.' (1088)

3. Todeyya: 'Is he without desire or is he longing, is he possessed of understanding or is he forming himself an understanding? Explain this to

---

[1] Hura*m* Gotamasâsanâ ti pubbatara*m*. Commentator.

[2] B reads ye satâ instead of tedasâ.

me, O thou all-seeing one, that I may know a Muni, O Sakka.' (1089)

4. Buddha: 'He is without desire, he is not longing, he is possessed of understanding, and he is not forming himself an understanding; know, O Todeyya, that such is the Muni, not possessing anything, not cleaving to lust and existence.' (1090)

Todeyyamâ*n*avapu*kkh*â is ended.

---

11. KAPPAMÂ*N*AVAPU*KKH*Â.

1. 'For those who stand in the middle of the water,'—so said the venerable Kappa,—'in the formidable stream that has set in, for those who are overcome by decay and death, tell me of an island, O venerable man, and tell thou me of an island that this (pain) may not again come on [1].' (1091)

2. 'For those who stand in the middle of the water, O Kappa,'—so said Bhagavat,—'in the formidable stream that has set in, for those overcome by decay and death, I will tell thee of an island, O Kappa. (1092)

3. 'This matchless island, possessing nothing (and) grasping after nothing, I call Nibbâna, the destruction of decay and death [2]. (1093)

4. 'Those who, having understood this, are thoughtful (and) calm, because they have seen the Dhamma, do not fall into the power of Mâra, and are not the companions of Mâra.' (1094)

Kappamâ*n*avapu*kkh*â is ended.

---

[1] B reads disam for dîpam.

[2] Aki*ñk*anan ti ki*ñk*anapa*t*ipakkha*m*, anâdânan ti âdânapa*t*ipakkha*m*, ki*ñk*anâdânavûpasaman ti vutta*m* hoti. Commentator.

12. *G*ATUKA*NN*IMÂ*N*AVAPU*KKH*Â.

1. 'Having heard of a hero free from lust,'—so said the venerable *G*atuka*nn*in,—'who has crossed the stream, I have come to ask him who is free from lust; tell me the seat of peace, O thou with the born eye (of wisdom), tell me this truly, O Bhagavat. (1095)

2. 'For Bhagavat wanders about after having conquered lust as the hot sun (conquers) the earth by its heat; tell the Dhamma to me who has (only) little understanding, O thou of great understanding, that I may ascertain how to leave in this world birth and decay.' (1096)

3. 'Subdue thy greediness for sensual pleasures, O *G*atuka*nn*in,'—so said Bhagavat,—'having considered the forsaking of the world as happiness, let there not be anything either grasped after or rejected by thee. (1097)

4. 'What is before thee, lay that aside; let there be nothing behind thee; if thou wilt not grasp after what is in the middle, thou wilt wander calm[1]. (1098)

5. 'For him whose greediness for name and form is wholly gone, O Brâhma*n*a, for him there are no passions by which he might fall into the power of death.' (1099)

*G*atuka*nn*imâ*n*avapu*kkh*â is ended.

13. BHADRÂVUDHAMÂ*N*AVAPU*KKH*Â.

1. 'I entreat the wise (Buddha), the houseless, who cuts off desire,'—so (said) the venerable Bhadrâvudha,—'who is free from commotion, forsakes joy, has

[1] Comp. supra, Attada*nd*asutta, v. 15.

crossed the stream, is liberated, and who leaves time behind; having heard the chief's (word), they will go away from here. (1100)

2. 'Different people have come together from the provinces, longing (to hear) thy speech, O hero; do thou expound it thoroughly to them, for this Dhamma is well known to thee.' (1101)

3. 'Let one wholly subdue the craving of grasping (after everything), O Bhadrâvudha,'—so said Bhagavat,—'above, below, across, and in the middle; for whatever they grasp after in the world, just by that Mâra follows the man. (1102)

4. 'Therefore, knowing this, let not the thoughtful Bhikkhu grasp after anything in all the world, considering as creatures of desire this generation, sticking fast in the realm of death.' (1103)

Bhadrâvudhamâ*n*avapu*kkh*â is ended.

---

14. UDAYAMÂ*N*AVAPU*KKH*Â.

1. 'To Buddha who is sitting meditating, free from pollution,'—so said the venerable Udaya,—'having performed his duty, who is without passion, accomplished in all things (dhamma), I have come with a question; tell me the deliverance by knowledge, the splitting up of ignorance.' (1104)

2. '(It consists in) leaving lust and desire, O Udaya,'—so said Bhagavat,—'and both (kinds of) grief, and driving away sloth, and warding off misbehaviour. (1105)

3. 'The deliverance by knowledge which is purified by equanimity and thoughtfulness and preceded

by reasoning on Dhamma I will tell thee, the splitting up of ignorance.' (1106)

4. Udaya: 'What is the bond of the world, what is its practice? By the leaving of what is Nibbâna said to be?' (1107)

5. Buddha: 'The world is bound by pleasure, reasoning is its practice; by the leaving of desire Nibbâna is said to be.' (1108)

6. Udaya: 'How does consciousness cease in him that wanders thoughtful? Having come to ask thee, let us hear thy words.' (1109)

7. Buddha: 'For him who both inwardly and outwardly does not delight in sensation, for him who thus wanders thoughtful, consciousness ceases.' (1110)

Udayamâ*n*avapu*kkh*â is ended.

---

15. POSÂLAMÂ*N*AVAPU*KKH*Â.

1. 'He who shows the past (births, &c.),'—so said the venerable Posâla,—'who is without desire and has cut off doubt, to him who is accomplished in all things (dhamma), I have come supplicatingly with a question. (1111)

2. 'O Sakka, I ask about his knowledge who is aware of past shapes, who casts off every corporeal form, and who sees that there exists nothing either internally or externally; how can such a one be led (by anybody)?' (1112)

3. 'Tathâgata, knowing all the faces of consciousness, O Posâla,'—so said Bhagavat,—'knows (also) him who stands delivered, devoted to that (object). (1113)

4. 'Having understood that the bonds of pleasure do not originate in nothingness (?), he sees clearly in this (matter), this (is) the knowledge of a perfect, accomplished Brâhma*n*a.' (1114)

Posâlamâ*n*avapu*kkh*â is ended.

16. MOGHARÂ*G*AMÂ*N*AVAPU*KKH*Â.

1. 'Twice have I asked Sakka,'—so said the venerable Mogharâ*g*an,—'but the clearly-seeing has not explained it to me; if the divine Isi is asked for the third time, he will explain it, so I have heard. (1115)

2. 'There is this world, the other world, Brahman's world together with the world of the gods; I do not know thy view, the famous Gotama's (view). (1116)

3. 'To this man who sees what is good I have come supplicatingly with a question: How is any one to look upon the world that the king of death may not see him?' (1117)

4. 'Look upon the world as void, O Mogharâ*g*an, being always thoughtful; having destroyed the view of oneself (as really existing), so one may overcome death; the king of death will not see him who thus regards the world[1].' (1118)

Mogharâ*g*amâ*n*avapu*kkh*â is ended.

[1] Comp. Dhp. v. 170.

17. PIṄGIYAMÂ*N*AVAPU*KKH*Â.

1. 'I am old, feeble, colourless,'—so said the venerable Piṅgiya,—'my eyes are not clear, my hearing is not good; lest I should perish a fool on the way, tell me the Dhamma, that I may know how to leave birth and decay in this world.' (1119)

2. 'Seeing others afflicted by the body, O Piṅgiya,'—so said Bhagavat,—'(seeing) heedless people suffer in their bodies;—therefore, O Piṅgiya, shalt thou be heedful, and leave the body behind, that thou mayest never come to exist again.' (1120)

3. Piṅgiya: 'Four regions, four intermediate regions, above and below, these are the ten regions; there is nothing which has not been seen, heard, or thought by thee, and (is there) anything in the world not understood (by thee)? Tell (me) the Dhamma, that I may know how to leave birth and decay in this world.' (1121)

4. 'Seeing men seized with desire, O Piṅgiya,'—so said Bhagavat,—'tormented and overcome by decay,—therefore thou, O Piṅgiya, shalt be heedful, and leave desire behind, that thou mayest never come to exist again.' (1122)

Piṅgiyamâ*n*avapu*kkh*â is ended.

This said Bhagavat, living in Magadha at Pâsâ*n*aka *K*etiya (the Rock Temple). Sought by sixteen Brâhma*n*as, the followers (of Bâvarî, and) questioned by each of them in turn, he responded to the questions. If a man, having understood the meaning and tenor of each question, lives according to the

Dhamma, then he will go to the further shore of decay and death, for these Dhammas lead to the further shore, and therefore this order of Dhamma was called 'the way to the other shore.'

1, 2. A*g*ita, Tissametteyya, Pu*nn*aka and Mettagû, Dhotaka and Upasîva, Nanda and Hemaka, the two Todeyya and Kappa, and the wise *G*atuka*nn*in, Bhadrâvudha and Udaya, and also the Brâhma*n*a Posâla, and the wise Mogharâ*g*an, and Piṅgiya the great Isi, (1123, 1124)

3. These went up to Buddha, the Isi of exemplary conduct; asking subtle questions they went up to the supreme Buddha. (1125)

4. Buddha, being asked, responded to their questions truly, and in responding to the questions the Muni delighted the Brâhma*n*as. (1126)

5. They, having been delighted by the clearly-seeing Buddha, the kinsman of the Âdi*kk*as, devoted themselves to a religious life near the man of excellent understanding. (1127)

6. He who lived according to what had been taught by Buddha (in answer) to each single question, went from this shore to the other shore. (1128)

7. From this shore he went to the other shore entering upon the most excellent way; this way is to lead to the other shore, therefore it is called 'the way to the other shore.' (1129)

---

8. 'I will proclaim accordingly the way to the further shore,'—so said the venerable Piṅgiya;—'as he saw it, so he told it; the spotless, the very wise, the passionless, the desireless lord, for what reason should he speak falsely? (1130)

9. 'Well! I will praise the beautiful voice of (Buddha), who is without stain and folly, and who has left behind arrogance and hypocrisy. (1131)

10. 'The darkness-dispelling Buddha, the all-seeing, who thoroughly understands the world[1], has overcome all existences, is free from passion, has left behind all pain, is rightly called (Buddha), he, O Brâhma*n*a, has come to me. (1132)

11. 'As the bird, having left the bush, takes up his abode in the fruitful forest, even so I, having left men of narrow views, have reached the great sea, like the ha*m*sa. (1133)

12. 'Those who before in another world explained the doctrine of Gotama, saying, "So it was, so it will be," all that was only oral tradition, all that was only something that increased my doubts. (1134)

13. 'There is only one abiding dispelling darkness, that is the high-born, the luminous, Gotama of great understanding, Gotama of great wisdom, (1135)

14. 'Who taught me the Dhamma, the instantaneous, the immediate, the destruction of desire, freedom from distress, whose likeness is nowhere[2].' (1136)

15. Bâvarî: 'Canst thou stay away from him even for a moment, O Piṅgiya, from Gotama of great understanding, from Gotama of great wisdom, (1137)

16. 'Who taught thee the Dhamma, the instantaneous, the immediate, the destruction of desire, freedom from distress, whose likeness is nowhere?' (1138)

---

[1] Lokantagû.

[2] Yo me dhammam adesesi
Sandi*tth*ikam akâlika*m*
Ta*n*hakkhayam anîtika*m*
Yassa n' atthi upamâ kva*k*i.

17. Piṅgiya: 'I do not stay away from him even for a moment, O Brâhma*n*a, from Gotama of great understanding, from Gotama of great wisdom, (1139)

18. 'Who taught me the Dhamma, the instantaneous, the immediate, the destruction of desire, freedom from distress, whose likeness is nowhere. (1140)

19. 'I see him in my mind and with my eye, vigilant, O Brâhma*n*a, night and day; worshipping I spend the night, therefore I think I do not stay away from him. (1141)

20. 'Belief and joy, mind and thought incline me towards the doctrine of Gotama; whichever way the very wise man goes, the very same I am inclined to. (?) (1142)

21. 'Therefore, as I am worn out and feeble, my body does not go there, but in my thoughts I always go there, for my mind, O Brâhma*n*a, is joined to him. (1143)

22. 'Lying in the mud (of lusts) wriggling, I jumped from island to island; then I saw the perfectly Enlightened, who has crossed the stream, and is free from passion.' (1144)

23. Bhagavat[1]: 'As Vakkali was delivered by faith, (as well as) Bhadrâvudha and Â*l*avi-Gotama,

---

[1] At the conclusion of this (i. e. the preceding) gâthâ, Bhagavat, who stayed at Sâvatthî, when seeing the maturity of the minds of Piṅgiya and Bâvarî, shed a golden light. Piṅgiya, who sat picturing Buddha's virtues to Bâvarî, having seen the light, looked round, saying, 'What is this?' And when he saw Bhagavat standing, as it were, before him, he said to the Brâhma*n*a Bâvarî: 'Buddha has come.' The Brâhma*n*a rose from his seat and stood with folded hands. Bhagavat, shedding a light, showed himself to the Brâhma*n*a, and knowing what was beneficial for both, he said this stanza while addressing Piṅgiya. Commentator.

so thou shalt let faith deliver thee, and thou shalt go, O Piṅgiya, to the further shore of the realm of death[1].' (1145)

24. Piṅgiya: 'I am highly pleased at hearing the Muni's words; Sambuddha has removed the veil, he is free from harshness, and wise. (1146)

25. 'Having penetrated (all things) concerning the gods, he knows everything of every description; the Master will put an end to all questions of the doubtful that (will) admit (him). (1147)

26. 'To the insuperable, the unchangeable (Nibbâna), whose likeness is nowhere, I shall certainly go; in this (Nibbâna) there will be no doubt (left) for me, so know (me to be) of a dispossessed mind.' (1148)

Pârâyanavagga is ended.

Suttanipâta is ended.

---

[1] Yathâ Vakkalithero saddhâdhimutto ahosi saddhâdhuren' eva arahatta*m* pâpu*n*i evam eva tvam pi mu*ñk*assu saddha*m* tato saddhâya adhimu*kk*anto sabbe sa*m*khârâ ani*kk*â 'ti âdinâ nayena vipassana*m* ârabhitvâ ma*kk*udheyyassa pâra*m* nibbâna*m* gamissasîti arahattaniku*l*ena desana*m* ni*tth*apesi. Commentator.

INDEX.

The figures of this Index refer to the pages of the Translation, and the numerals to the Introduction.

TRANSLITERATION OF ORIENTAL ALPHABETS ADOPTED FOR THE TRANSLATIONS OF THE SACRED BOOKS OF THE EAST.

CONSONANTS.	MISSIONARY ALPHABET. I Class.	II Class.	III Class.	Sanskrit.	Zend.	Pehlevi.	Persian.	Arabic.	Hebrew.	Chinese.
Gutturales.										
1 Tenuis	k	...	....	क	𐬐	𐭪	ك	ك	כּ	k
2 „ aspirata	kh	...	....	ख	𐬑	𐭧	...	...	כ	kh
3 Media	g	...	....	ग	𐬔	𐭢	گ	...	גּ	...
4 „ aspirata	gh	...	....	घ	𐬖	𐭢	...	...	ג	...
5 Gutturo-labialis	q	...	....	...	....	...	ق	ق	ק	...
6 Nasalis	ṅ (ng)	...	....	ङ	{𐬧 (ng) 𐬣 (N)}	...	...	...	...	...
7 Spiritus asper	h	...	....	ह	𐬵 (𐬓 *hv*)	𐭧	ه	ه	ה	h, hs
8 „ lenis	'	...	....	...	....	...	ا	ا	א	...
9 „ asper faucalis	'h	...	....	...	....	...	ح	ح	ח	...
10 „ lenis faucalis	'h	...	....	...	....	...	ع	ع	ע	...
11 „ asper fricatus	...	*'h*	....	...	....	...	خ	خ	ח	...
12 „ lenis fricatus	...	*'h*	....	...	....	...	...	...	...	...
Gutturales modificatae (palatales, &c.)										
13 Tenuis	...	*k*	....	च	𐬗	𐭰	چ	...	...	*k*
14 „ aspirata	...	*kh*	....	छ	....	...	...	...	...	*kh*
15 Media	...	*g*	....	ज	𐬘	𐭰	ج	ج	...	...
16 „ aspirata	...	*gh*	....	झ	....	...	ژ	ژ	...	...
17 „ Nasalis	...	*ñ*	....	ञ	....	...	...	...	...	...

CONSONANTS (*continued*).	MISSIONARY ALPHABET. I Class.	II Class.	III Class.	Sanskrit.	Zend.	Pehlevi.	Persian.	Arabic.	Hebrew.	Chinese.
18 Semivocalis	y	. . .	. . . .	य	𐬫, init. 𐬪 𐬌	[illegible]	ي	ي	י	y
19 Spiritus asper	. . .	(ý)	. . . .	. . .	. . . .	. . .	. . .	. . .	. . .	. . .
20 „ lenis	. . .	(ỳ)	. . . .	. . .	. . . .	. . .	. . .	. . .	. . .	. . .
21 „ asper assibilatus . .	. . .	*s*	. . . .	श	𐬱	[illegible]	ش	ش	. . .	. . .
22 „ lenis assibilatus . .	. . .	*z*	. . . .	. . .	𐬲	[illegible]	ژ	. . .	. . .	*s*
Dentales.										
23 Tenuis	t	. . .	. . . .	त	𐬙	[illegible]	ت	ت	תּ	t
24 „ aspirata	th	. . .	. . . .	थ	𐬚	. . .	. . .	. . .	ת	th
25 „ assibilata	. . .	. . .	TH	. . .	. . . .	. . .	ث	ث	. . .	. . .
26 Media	d	. . .	. . . .	द	𐬛	و	د	د	דּ	. . .
27 „ aspirata	dh	. . .	. . . .	ध	𐬜	. . .	. . .	. . .	ד	. . .
28 „ assibilata	. . .	. . .	DH	. . .	. . . .	. . .	ذ	ذ	. . .	. . .
29 Nasalis	n	. . .	. . . .	न	𐬥	ا	ن	ن	נ	n
30 Semivocalis	l	. . .	. . . .	ल	. . . .	[illegible]	ل	ل	ל	l
31 „ mollis 1	. . .	*l*	. . . .	ळ	. . . .	. . .	. . .	. . .	. . .	. . .
32 „ mollis 2	. . .	. . .	L	. . .	. . . .	. . .	. . .	. . .	. . .	. . .
33 Spiritus asper 1	s	. . .	. . . .	स	𐬯	[illegible]	س(ث)	س	שׂ	s
34 „ asper 2	. . .	. . .	s (ʃ)	. . .	. . . .	. . .	. . .	. . .	ס	. . .
35 „ lenis	z	. . .	. . . .	. . .	𐬰	[illegible]	ز (ذ)	ز	ז	z
36 „ asperrimus 1	. . .	. . .	z (ʒ)	. . .	. . . .	. . .	ص	ص	צ	ʒ, ʒh
37 „ asperrimus 2	. . .	. . .	ẓ (ʒ)	. . .	. . . .	. . .	ض	. . .	. . .	. . .

Dentales modificatae (lingualos, &c.)										
38 Tenuis	...	*t*	...	ट	...	...	ط	ط	ט	...
39 „ aspirata	...	*th*	...	ठ	...	...	ظ	ظ	...	...
40 Media	...	*d*	...	ड	𐬜	[illegible]	...	...	...	...
41 „ aspirata	...	*dh*	...	ढ	...	...	...	ض	...	...
42 Nasalis	...	*n*	...	ण	𐬣	...	...	...	...	...
43 Semivocalis	r	...	...	र	𐬭	[illegible]	ر	ر	ר	...
44 „ fricata	...	*r*	...	...	...	...	...	...	...	*r*
45 „ diacritica	...	...	R	...	...	...	...	...	...	...
46 Spiritus asper	sh	...	...	ष	𐬴	[illegible]	...	...	...	sh
47 „ lenis	zh	...	...	...	...	...	...	...	...	...
Labiales.										
48 Tenuis	p	...	...	प	𐬞	[illegible]	پ	...	פּ	p
49 „ aspirata	ph	...	...	फ	...	...	...	...	פ	ph
50 Media	b	...	...	ब	𐬠	[illegible]	ب	ب	בּ	...
51 „ aspirata	bh	...	...	भ	...	...	...	...	ב	...
52 Tenuissima	...	*p*	...	...	...	...	...	...	...	...
53 Nasalis	m	...	...	म	𐬨	[illegible]	م	م	מ	m
54 Semivocalis	w	...	...	...	cu	...	...	...	...	w
55 „ aspirata	hw	...	...	...	...	...	...	...	...	...
56 Spiritus asper	f	...	...	...	𐬟	[illegible]	ف	ف	...	f
57 „ lenis	v	...	...	व	»	ı, e	و	و	ו	...
58 Anusvâra	...	*m*	...	अं	𐬅 ä	...	...	...	...	...
59 Visarga	...	*h*	...	अः	...	...	...	...	...	...

VOWELS.	MISSIONARY ALPHABET. I Class.	II Class.	III Class.	Sanskrit.	Zend.	Pehlevi.	Persian.	Arabic.	Hebrew.	Chinese.
1 Neutralis	0	...	....	...	....	...	...	...	ְ	ă
2 Laryngo-palatalis	ĕ	...	....	...	....	...	...	...	...	...
3 „ labialis	ŏ	...	....	...	....	ا fin.	...	...	...	...
4 Gutturalis brevis	a	...	....	अ	𐬀	𐭠 init.	ـَ	ـَ	ַ	a
5 „ longa	â	(a)	....	आ	𐬁	𐭠	ـَا	ـَا	ָ	â
6 Palatalis brevis	i	...	....	इ	𐬌	...	ـِ	ـِ	ִ	i
7 „ longa	î	(i)	....	ई	𐬍	ی	ـِي	ـِي	ִי	î
8 Dentalis brevis	*li*	...	....	ऌ	....	...	...	...	...	...
9 „ longa	*lî*	...	....	ॡ	....	...	...	...	...	...
10 Lingualis brevis	*ri*	...	....	ऋ	....	...	...	...	...	...
11 „ longa	*rî*	...	....	ॠ	....	...	...	...	...	...
12 Labialis brevis	u	...	....	उ	𐬎	...	ـُ	ـُ	ֻ	u
13 „ longa	û	(u)	....	ऊ	𐬏	ו	ـُو	ـُو	וּ	û
14 Gutturo-palatalis brevis	e	...	....	...	𐬈(e) 𐬉(e)	...	...	...	ֶ	e
15 „ longa	ê (ai)	(e)	....	ए	𐬉, 𐬊	ی	...	...	ֵ	ê
16 Diphthongus gutturo-palatalis	âi	(ai)	....	ऐ	....	...	ـَيْ	ـَيْ	...	âi
17 „ „	ei (ĕi)	...	....	...	....	...	...	...	...	ei, êi
18 „ „	oi (ŏu)	...	....	...	....	...	...	...	...	...
19 Gutturo-labialis brevis	o	...	....	...	𐬊	...	...	...	ָ	o
20 „ longa	ô (au)	(o)	....	ओ	𐬋	ו	...	...	וֹ	...
21 Diphthongus gutturo-labialis	âu	(au)	....	औ	𐬀𐬊 (*au*)	...	ـَوْ	ـَوْ	...	âu
22 „ „	eu (ĕu)	...	....	...	....	...	...	...	...	...
23 „ „	ou (ŏu)	...	....	...	....	...	...	...	...	...
24 Gutturalis fracta	ä	...	....	...	....	...	...	...	...	...
25 Palatalis fracta	ï	...	....	...	....	...	...	...	...	...
26 Labialis fracta	ü	...	....	...	....	...	...	...	...	ü
27 Gutturo-labialis fracta	ö	...	....	...	....	...	...	...	...	...